BETWEEN DEATH AND REBIRTH

IN RELATION TO COSMIC FACTS

BETWEEN DEATH AND REBIRTH
IN RELATION TO COSMIC FACTS

Ten lectures given in Berlin between
5 November 1912 and 1 April 1913

TRANSLATED BY E. H. GODDARD, D. S. OSMOND
AND FREDERICK AMRINE

EDITED BY FREDERICK AND MARGOT AMRINE

INTRODUCTION BY FREDERICK AMRINE

RUDOLF STEINER

RUDOLF STEINER PRESS

CW 141

Rudolf Steiner Press
Hillside House, The Square
Forest Row, RH18 5ES

www.rudolfsteinerpress.com

Published by Rudolf Steiner Press 2021

Originally published in German under the title *Das Leben zwischen dem Tode und der neuen Geburt im Verhältnis zu den kosmischen Tatsachen* (volume 141 in the *Rudolf Steiner Gesamtausgabe* or Collected Works) by Rudolf Steiner Verlag, Dornach. Based on shorthand notes that were not reviewed or revised by the speaker. This authorized translation is based on the fifth German edition (1997), edited by H. R. Niederhäuser

Published by permission of the Rudolf Steiner Nachlassverwaltung, Dornach

© Rudolf Steiner Nachlassverwaltung, Dornach, Rudolf Steiner Verlag 1997

This translation © Rudolf Steiner Press 2021

A catalogue record for this book is available from the British Library

ISBN 978 1 85584 593 0

Cover by Morgan Creative
Typeset by Symbiosys Technologies, Vishakapatnam, India
Printed and bound by 4Edge Ltd., Essex

Contents

LECTURE 1
BERLIN, 5 NOVEMBER 1912

All the forces of the soul must be activated if the essence of anthroposophy is to be grasped. Subjects must be studied constantly from new perspectives. Since the last third of the nineteenth century, the soul need only be duly prepared and revelations will flow from the spiritual world. Activity in the physical world, quietude in the spiritual world. Since 1899, spiritual influences must take effect inwardly instead of being occasioned by outer events. These lectures will deal chiefly with the life after death when the Kamaloka period is over. After death, relationships between individuals continue as they were during life on Earth. Homer's seership. Michelangelo and the Medici tombs in Florence. Our attitude to spiritual knowledge can establish the seeds of a true morality. Companionship or isolation in the planetary spheres after death depend upon moral and religious attitudes of soul in earthly life. For karmic adjustments, return into the physical body is essential.

LECTURE 2
BERLIN, 20 NOVEMBER 1912

Consciousness of the 'I' acquired as the result of contacts and collisions with the external world and with the body when waking from sleep. Between birth and death a human being may reduce the value of his 'I' as the result of causing suffering to others. Effects of the destruction thus caused remain in one's astral, etheric and physical bodies; the forces able to repair the damage to these sheaths cannot be drawn from the Earth but only from the planetary spheres after death. Particular qualities acquired on Earth determine whether companionship or isolation will be experienced by the soul after death when passing through the spheres of Mercury, Venus, Sun, Mars, Jupiter, Saturn. Experiences during initiation closely akin to those undergone during the life after death. Understanding of every human soul without distinction of creed necessary for initiation as it is in the Sun sphere.

The meeting between Abraham and Melchizedek contains a deep secret of the evolution of humanity. The distinction between Christianity and other faiths. The Mystery of Golgotha was fulfilled for all human beings, not only for those who call themselves Christians. 'Ye shall be as Gods'—difference in implications of these words if uttered by Lucifer or Christ. Forces needed for renewal of the etheric body in the next incarnation must be drawn from the solar sphere, for renewal of the astral body from the other planetary spheres.

Pages 19-35

LECTURE 3
BERLIN, 3 DECEMBER 1912

Relationships established during existence on Earth cannot, to begin with, be changed during the life after death. From the possible suffering caused by this realization the power is acquired to change conditions in later karma. Those living on Earth are able to have a great influence on those who have died. Reading to the dead. Opposition to anthroposophy in the upper consciousness may take the form of longing for it in the subconsciousness. Necessity of mediation between the physical world and the spiritual world. Possibilities that do not become reality on the physical plane exist as forces and effects in the spiritual world. Actual experiences are only a fractional part of the possibilities. The purpose of anthroposophy is fulfilled in the creation of an actual link between the physical and spiritual worlds. The relation of the soul to the body. Analogy of the plant and its connection with the Sun. The human being belongs to the Universe, not only to the Earth. Only during the last four centuries has consciousness of this connection been lost. The Christ Impulse imparts feeling of kinship with the macrocosm. A twelfth-century allegory. Reference to Chapter IV in the book *Esoteric Science*.

Pages 36-50

LECTURE 4
BERLIN, 10 DECEMBER 1912

After death the human being draws forces from the stellar world to the extent to which he developed moral and religious qualities during life on Earth. Humans are not meant to witness what happens to them during sleep, i.e. the restoration of forces used up during waking life. Processes of cognition lie within the field of human's consciousness, but the life-giving process does not. The expulsion from Paradise. The purpose of life between death and rebirth is that forces may be drawn from the stellar world for shaping the following incarnation. Difference between the life after death and the condition of sleep is fundamentally one of consciousness only. Direct astronomical vision in ancient Egypt, but no logical thinking. In the Graeco-Latin epoch there was only remembrance of what had formerly been direct vision. By the time of Copernicus human beings had eyes only for physical globes in space. Kepler's spiritual insight into the connection of certain events with heavenly constellations. Anthroposophy is a torch by which the spiritual world is illumined for us from a certain time onwards during life after death. Forces once drawn from the stellar worlds must now be drawn from human beings' own souls. This is the mission of the Earth.

LECTURE 5

BERLIN, 22 DECEMBER 1912

A special lecture given 'as a kind of Christmas gift' on the subject of Christian Rosenkreutz and Gautama Buddha: their missions and achievements in the spiritual history of mankind.

LECTURE 6

BERLIN, 7 JANUARY 1913

In our fifth post-Atlantean epoch, the sixth is prepared in the souls of human beings by increasing understanding of the Christ Impulse and of the Mystery of the Holy Grail. The latter is connected with the mission of Buddha in the Mars sphere referred to in the preceding lecture. Of the members of the human being it is the 'I' or ego which, basically speaking, passes through all the periods of existence between birth and death and death and rebirth. But this 'I' must not be confused with the 'I' recognized in earthly life. The true 'I' is the actor in the processes of learning to walk, to speak and to think. There is a natural correspondence between the true human form and those faculties. The human form stems from the Spirits of Form. These Spirits are opposed by backward luciferic Spirits who suppress the consciousness proper to the ego. The bodily organs are pervaded by the Spirits of Form quite differently in each case. Contrast between the head and the rest of the physical body. At a certain stage of development, physical mobility can be held still while complete mobility of the corresponding etheric organs is maintained. Between death and rebirth man experiences the higher 'I' of which he is unconscious during earthly life between birth and death.

LECTURE 7

BERLIN, 14 JANUARY 1913

Cyclic seven-year periods in life. Coming of the second teeth marks the culmination of the formative process which works from within the human being. Growth, however, continues until checked by forces working from outside (see diagram). The work of the 'regular' Hierarchies and of the luciferic beings belonging to those Hierarchies. Essential changes take place in the course of time both in life on Earth and after death. 'Public opinion' and its influence. St Paul's profound esoteric knowledge exemplified in his teaching of the 'first Adam' and the 'second Adam'. Progressive dimness of the human life of soul after death until the Mystery of Golgotha, when the new impulse was given to spiritual life. The Baptism by John the Baptist and its effects. In the life of soul, human beings were under the leadership of the Third Hierarchy to a far greater extent than was the case after the Mystery of Golgotha. The power and influence of the luciferic beings have no significance in human life after death. The effect of Buddha's influence in the Mars sphere. In the future it will be characteristic of those who are to become spiritual leaders on Earth that a fundamental change takes place in their whole character when they have reached a certain age. This is the result of the Buddha's influence in the Mars sphere during their life between death and rebirth. Rosicrucianism has always recognized this.

Pages 88-104

LECTURE 8
BERLIN, 11 FEBRUARY 1913

The greatest mysteries of existence are within humans themselves. The thoughts conceived by divine and spiritual beings in the past live on in the present mineral, plant, and animal kingdoms, just as our memories continue into our present life. With our memory we grasp a tiny corner of creation, namely what has passed over from creation into existence. From the viewpoint of sleep we behold what is hidden from waking life. Results of destructive processes during waking life are repaired during sleep. Processes of destruction in the organism are the precondition of the life of soul. Experiences during the life between death and new birth. At a certain point there is a reversal of vision. Everything that was outside us in life on Earth becomes our inner world. Preparation of the body of the future earthly existence. When the soul encounters in the spiritual world that which bears a new life germinally within it, this is an experience of the moment of the last death in reverse. Vision of spiritual realities gradually lost by human souls in the course of evolution. Human beings are now beginning to be interested only in what is sub-sensory, e.g. vibrations, wavelengths, the working of forces. The mission of anthroposophy is to counter the withering of our inner spirituality.

Pages 105-118

LECTURE 9

BERLIN, 4 MARCH 1913

Spiritual investigation discloses that the supersensible forces needed by humans in order to mould their bodies and also our destiny are received by us from the beings of the Hierarchies whom we contact between death and rebirth. Rejection of spiritual ideas in earthly life means loneliness and darkness in the spiritual world after death, also inability to mould the physical organs efficiently for the next incarnation. Individuals after death are approached by luciferic or ahrimanic beings according to their attitude to spiritual knowledge whilst on Earth. The power exercised by ahrimanic beings during a soul's life after death can be recognized in characteristics of three successive incarnations. An example: egotistic mysticism in one life, hypochondria in the next, defective thinking in the third. Acting out of love rather than merely out of a sense of duty enables contact to be made after death with spiritual beings who send down to the physical world forces that promote health. Life in the spiritual world depends upon the mode of our life in the physical body on Earth. Relationship with the Buddha can be established during the life between death and rebirth, even if there had been no contact in earthly life, but this remains an exceptional case. Nothing can replace the significance of our connection with the Earth. Words of Leonardo da Vinci. Anthroposophy can bridge the gulf between the living and the dead.

LECTURE 10

BERLIN, 1 APRIL 1913

Reference to the book *Theosophy*, Chapter III on 'The Soul World', 'The Soul in the Soul World after Death', 'The Spiritland', 'The Spirit in Spiritland after Death'. These descriptions are more closely related to inner conditions of the soul, whereas in the present course of lectures the descriptions are of great cosmic conditions and the functions of the planetary spheres. Experiences of the soul after death in Kamaloka and final discarding of longings connected with earthly life. Passage through the planetary spheres. Quotation from the book *Theosophy* with special reference to experiences in the region of Mars and the mission of Buddha. At the beginning of the seventeenth century, Brahmanism was absorbed into Buddhism in the cultural life of India. Events on Earth are reflected images of happenings in the heavens. The fruits of the soul's experiences beyond the Saturn sphere between death and rebirth make progress of culture on Earth possible. The stream of spirituality which has its centre of gravity in the Mystery of Golgotha comes from Old Sun. The death on Golgotha was only seemingly a death; in reality it was the birth of the Soul of the Earth.

PUBLISHER'S NOTE

At the time Rudolf Steiner gave these lectures, he was developing his anthroposophy under the auspices of the Theosophical Society, of which he was the head of the German Section. Thus he used the words 'theosophy' and 'theosophical'. However, from the beginning these terms were used in the sense of his own research, which he referred to as anthroposophy. On account of a later statement by Rudolf Steiner, these terms in the Collected Works have generally been replaced by 'spiritual science', 'anthroposophy', or 'anthroposophical'.

Expansion of soul after death: ☽ → ☿ → ♀

→ ☉ → ♂ → ♃ → ♄
↓   ↓   ↓
solar   strengthening
impulses   of solar
(etheric   impulses. Helps avoid dimming ☿
body)   of consciousness.

p.64 "If a especially beyond the sphere of the sun it is impossible for consciousnesses to be kindled if during our life on earth we have made no attempt to raise to the level of waking consciousness the concepts lying in the depths of the soul." Knowledge of anthroposophy between birth & death becomes an illuminating torch at a certain point between death & rebirth.

MARS BARS: Strengthening the heart & forces of the soul.

p.81 Except for an extract the astral body is shed after the period of Kamaloka. These seeds are able to be further transformed between death/rebirth. But in its innermost nature the "I" remains unchanged.

p.92 Seeds of physical body from Thrones – Spirits of Will
"   " etheric   "   "   Spirits of Wisdom
"   " astral   "   "   "   " Movement
"   " "I"   "   "   "   " Form

p.102. Transf of warlike Mars traits to traits of freedom & independence.

p.103 The backward spirits are utilised to constitute the opposite pole to the spirits who have progressed to further stages.

p.110: Old Saturn – foundation of physical body
"   " Sun –   "   "   " etheric
"   " Moon – foundation of astral body
"   ○ Earth –   "   "   " "I"

Introduction

T HIS cycle of lectures raises, to my mind, two salient issues. One is very much a matter of public interest and public debate: namely, whether Rudolf Steiner was a racist and a nationalist. The other is more an internal issue for anthroposophists that seems to have been settled, but I would like to unsettle it. That is the question of the relationship between Rudolf Steiner and Freud.

Between Death and Rebirth offers abundant direct evidence bearing on the former question, but only indirect evidence bearing on the latter. Nevertheless, this is a good occasion to address both issues. Both questions deserve much fuller treatment than will be possible here: please consider what follows a down payment on more extensive studies that will be forthcoming.

Was Rudolf Steiner a Racist?

At time of writing (2021), this is undoubtedly the most burning question facing anthroposophists. Paradoxically, I see the focus on this issue as something positive. It is a chance to clarify an important question that anthroposophy has raised. It is also a sign of anthroposophy's growing prominence, that anthroposophy is beginning to enter the mainstream. The mainstream is an arena of contestation, and the first signal that one has arrived is typically that one is attacked.

I will not try to answer this question definitively; it is far too complex. Much depends on whether one views racism in relative or absolute terms. Steiner was born in 1861. Viewed absolutely, there are probably only a dozen figures in this generation, and fewer if any in earlier generations, who were *not* racist. To take a notable example, Abraham Lincoln fails to clear this bar. Then the question becomes whether one really wants to dismiss—to 'cancel'—the individual in question entirely on the basis of a few racist remarks, despite their many positive contributions. My own stance on this issue is decidedly relativist. After all, it seems more than a little arrogant to assume that effectively nobody was virtuous in this regard in the past, while we have attained the correct and final answer. What appears virtuous today will undoubtedly be seen as deficient in retrospect at some indeterminate time in the future. There is no room for supposed absolutes. But I realize that I would have to work very hard to make this case persuasive, and I will not try to accomplish that here.

What I will try to do, however, is to answer this question on the evidence provided by *Between Death and Rebirth*. And here we find ourselves in a fortunate situation. The evidence is overwhelming that Steiner was not only not a racist, but that he was arguably among the *most progressive* figures of his generation.

Relevant passages can be found throughout the cycle, but let us simply focus on Lecture Two, which offers important statements on this issue from the perspective of the life after death. Let us take three quotes, which are quite self-explanatory:

> Humanity today is still divided into groups determined by their religious tenets and views of the world. But it is through what is thereby formed in our souls that we prepare our understanding of and possibility for contacts in the sphere of Venus. Hindu, Chinese, Islamic, or Christian religions prepare the soul in such a way that in the sphere of Venus it will understand and be attracted to those individuals whose souls have been moulded by the same religious tenets. Esoteric investigation shows clearly that whereas today, humans on Earth are divided by race, descent, and so forth, and can be distinguished by these factors—although this will change in the future and has already begun to do so—in the sphere of Venus, in which we live together with other human beings, there are no such divisions.

If we are to fare well in the solar sphere between death and a new birth, it is essential to be able to understand not merely one particular group of human beings, but to understand and find points of contact with all human souls. In the solar sphere, we feel isolated, like hermits, if the prejudices of one particular faith render us incapable of understanding a human being whose soul has been filled with the principles of a different faith. An individual who on the Earth regarded only one particular religion as valuable is incapable in the solar sphere of understanding adherents of other religions.

It is therefore essential that initiation should be preceded by a thorough understanding of every religious faith spread over the Earth, and also an understanding of what is taking place in every individual soul, regardless of the creed or system of thought to which they adhere. Otherwise, whatever has not been met with understanding becomes a source of suffering, as if towering mountains were threatening to crash down upon us; as if explosions were discharging their whole force upon us. Whatever lack of understanding has been shown to human beings on Earth due to our own narrow prejudices has this effect in the spiritual worlds.

So clearly our aspirational ideal is to understand and appreciate all human beings without prejudice of any kind. Even on Earth, the division into races is becoming less and less relevant, and will disappear completely at some unspecified point in the future. Indeed, this ideal needs very much to be fulfilled, with dire consequences attending on those who fail. Here Steiner's take on race could not be more unambiguous. He was surely one of the most enlightened thinkers of his generation.

Was Rudolf Steiner a German Nationalist?

This question is far simpler, and I do not hesitate to make a definitive pronouncement. Steiner is absolutely not a German nationalist.

The case can be made very simply and effectively by scanning his major works for the word: 'deutsch'. Surely readers will agree that someone who never refers to his nationality can hardly be accused of being a nationalist. (True, Steiner was born in Austria, and ended his life in Switzerland; but throughout his entire theosophical and anthroposophical career, he was based in Germany or just across the border in Dornach, and he had identified strongly with the German faction in the 'culture wars' while residing in Austria.)

Let us begin by scanning the four 'basic books' of anthroposophy. In *The Philosophy of Freedom*, we find precisely one occurrence of the word *deutsch*, and that is in a footnote to another book—i.e. someone else's work—with that word in the title. *How to Know Higher Worlds* contains *no occurrences*. *Theosophy* contains four, but two are footnotes to other works; one is a characterization of another philosopher as 'German'; and the last refers to the German language. In the massive tome *Esoteric Science* there are five mentions: four in footnotes to other books, and one a reference to the territory millennia previous that now is occupied by Germany. That is it.

Now let us go to the other end of the spectrum, to two late projects that are inarguably central to Steiner's *oeuvre*: the six volumes of *Karmic Relationships* and the *Anthroposophical Leading Thoughts*. The project of *Karmic Relationships*, comprising no less that 82 separate lectures, contains a smattering of occurrences, all innocuous. Many are footnoted references to others' publications, and several refer to aspects of the thought of the many figures whose karma Steiner discusses. An especially interesting cluster can be found in Vol. 3, where Steiner discusses at some length the interesting case of young children who do not yet know or care about their nationality. The *Anthroposophical Leading Thoughts* show only one occurrence, and that is again in a footnote referencing someone else's work.

I think this can stand as a representative sample of Steiner's most important work. Sceptics are invited to scan Steiner's other works, as I have done. This can be accomplished relatively easily using the Russian-language website: http://bdn-steiner.ru/modules. php?name=Ga, where all books and cycles are available in the original German in pdf form. Simply scan each for 'deutsch'.

So how can this charge have ever been raised in the first place? I think that it was mounted chiefly by Peter Staudenmaier in his book of 2014.[1] In addition to publishing this substantial work with a reputable press, Staudenmaier has been quite a noisy (and much less balanced) presence on the Internet. I think it is fair to say that he has become a spokesman for opposition to Steiner.

I feel highly ambivalent about this book. (Nothing further will be said here about his various Internet exploits.) Staudenmaier's study is not chiefly about Steiner himself, but rather mostly about various other anthroposophists' relationship to fascism in the years after Steiner died in 1925. I have not yet verified all the many footnotes, but suffice it to say that this work is apparently well researched, and even if only half of what he claims is true, then these years were a very dark episode indeed for anthroposophy. Perhaps paradoxically, I view this as a great service to the anthroposophical movement, which needs to face squarely the misdeeds of many anthroposophists during these years.

Only the first section of the book, a quarter at most, is about Steiner himself. Here my response is very different. Steiner is characterized in a way that must be fundamentally rejected. Staudenmaier charges Steiner with having been a German nationalist. Yet nowhere is Steiner quoted to that effect; instead, Staudenmaier quotes various anthroposophists who claimed that Steiner was the 'savior of the German nation' and so forth. That anthroposophists viewed Steiner in this way was highly unfortunate, but it was also clearly an inaccurate assessment of Steiner's contributions.

Staudenmaier states, for example, on p. 20: 'The mature Steiner looked askance at what he termed "national chauvinism," but his viewpoint was itself embedded in a series of nationalist assumptions about the spiritual mission of Germany'. This passage is marked with a footnote that cites a reference for the positive half of the assessment, but Staudenmaier cites no reference for the negative half. Chapter One, entitled 'Germany's Savior,' Rudolf Steiner on Race and Redemption', begins by arguing that 'At the height of his public renown in the early 1920s, Rudolf Steiner's followers referred to him as "Germany's Savior," confident that future generations would one day view the founder of anthroposophy with awe'. Or later in the same chapter: 'Steiner's apotheosis as "Germany's Savior" and his transition to a messianic figure in the eyes of his followers crested in the chaotic aftermath of World War One' [30].

And on page 36: 'This is the intellectual backdrop against which his later anthroposophical followers cast him as Germany's would-be Savior'.

One wonders whether this seeming sleight-of-hand could be anything less than deliberate. Is it possible for Staudenmaier actually to have read Steiner dispassionately and to have arrived at this conclusion? The result seems to be an act of academic mischief, and I am surprised that his book passed peer review.

Ships in the Night

There are numerous strikingly Freudian passages throughout this cycle of lectures, but it should suffice to quote solely from Lecture Three:

> Let us think of two friends living on Earth, one of whom comes into contact with anthroposophy at a certain time and becomes an anthroposophist. It may happen that because of this, the friend rages against anthroposophy. You may have known such a case. If the friend had been the first to find anthroposophy, they might themselves have become a very good adherent! Such things certainly happen, but we must realize that they are very often clothed in maya. Consequently it may happen that the one who rages against anthroposophy because the friend has become an adherent is raging in their surface consciousness only, in their ego-consciousness. In their astral consciousness, in their sub-consciousness, they may very likely not share in the antipathy. Without realising it, they may even be longing for anthroposophy. In many cases it happens that aversion in the upper consciousness takes the form of longing in the sub-consciousness. It does not necessarily follow that an individual feels exactly what they express in their upper consciousness.
>
> Impressions are also produced in our soul, either of sympathy or antipathy. Even trifling reflection can teach us that we are living as it were on the surface of the sea without the faintest idea of what is down below on the seabed. As we pass through life, we get to know external reality only.
>
> If you were to observe your dream-life more closely, or the strange moments of transition from waking life to sleep or from sleep to waking

life, if you were to observe with greater exactitude certain dreams which are often quite inexplicable, in which certain things that happen to you appear in a dream-picture or vision, you would find that these inexplicable pictures indicate something that might have happened and was prevented only because other conditions, or hindrances, intervened. A person who through meditation or some other means makes their thinking more mobile, will have moments in their waking life during which they will feel that they are living in a world of possibilities; this may not be in the form of definite ideas, but of feelings.

In many places throughout his lectures, Steiner dismisses Freud, sometimes brusquely. Yet without mentioning Freud, he often argues in a surprisingly Freudian vein, as here. Thus I would suggest that the negative assessment of Freud upon which anthroposophists have generally settled needs very much to be re-evaluated. It may be that Steiner misunderstood how close to Freud he actually was. Let us put the two men side-by-side.

Freud and Steiner were of course rough contemporaries. (Freud was five years older.) Both were residents of Vienna. Most importantly, each sought to raise the unconscious to consciousness, expanding the notion of science as such. But the parallels run even deeper.

Both Freud and Steiner went out of their way to attend lectures by Franz Brentano at the University of Vienna, and both admired Brentano intensely. Freud attended no less than five courses of lectures by Brentano. When Brentano died in 1917, Steiner would write a lengthy obituary in which he claimed that Brentano's philosophy had been close to anthroposophy in many regards.

Moreover, the private circles in which Steiner was moving overlapped with Freud's professional circles. From 1876 until 1882, Freud worked in von Brücke's laboratory together with Josef Breuer. In 1885, Freud took advantage of an extraordinary scholarship he had won to study with Charcot in Paris for five months. On returning to Vienna, he developed a great interest in Breuer's 'talking cure', and Breuer generously shared his patients with Freud while Freud devoted many years to laboriously building up his own practice. In 1887, Freud displayed his great affection for Breuer's wife, Mathilde, by naming his first child after her. Eventually, Freud co-authored with Breuer his first book, *Studies on Hysteria*, in 1895, which included the famous case study on Anna O.

Meanwhile, Steiner was moving in Jewish circles in Vienna. He lived from 1884 to 1890 with the family of Ladislaus and Pauline Specht, who were prominent Jews, and he felt especially close to the wife. Steiner assumed care of their severely challenged son, and worked a minor miracle by bringing the boy, who was considered uneducable, to the point at which he graduated from *Gymnasium*, and eventually became a doctor. (The lessons Steiner learned from this episode would prove invaluable later, when he developed Waldorf pedagogy.)

Pauline Specht had known Josef Breuer all her life, and she took Steiner along many times to the Breuer's salon. We know that Freud attended the salon as well. So Freud and Steiner surely must have met, and they were both so obviously brilliant that they cannot simply have ignored one another. Moreover, Steiner's success in treating the younger Specht would surely have interested Freud very much, given that he was also exploring alternative modes of healing pathological conditions. Strangely, however, I have been able to find no record of any such encounter! This is a very great puzzle. As early as 1891, Freud's relationship with Breuer began to change, and by 1894, scientific contacts with Breuer had ceased. Eventually, there was an irrevocable split between Freud and Breuer, undoubtedly caused by Breuer's unwillingness to go along with Freud in ascribing to sexuality a major role in explaining various behaviours. And indeed, Steiner often echoes Breuer in his later discussions of psychoanalysis. But this cannot have been the reason for Freud and Steiner failing to meet: Steiner left Vienna for Weimar in 1890.

Steiner and Freud seem to have passed one another like ships in the night. But I would contend that they were natural allies, who each had a great deal to learn from the other. The standard line of interpretation is that Freud never abandoned his training, which had been thoroughly materialistic, and that he was notoriously adverse to occultism.[2] There is some truth to this: perhaps it was because science seemed to Freud antithetical to spirituality in all its forms; he simply could not imagine what Steiner would go on to develop as 'spiritual science'. But his early and enthusiastic reception of Charcot, who was the antithesis of a materialist in every regard, should already have led scholars to be highly sceptical of this one-sided interpretation. Steiner could have helped Freud to rid himself of scepticism in esoteric matters once and for all. More specifically, he could have steered Freud from the relatively limited perspective of a *personal* unconscious to recognize the existence of a macrocosmic unconscious—what one might call 'the unconscious of nature'. Which is to say, the spirit.

For his part, Freud could have brought at least three things to the table. First, although of course Freud was not Steiner's equal as a clairvoyant, he was very much Steiner's equal in the penetration and rigour of his thinking. It is easy to imagine Steiner and Freud bringing out the very best in each other. Secondly, Freud had an enormous stylistic gift generally, and a gift for popularization in particular. After all, Freud won the prestigious Goethe Prize, and he was a finalist for the Nobel Prize *in literature*. He is widely considered one of the finest German prose stylists. With all due respect, this was not Steiner's strong suit. Finally, because Steiner eventually had to collaborate with the theosophists after trying a number of different avenues, his spiritual psychology was framed in the alien discourse of theosophy, which made it nigh impossible to build bridges to the nascent field of psychology. Freud could have given him a much more suitable vocabulary.

I have quoted Lecture Three as an example of ways in which Steiner was close to Freud. We can also quote many passages from Freud that are surprisingly close to Steiner. Chapter 7 of *The Interpretation of Dreams* contains numerous instances where Freud repeatedly gropes his way right to the threshold of anthroposophy.

The first is the concept of 'unconscious purposive ideas'. Like Steiner, Freud declares that the conscious, rational part of our thinking is only the tip of the iceberg. More importantly, thinking is shown to be anything but brain-bound. Rather, it expands beyond the conscious self into a realm that is only apparently indeterminate. In fact, unconscious ideas are always *purposive*:

> For it is demonstrably wrong to say that we are being borne along an aimless flow of ideas when we relax our reflectiveness and let the involuntary ideas come to the surface, as we do when we are interpreting dreams. It can be shown that the only purposive ideas we are able to relinquish are the ones known to us, and the moment they cease, unknown—or, as we would loosely say, unconscious—purposive ideas take over and then determine the course taken by the involuntary ideas. There is no way that our own influence on the life of our psyche can bring about a kind of thinking without purposive ideas, nor am I acquainted with any state of psychical disorder that might do so. In this respect the psychiatrists have dispensed with the stability of the psyche's interconnected structure much too soon. [343-344]

In another extraordinary passage, Freud attempts to locate the psyche *apart from anatomical considerations*, which is to say: spiritually, not materially. He compares the psyche to a compound microscope or telescope:

> The idea it puts at our disposal is that of *location in the psyche*. Let us put aside into the fact that the psychical apparatus we are dealing with here is also familiar to us an anatomical specimen; and let us take care to avoid being tempted to define the psychical location in broadly anatomical terms. We shall remain on psychological terrain, bearing in mind only to follow the requirement that we should think of the instrument serving the functions of the psyche as acting like a compound microscope, say, or a photographic apparatus. The psychical location then corresponds to a place within this apparatus where one of the preliminary stages of the image comes about. In the microscope and telescope, as we know these are partly hypothetical locations, places where no tangible component of the apparatus is sited. [349]

Moreover, Freud achieves an astonishing insight into the relationship between dreams and what Steiner calls 'atavistic clairvoyance'.

They are a remnant of an older form of consciousness, to which we regress during the night:

> The dream, which fulfills its wishes along short, regressive paths, has preserved for us a mere sample of the psychical apparatus's *primary*—discarded—way of functioning, discarded, that is, as inexpedient. It seems banished to the night, that once governed our waking, when the life of the psyche was still young and helpless, rather as we find the primitive adult weapons, the bow and arrow, which the human race has laid aside, in the nursery still. *Dreaming is a part of the—surmounted—childhood life of the psyche.* [370]

There are a vast number of passages in Freud and Steiner that could be juxtaposed. Perhaps this brief treatment is enough to reopen the question of Freud's and Steiner's close relationship.

*

Freud eventually became famous, but that fame brought a host of annoyances. One was that Freud was constantly being asked by reporters for a one-sentence explanation of psychoanalysis. Finally, he came up with: '*Es soll Ich werden*'; 'Id shall become ego'—i.e., the unconscious shall become conscious. Would this not stand as a suitable short characterization of anthroposophy as well?

Frederick Amrine
July 2021

p. 46 The ego consciousness & astral body belong to the same cosmic sphere to which the sun belongs & not to the earth at all.

Ibid. The human ego & astral body have made themselves independent of the forces in space, and they go their own way.

Spiritual Hierarchies

1 Thrones
2 Cherubim } 1st hierarchy   Spirits of Will
3 Seraphim

4 Exousiai
5 Dynameis } 2nd hierarchy   Spirits of Form
6 Kyrioteten   Spirits of Movement
                             Spirits of Wisdom

7 Angeloi / Principalities
8 Archangels   } 3rd hierarchy
9 Angels

P.131 } Mediating to disincarnate souls.
P.133 }

P. 92   Thrones (will) → Physical body – Saturn
        Spirits of Wisdom (2nd hierarchy) → etheric
                              body – Sun
        Spirits of Movement → astral body – Moon
        Spirits of form – "||" body – Earth

p. 140 Mars is the 1st region of Devachan.

LECTURE 1

BERLIN, 5 NOVEMBER 1912

I AM very glad to be able to speak here again after a comparatively long absence. Those of you who were present at our meeting in Munich earlier this year[3] or have heard something about my *Mystery Play*,[4] *The Guardian of the Threshold*, will have realized what the attitude of the soul must be if an adequate conception is to be acquired of the content of anthroposophy or, let us say, of esotericism.

Various things have been said previously about the luciferic and ahrimanic beings.[5] The aim of *The Guardian of the Threshold* was to show that the essential nature of these beings could be revealed only by studying them very gradually and from many different aspects. It is not enough to form a simple concept or give an ordinary definition of these beings—popular as such definitions are. My purpose was to show from as many different sides as possible the part played by these beings in human lives. The play will also have helped you to realize that there must be complete truthfulness and deep seriousness when speaking of the spiritual worlds. This, after all, has been the keynote of the lectures I have given here. It must be emphasized all the more strongly at the present time because there is so little recognition of the seriousness and value of genuine anthroposophical endeavours. If there is one thing that I have tried to emphasize in the lectures given over the years, it is that you should embark upon all your anthroposophical efforts in this spirit of truthfulness and earnestness, and become thoroughly conscious of their significance in cosmic existence as a whole, in the evolutionary process of humanity, and in the spiritual content of our present age. It cannot be emphasized too often that the essence of anthroposophy cannot be grasped with the help of a few simple concepts or a theory briefly propounded, let alone a programme. The forces of the entire soul must be involved. But life itself is a process of becoming, of development. Someone might argue that we can hardly be expected to ally ourselves with the anthroposophical movement if we are immediately faced with a demand for self-development and told that we can only hope to penetrate slowly and gradually to the essence of anthroposophy. We might ask how we can decide to join something for which we can prepare only slowly? The rejoinder to this would be that before humans can climb to the highest summit of development, we already have in our heart and in our soul the sense of truth which has led us as a whole to strive for such development, and we need only devote ourselves open-mindedly to the sense of the truth, with the will for truth that lies in the depths of our souls unless prejudices have led us astray. We must avoid empty theories and high-sounding programmes. We are able to sense truth where it genuinely exists. Honest criticism is therefore always possible, even if someone is only at the very beginning of the path of attainment. This, however, does not preclude us from attributing supreme importance to anthroposophical endeavour.

In our present age there are many influences which divert us from the natural feeling for truth that is present in our souls. Over the years it has often been possible to indicate these misleading influences and I need not do it again today. My purpose is to emphasize how necessary it is—even if there is already some knowledge of anthroposophy—to approach and study things again and again from constantly new sides. One example of what I mean is our study of the four Gospels. This autumn I brought these studies to a conclusion with a course of lectures on the Gospel of St Mark.[6] These studies of the four Gospels may be taken as a prime example of the way in which the great truths of existence must be approached from different sides. Each Gospel affords an opportunity to view the Mystery of Golgotha[7] from a different angle, and indeed we cannot begin really to know anything essential about this Mystery until we have studied it from the four different viewpoints presented in the four Gospels.

In what way have our studies over the last ten or twelve years demonstrated this? Those of you who want to be clear about this need only turn to my book *Christianity as Mystical Fact*,[8] the content of which was first given in the form of lectures, before the German Section of the Theosophical Society was founded [in 1902]. Anyone who studies this book seriously will find that it already contained the gist of what I have since said over the course of years about the Mystery of Golgotha and the four Gospels. Nothing, however, would be more unjustified than to believe that by knowing the contents of that book you would *ipso facto* have an adequate understanding of the Mystery of Golgotha. All the lectures given since the book appeared have been the necessary and natural outcome of that original spiritual study; nowhere are they at variance with what has developed from the embryo of *Christianity as a Mystical Fact*. It has furthermore been possible to open up new ways for contemplating the Mystery of Golgotha, thus enabling us to penetrate more and more deeply into its significance. The attempt has been made to substitute direct, vital participation in the spiritual facts for concepts, theories, and abstract speculations. And if, in spite of it all, a feeling of a certain lack still exists—namely, that one cannot always give everything necessary—this lack is due to something that is inevitable on the physical plane, namely, the time factor. It is just not possible always to give something at a specific time. Hence I have always presumed of your soul [*Gemüt*][9] that you would have patience and wait for matters to develop gradually. This is also an indication of how what I have to say to you during this coming winter should be understood.

In the course of years we have spoken a great deal of the life between death and a new birth. The same subject will, however, be dealt with in the forthcoming lectures,[10] the reason being that during this last summer and autumn it has been my task to undertake further spiritual research into this realm and to present an aspect of the subject which could not previously be dealt with. Only now is it possible to consider certain matters which bring home the profound moral significance of the supra-sensible truths pertaining to this realm. In addition to all other demands to which only very brief reference has been made, there is one which in this vain and arrogant age is a cause of offence to numbers of individuals. But we must not allow this to deter us from the earnestness and respect for truth that are due to our movement. The demand will continue to be made that by dint of earnest, intimate efforts we shall learn to be receptive to knowledge brought from the spiritual world.

For some years now the relationship of human beings living on the physical plane to the spiritual worlds has changed from what it was through almost the whole of the nineteenth century. Until the last third of that century, we had little access to the spiritual worlds; it was necessary for evolution that only a little of the content of those worlds should flow into the human soul. But now we are living in an age when the soul needs only to be receptive and duly prepared, and then revelations from the spiritual worlds will be able to flow into it. Individual souls will become more and more receptive and, being aware of their task in the present age, they will find this inflow of spiritual knowledge to be a reality. Hence the further demand is made that anthroposophists shall not turn deaf ears to what can make its way into the soul today from the spiritual worlds. Before entering into the main theme of these lectures, I want to speak of two characteristics of the spiritual life to which special attention must be paid.

Between death and a new birth, humans experience the realities of the spiritual world in a very definite way. But we also experience these realities through initiation; we experience them too if our soul is prepared during our life in the physical body in a way that enables us to participate in the spiritual worlds. We have often spoken about such matters. Hence it is true to say that what takes place between death and the new birth—which is, in fact, existence in the spiritual world—can be revealed through initiation.

Attention must be paid to two points which emerge from what has often been said here; they are essential not only to experience of the spiritual worlds, but also to the right understanding of communications received from these worlds. The difference between conditions in the spiritual world and the physical world has often been emphasized, and also the fact that when the soul enters the spiritual world, it finds itself in a sphere in which it is essential to become accustomed to a great deal that is the exact opposite of conditions in the physical world. Here is one example. If, on the physical plane, something is to be brought about by us, we have to be active, to use our hands, to move our physical body from one place to another. Activity on our part is necessary if we are to bring about something in the physical world. In the spiritual worlds, exactly the opposite holds good. I am speaking always of the present epoch. If something is to happen through us in the spiritual worlds, however, it must be achieved through inner calm, inner tranquility; in the spiritual worlds the capacity to await events with tranquility corresponds to busy activity on the physical plane. The less we bestir ourselves on the physical plane, the less we can bring about; the more active we are, the more can happen. In the spiritual world, on the other hand, the calmer our soul can become, the more all inner restlessness can be avoided, the more we shall be able to achieve. It is therefore essential to regard whatever comes to pass as something bestowed upon us by grace, something that comes to us as a blessing because we have deserved it as the fruit of inner tranquility. Let me give you an example.

I have often said that anyone possessed of spiritual knowledge is aware that 1899 was a very significant year; it was the end of a period of 5,000 years in human history, the so-called Lesser Kali Yuga.[11] Since that year it has become necessary to allow the spiritual to come to us in a way differing from what was previously usual. I will give you a concrete example. In the early twelfth century, a man named *Norbert*[12] founded a religious order in the West. Before the idea of founding the order came to him, Norbert was a loose-living man, full of sensuality and worldly impulses. One day something very unusual happened to him: he was struck by lightning. This did not prove fatal, but his whole being was transformed. There are many such examples in history. The inner connection between Norbert's physical body, etheric body, astral body, and ego was changed by the force contained in the lightning. It was then that he founded his Order, and although, as in so many other cases, it failed to fulfil the aims of its founder, in many respects it did good at the time. Such 'chance' events, as they are called nowadays, have been numerous. But this was not a chance happening; it was an event of cosmic karma. The man was chosen to perform a task of special importance and to make this possible, particular bodily conditions had to be created. An outer event, an external influence, was necessary.

Since the year 1899, such influences on our souls have to be purely inner influences, not exerted from outside. Not that there was an abrupt transition; but since the year 1899, influences exerted on human souls must more and more take effect inwardly. You may remember what I once said about Christian Rosenkreutz[13]—that when he wishes to call a human soul to himself, it is a more inward call. Before 1899, such calls were made by means of outer events; since that year they have become more inward. Intercourse between human souls and the higher Hierarchies[14] will become more and more dependent upon inner exertions, and we will have to apply the deepest, most intimate forces of our souls in order to maintain this intercourse with the entities of the Hierarchies.

What I have just described to you as an incisive point in life on the physical plane has its counterpart in the spiritual world—visibly for one who is a seer—in much that has taken place between the beings of the higher Hierarchies. At this time in particular there were certain tasks which it was incumbent upon the beings of the Hierarchies to carry out among themselves, but one particular condition must be noted. The beings whose task in the spiritual worlds was to bring about the ending of Kali Yuga needed something from our Earth, something taking place on our Earth. It was necessary that certain souls who are sufficiently mature should be knowledgeable about this change, or at least that such souls should be able to envisage[15] it. For just as on the physical plane we need a brain in order to develop consciousness, so do the beings of the Hierarchies need human thoughts wherein their deeds are reflected. Thus our world is also necessary for the spiritual world; it co-operates with the spiritual world and is an essential factor—but it must co-operate in the right way. Those who were ready previously or are ready now to participate in this activity from the human side, would not have been right then, nor would they be right now, to agitate in the way that is customary on the physical plane for the furtherance of something that is to take place in the spiritual world. We do not help the spirits of the higher Hierarchies by busy activity on the physical plane, but primarily by having some measure of understanding of what is to happen; then, in restfulness and concentration of soul, we should await a revelation of the spiritual world. What we can contribute is the inner quietude we can achieve, the attitude of soul we can induce in ourselves to await this bestowal of grace.

Thus, paradoxical as it may seem, our activity in the higher worlds depends upon our own inner tranquility; the calmer we can become, the more will the facts of the spiritual world be able to come to expression through us. Hence it is also necessary, if we are to participate effectively in a spiritual movement, to be able to develop this mood of tranquility. And in the anthroposophical movement, it would be especially desirable for its adherents to endeavour to achieve this inner tranquility, this consciousness of grace in their attitude to the spiritual world.

Among the various activities in which we are engaged on the physical plane it is really only in the domain of artistic creation, or where there is a genuine striving for knowledge or for the advancement of a spiritual movement, that these conditions hold good. Artists will assuredly not create the best work of which their gifts are capable if they are perpetually active and impatient to make progress. They will produce their best work if they can wait for the moment when grace is vouchsafed to them and if they can abstain from activity when the spirit is not speaking. And those who attempt to formulate it out of concepts already familiar to them will quite certainly attain no higher knowledge. Higher knowledge can be attained only by those who are able to wait quietly, with complete resignation, when confronted by a problem or riddle of existence, and who say to themselves: I must wait until the answer comes to me like a flash of light from the spiritual worlds. Again, those who rush from one person to another, trying to convince them that some particular spiritual movement is the only genuine one, will certainly not be setting about this in the right way; they should wait until those souls they approach have recognized the urge in themselves to seek the truths of the spiritual world. That is how we should respond to any illumination shining down into our physical world; but it is particularly true of everything that we can ourselves bring about in the spiritual world. It may truly be said that even the most practical accomplishments in that realm depend upon the establishment of a certain state of tranquility.

Now I want to speak about so-called psychic or spiritual healing. Here again it is not the movements or manipulations carried out by the healer that are of prime importance; they are necessary, but only as preparation. The aim is to establish a condition of rest, of balance. Whatever is outwardly visible in a case of spiritual healing is only the preparation for what the healer is trying to do; it is the final result that is of importance. In such a case the situation is like weighing something on a pair of scales: first, we put in the one scale what we want to weigh; in the other scale we put a weight and this sets the beam moving to right and left. But it is only when equilibrium has been established that we can read the weight. Something similar is true of actions in the spiritual worlds.

In respect of knowledge, of perception, however, there is a difference. How does perception come about in everyday life on the physical plane? Everyone is aware that with the exception of certain spheres of the physical plane, objects present themselves to us from morning until evening during the waking life of day; from minute to minute new impressions are made upon us. It is only in exceptional circumstances that we, on our side, seek for impressions and do with objects what otherwise they do to us. This, however, is already near to being a searcher for knowledge. Spiritual knowledge is a different matter. *We ourselves* must set before our soul whatever is to be presented to it. Whereas we must be absolutely *quiescent* if anything is to come about, to happen through us in the spiritual world, we must be uninterruptedly *active* if we really desire to understand something in the spiritual world. Connected with this is the fact that many people who would like to be anthroposophists find that the knowledge we are trying to promote here is too baffling for them. Many of them complain: in anthroposophy one has to be always learning, always pondering, always busy! But without such efforts it is not possible to acquire any understanding of the spiritual worlds. The soul must make strenuous efforts and contemplate everything from many sides. Mental pictures[16] and concepts of the higher worlds must be developed through steady, tranquil work. In the physical world, if we want to have, say, a table, we must acquire it by active effort. But in the spiritual world, if we want to acquire something, we must develop the necessary tranquility. If anything is to happen, it emerges from the twilight. But when it is a matter of knowing something, we must exert every possible effort to create the necessary Inspirations. If we are to 'know' something, effort is essential; the soul must be inwardly active, move from one Imagination to another, one Inspiration to another, one Intuition to another. We must create the whole structure; nothing will come to us that we have not ourselves produced in our search for knowledge. Thus conditions in the spiritual world are exactly the opposite of what holds good in the physical world.

I have had to give this introduction in order that we may agree together, firstly, as to how certain facts are discovered, but secondly, how they can be understood as more is said of them. In these lectures I shall deal less with the life immediately following death—known to us under the name of Kamaloka[17]—the essential aspects of which are already familiar to you. We shall be more concerned to study from somewhat new points of view those periods in the life after death which follow the period of Kamaloka.

First of all it is important to describe the general character of that life. The first stage of higher knowledge is what may be called the 'Imaginative' life, or life filled with true, genuine visions. Just as in physical life we are surrounded by the world of colours, sounds, scents, tastes, and representations which we form for ourselves by means of our intellect, so in the spiritual world we are surrounded by 'Imaginations'—which can also be called 'visions'. But we must realize that these Imaginations or visions, when they are true in the spiritual sense, are not the imagery of dreams, but realities. Let us take a definite case.

When humans have passed through the portal of death, they come into contact with those who died before them, and with whom

Just as Jung saw in his NDE

they were connected in some way during life. During the period between death and a new birth we are actually together with those who belong to us. Just as in the physical world we become aware of objects by seeing their colours, hearing their sounds and so on, in the same way we are surrounded after death, figuratively speaking, by a cloud of visions. Everything around us is vision; we ourselves are visions in that world, just as here on Earth we are flesh and bone. But this vision is not a dream; we know that it is reality. When we encounter someone who is dead and with whom we previously had some connection, he too is 'vision'; he is enveloped in a cloud of visions. But just as on the physical plane we know that the colour 'red' comes, let us say, from a red rose, on the spiritual plane we know that the 'vision' comes from the spiritual being of someone who passed through the portal of death before us. But here I must draw your attention to a particular aspect, especially as it is experienced by everyone who is living through this period after death. Here on the physical plane it may, for example, be the case that at least as far as we can judge, we ought to have loved some individual but have loved him too little; we have, in fact, deprived him of love or have hurt him in some way. In such circumstances, if we are not stony-hearted, the idea may occur to us that we must make reparation. When this idea comes to us it is possible to compensate for what has happened. On the physical plane, we can modify the previously existing relationship, but during the period immediately following Kamaloka, we cannot. From the very nature of the encounter we may well be aware that we have hurt the person in some way or deprived that person of the love we ought to have shown; we may also wish to make reparation, but we cannot. During this period all we can do is to continue the relationship which existed between us before death. We perceive what was amiss, but for the time being we can do nothing to make amends. In this world of visions which envelops us like a cloud, we cannot alter anything. We look at it, but we cannot change anything. The relationship we had with an individual who died before us remains, and we continue to live it out. This is often one of the more painful experiences also associated with initiation. Persons experience much more deeply the significance of their relation to the physical plane than they were able to do with their eyes or their intellect, but for all that they cannot directly change anything. This, in fact, constitutes the pain and martyrdom of spiritual knowledge, in so far as it is self-knowledge and relates to our own life. And so it is also after death. After death, relationships between individuals remain and continue as they were during earthly life.

When recently this fact presented itself to my spiritual sight with tremendous force, something further occurred to me. During my life I have devoted a great deal of study to the works of Homer[18] and have tried to understand many things contained in these ancient epics. On this particular occasion I was reminded of a certain passage. Homer, by the way, was called by the Greeks the 'blind' Homer, thus indicating his spiritual seership. In speaking of the realm through which we journey after death, Homer calls it the 'realm of the shades in which no change is possible'. Here once again I realized anew that we can rightly understand much that is contained in the great masterpieces and revelations of humanity only by drawing upon the very depths of spiritual knowledge. Much of what will lead to an understanding of humanity as a whole must depend upon a new recognition of those great ancestors whose souls were radiant with spiritual light. Any sensitive soul will be moved by the recognition that this ancient seer was able to write as he did only because the truth of the spiritual world shone into his soul! Here begins the true reverence for the divine and spiritual forces which stream through the world, and especially through our hearts and souls. This attitude makes it possible to realize how the progress and development of the world are furthered. A very great deal that is true in the deepest sense is contained in the works of those whose gifts were on a level with those of Homer. This truth, which was once directly revealed to an ancient, dreamlike clairvoyance, has now been lost and must be regained on the path leading to spiritual knowledge.

In order to substantiate still further this example of what has been bestowed upon humanity by creative genius, I will now speak of something else as well. There was a certain truth which I strongly resisted when it first dawned upon me, which seemed to me to be paradoxical, but which I was eventually bound to recognize through inner necessity. Thus I should speak of what happened.

The spiritual investigation on which I was engaged at that time was also connected with the study of certain works of art. I had to contemplate these works of art. Among them was one which I had previously seen and studied, although a particular aspect of it had not struck me before. I am speaking now of the Medici tombs in the chapel designed and built in Florence by Michelangelo.[19] Two members of the Medici family, of whom no more need be said at present, were to be immortalized in statues. But Michelangelo added four so-called 'allegorical' figures, named at his suggestion, 'Dawn' and 'Dusk' [see Plate 1], 'Day' and 'Night' [see Plate 2]. 'Day' and 'Night' were placed at the foot of one statue; 'Dawn' and 'Dusk' at the foot of the other. Even if you have no particularly good reproductions of these allegorical figures, you will easily be able to verify what I have to say about them.

We will begin with 'Night', the most famous of the four. In guidebooks you can read that the postures of the limbs in the recumbent figure of 'Night' are unnatural, that no human being could sleep in that position; and therefore the figure cannot be a good symbolic presentation of 'Night'. But now let me say something else. Suppose we are looking at the allegorical figure of 'Night' with clairvoyant vision. We can then say to ourselves: When we are asleep, our ego and astral body have left the physical and etheric bodies.[20] It is conceivable that someone might visualize a particular posture which most accurately portrays that of the etheric body when the astral body and ego have withdrawn. As we go about during the day, our gestures and movements are conditioned by the fact that the astral body and ego are within the physical and etheric bodies. But at night the astral body and ego are outside, and the etheric body alone is in the physical body. The etheric body then unfolds its own activity and mobility, and thus adopts a certain gesture. The impression may well be that there is no more fitting portrayal of the free reign of the etheric body than that achieved by Michelangelo in this figure of 'Night'. In point of fact, the movement is conveyed with such precision that no more appropriate presentation of the etheric body under such circumstances can be imagined.

Now let us turn to the figure of 'Day'. Then we can say the following. Suppose we could induce in humans a condition in which their astral and etheric bodies were as quiescent as possible and the ego especially active. No posture could be more fitting for the activity of the ego than that portrayed by Michelangelo in the figure of 'Day'. The postures are not allegorical but drawn directly and realistically from life. The artist has succeeded in capturing, as it were, for earthly eternity the postures which in the evolutionary process most aptly express the activity of the ego and the activity of the etheric body.

We come now to the other figures. First let us take that of 'Dusk'. If we think of how, in a healthily developed human being, the etheric body emerges and the physical body relaxes—as also happens when death overtakes us—but if we think, not of actual death but of the emergence of the etheric body, the astral body, and the ego from the

1. Medici Chapel, 'Dusk' [left] and 'Dawn' [right]

2. Medici Chapel, 'Night and Day'

human physical body, we shall find that the posture then assumed by the physical body is accurately portrayed in the figure of 'Dusk'. Again, if we think of the inner activity of the astral body while there is diminished activity of the etheric body and ego, we shall find the most precise representation in Michelangelo's figure of 'Dawn'. So on the one side we have the portrayals of the activity of the etheric body and of the ego (in the figures of 'Night' and 'Day') and on the other side the portrayals of the physical and astral bodies (in the figures of 'Dusk' and 'Dawn').

As already said, at first I resisted this conclusion, but the more carefully I investigated, the more I was compelled to accept it. What I wanted to indicate here is how the artist is inspired by the spiritual world. Admittedly, in the case of Michelangelo the process was more or less unconscious, but in spite of that his creations could only have been produced by the radiance of the spiritual world shining into the physical! Esotericism does not lead to the destruction of works of art, but, on the contrary, to a much deeper understanding of them. As a result. a great deal of what passes for art today will in the future no longer do so. A number of people may be disappointed, but truth will gain. I could well understand the foundation of the legend that has grown up in connection with the most elaborate of these figures. The legend is that when Michelangelo was alone with the figure of 'Night' in the Medici Chapel in Florence, he could make the figure rise up and walk! I will not go further into this, but when we know that this figure gives expression to the 'life-body', the significance of the legend is obvious.

The same applies in many cases—in that of Homer, for instance. Homer speaks of the spiritual realm, a realm of the shades in which there can be no change or alteration. But when we study the conditions prevailing in the period of life following Kamaloka, we begin to have a new understanding of works of a divinely blessed man such as Homer. And a great deal will be similarly enriched through anthroposophy.

Useful as it may be to indicate these things, they are not of prime importance in actual life. Of prime importance is the fact that mutual relationships are continually being formed between one human and another. One individual's attitude towards another will be very different if he detects a spiritual quality in the other, or thinks of human beings as pictured by a materialistic view of life. The sacred riddle that every human being should be to us can only be sacred to our feelings and perceptions when we have something within our own soul that is able to throw spiritual light upon the other soul. By deepening our contemplation of cosmic secrets—with which the secrets of human existence are connected—we shall learn to understand the nature of the person standing before us; we shall learn to silence our preconceptions and to feel and recognize the true qualities of the individual in question. The most important light that anthroposophy can give will be the light it throws upon the human soul. Thereby sound social feelings, also those feelings of love which ought to prevail between us, will make their way into the world as a fruit of true spiritual knowledge. We shall recognize that our grasp of spiritual knowledge alone can help this fruit to grow and thrive. When Schopenhauer[21] said: 'To preach morality is easy; to establish morality is difficult', he was giving expression to true insight. After all, it is not so very difficult to discover moral principles, neither is it difficult to preach morality. But to quicken the human soul at the point where spiritual knowledge can germinate and develop into true morality capable of sustaining life—that is what matters. Our attitude to spiritual knowledge can also establish within us the seeds of a truly human morality of the future. The morality of the future will either be built on the foundations of spiritual knowledge—or it will not be built at all!

Love of truth requires that we acknowledge these things; it requires us to deepen our anthroposophical life; and above all to bear in mind what has been said today as an introductory fact, namely, that whereas *knowledge* demands *activity*, *action* in the spiritual world demands of us inner *tranquility*, in order that we may prove worthy of grace. You will now be able to understand that during the period between death and a new birth, when we are confronting another being, we can realize through the activity we then unfold whether we have deprived them of love or done anything to them that we ought not to have done. But, as I have said, during this period we cannot induce the tranquility of soul that is necessary if the wrong is to be righted. In the lectures this winter I shall be describing the period during which it is actually possible in the natural course of the life between death and a new birth to establish conditions in which change can be made possible—in other words, when a person's karma can be influenced in a certain way. We must, however, carefully distinguish between the point of time we have just been considering and the later period between death and a new birth when the tasks are different.

It remains to be said that there are certain conditions which will enable a human being to live through his existence after death in a favourable or an unfavourable way. It will be found that the mode of existence of two or more human beings after the period immediately following their life in Kamaloka depends largely upon their moral disposition on Earth. Humans who displayed good moral qualities on Earth will enjoy favourable conditions during the period immediately following Kamaloka; those who displayed defective morality will experience bad conditions.

I would like to sum up what I have been saying about the life after death in a kind of formula, although, since our language has been coined for the physical world and not for the spiritual world, it cannot be precise. One can only try to make it as exact as possible. If, then, there has been a good moral quality in our soul, we shall become 'sociable' spirits and enjoy companionship with other spirits, with other human beings or with spirits of the higher Hierarchies. The opposite is the case if a genuine moral quality has been lacking in us; we then become solitary spirits, spirits who find it extremely difficult to move away from the clouds of their visions. To feel thus isolated as a spiritual hermit is an essential cause of suffering after death. On the other hand it is characteristic of the companionship of which I have spoken, to be able to establish the connection with what is necessary for us. It takes a long time after death to live through this sphere, which in esotericism is called the sphere of Mercury.

The moral tone of the soul is naturally still decisive in the next sphere, the sphere of Venus; but new conditions then begin. In this sphere it is the religious disposition of the soul that is decisive. Individuals with a religious inner life will become sociable beings in the sphere of Venus, quite irrespective of the creed to which they belonged. On the other hand, individuals without any religious feelings are condemned in this sphere to complete spiritual self-absorption. Paradoxical though it may seem, I can only say that individuals with predominantly materialistic views and who scorn religious life, inevitably become spiritual hermits, each one living, as it were, confined in their own cell. Far from being an ironical comparison, it is true to say: all those who are supporters of 'monistic religion'[22]— that is to say, the opposite of true religion—will find themselves firmly imprisoned and be quite unable to find one another.

In this way, the mistakes and errors committed by the soul in earthly life are corrected. On the physical plane, errors correct themselves, but in the life between death and a new birth, errors and mistakes on Earth, and also our thoughts, become facts. In the process of initiation, too, thinking is a real fact, and if we were able to perceive it, an erroneous thought would stand there before us, not only in all its ugliness, but with all the destructive elements it contains. If people had no more than an inkling that many a thought signifies a destructive reality, they would soon turn away from many of the thoughts circulating in movements intent upon agitation. It is part of the martyrdom endured in the process of initiation that thoughts gather around us and stand there like solidified, frozen masses, which we cannot in any way dislodge, as long as we are out of the body. If we have formed an erroneous thought and then pass out of the body, the thought is there and we cannot change it. To change it we must go back into the body. True, memory of it remains, but even initiates are only able to rectify it when they are in the physical body. Outside the body, it stands there like a mountain. Only in this way can we become aware of the seriousness of the realities of life.

This will help you to understand that for certain karmic adjustments, a return into the physical body is essential. Our mistakes do indeed confront us during the life between death and a new birth; but our errors have to be corrected while we are in the physical body. In this way, compensation is made in the subsequent life for what happened in the previous life. But what must be recognized in all its strength and fallaciousness stands there, unchangeable to begin with, as in the case of things in the spiritual world according to Homer. Such knowledge of the spiritual world must penetrate into our souls and become perception and feelings, and as feelings they form the basis for a new conception of life. A monistic Sunday sermon[23] may expound any number of moral principles, but as time will show, those moral principles will produce very little change, because in the way they are presented the concepts can have a real effect only when we recognize that for a certain period after death whatever is a burden on our karma will confront us as a direct reality. We recognize the burden but it remains as it is; we cannot change it now; all we can do is to recognize and accept the burden fully and deepen our nature accordingly!

Such concepts enable our souls to have a genuine view of life. And then there will follow all that is necessary to further the progress of life along the paths laid down by the spiritual leaders of humanity. We shall thus move forward towards the goals that are set before us all.

Lecture 2

It has already been announced that our studies in these group meetings during the winter are to be concerned with the life between death and a new birth. Obviously, what will be said from a comparatively new point of view will become thoroughly clear only when the course of lectures has been given. It has to be taken for granted that a great deal will consist in the communications of findings from investigations carried out during recent months. Only as our studies progress can understanding become more complete. Let us, however, begin with a brief consideration of human nature and our constitution—a study that everyone can undertake themselves.

The most important and most outstanding fact revealed by an unprejudiced observation of human life is surely the existence of the human ego, the 'I'. A distinction must however be made between the genuine 'I' and consciousness of the 'I'. It must be clear to everyone that from the time children are born the 'I' is already active. This is obvious, long before children have any 'I'-consciousness, when in the language they use they speak of themselves as if they were another person. We have frequently considered these things. At about the third year of life (although of course there are children in whom this happens at an earlier age), children begin to have some consciousness of themselves and to speak of themselves in the first person. We know too that this third year (although it varies in many individuals) marks the limit before which, in later life, we are able to recall what our souls have experienced. There is thus a dividing line in the life of a human being: before it, there is no possibility of any clear and distinct experience of ourselves as an 'I'. After that point, we can experience ourselves as an ego, as 'I'; we find ourselves so at home in our 'I' that we can again and again summon up from our memory what our 'I' has experienced.

Now what does an unprejudiced observation of life teach us about the reason why children gradually pass from the stage when they have no experience of their egos to the stage when this experience comes to them? A clear observation of life can teach us that if from the earliest periods after birth children were never to come into any sort of collision with the outer world, they never could become self-conscious. You can discover for yourselves how often you become conscious of yourselves in later life. You have only to knock hard against the corner of a cupboard, and you will certainly be made aware of your self. This collision with the outside world tells you that you are an 'I', and you will hardly fail to be aware of that self when you have given yourself a nasty bruise! In the case of a child, these collisions with the outside world need not always cause bruises, but in essence their effect is similar—to some extent at least. When children stretch out their little hands and touch something in the outside world, this amounts to a slight collision, and the same holds good when children open their eyes and light falls upon them. It is actually by such contacts with the world outside that children become aware of their own identity. Indeed, their whole lives during these early years consist in learning to distinguish themselves from the world outside, and thus becoming aware of the self, the 'I', within them. When there have been enough of these collisions with the outside world, the children acquire self-consciousness and say 'I' of themselves. Once self-consciousness has been acquired, children's 'I' have to keep it alive and alert. The only possibility of this, however, is that collisions will continue to take place. These collisions with the world outside have completed their essential function once children have reached this stage when they say 'I' of themselves, and there is nothing further to be learnt by this means as far as the development of consciousness is concerned. However, unbiased observation, for instance, of the moment of waking will help everyone to realize that this 'I'-consciousness can be maintained only by means of 'collisions'.

We know that this self-consciousness, together with all the other experiences, including those of the astral body, vanishes during sleep and wakens again in the morning. This happens because as beings of soul and spirit, we return into our physical and etheric bodies. Again, collisions take place—now with the physical and etheric bodies. People who are able—even without any esoteric knowledge—to observe the life of the soul accurately, can have the following experience. When they wake in the morning, they will find that a great deal of what their memory has preserved rises again into their consciousness: representations, feelings, and other experiences rise up into consciousness from their own depths. If we investigate all this with exactitude—and that is possible without any esoteric knowledge, provided only there is some capacity for observing what the soul experiences—we shall find that what rises up into consciousness has a certain impersonal character. We can observe, too, that this impersonal character becomes more marked the longer ago the events in question took place—which means, of course, the less we are participating in them with our immediate self-consciousness. We may remember events which took place very long ago in our life, and when memory recalls them, we may feel that we have as little directly to do with them as we have with experiences in the outside world which do not particularly concern us. What is otherwise preserved in our memory tends continually to break loose from our self. The reason why, in spite of this, we find ourselves returning with all clarity into our consciousness each morning is that we come back into the same body. Through the resulting collision, our self-consciousness is awakened again each morning. Thus just as children develop consciousness of their selves by colliding with the external world, we keep that consciousness alert by colliding each morning with our inner being. This takes place not only in the morning, but throughout the day; our self-consciousness is kindled by the counter-pressure of our body. Our 'I' is implanted in the physical body, etheric body, and astral body, and is continually colliding with them. We can therefore say that we owe our self-consciousness to the fact that we press inwardly into our bodily constitution and experience the counter-pressure from it. We collide with our body.

You will readily understand that this must have the consequence that always results from collisions, namely that damage or injury is caused, even if it is not immediately noticed. Collisions of the 'I' with the bodily constitution cause slight injuries in the latter. It is indeed the case that we are continuously destroying our corporeality. Our self-consciousness could never develop if we were not perpetually colliding with our bodily make-up, and thereby destroying it. It is in fact the sum-total of these destructive events that ultimately brings about death in the physical world. Our conclusion has to be therefore that we owe the preservation of our self-consciousness to our own destructive activity, to the circumstance that we are able to destroy our organism perpetually.

In this way we are destroyers of our astral, etheric, and physical bodies. But because of this, our relation to those bodies is rather different from what it is to the 'I'. Everyday life itself makes it obvious that we can also work destructively upon the 'I', and we will now try to be clear as to how this may happen.

Our 'I' is something—never mind for the moment exactly what—that has a certain value in the world. We feel the truth of this, but it is in our power to reduce that value. How do we reduce the value of our 'I'? If we do harm to someone to whom we owe a debt of love, we shall actually at that moment have reduced the value of our 'I'. This is a fact that every human being can recognize. At the same time, we can realize that as humans never fulfil their ideal value, their 'I' is really occupied throughout life with reducing its own value, with bringing about its own destruction. However, as long as we remain poised in our own 'I', we have the constant opportunity in life to annul the destruction we have caused. We are capable of this even though we do not always manage to do it. Before we pass through the gate of death, we can make compensation in some form for undeserved suffering caused to another person. If you think about it you will realize that between birth and death it is possible for us to reduce the value of our 'I', but also ultimately to make good the destruction that has been brought about.

But in the case of the astral, etheric, and physical bodies, there is no possibility of being able to do this at the present stage of human evolution. We are unable to work consciously on these bodies, as we can do in the case of our 'I', because we are not, in the real sense, conscious in these members of our being. The destruction for which we are continually responsible remains in our astral, etheric, and physical bodies, but we are not in a position to repair it. It is easy to understand that if we were to come into a new incarnation with the forces of the astral, etheric, and physical bodies as they were at the end of our previous incarnation, those bodies would be useless. The content of the life of soul is always the source and the sum and substance of what comes to expression in the bodily constitution. The fact that at the end of life we have a brittle organism is evidence that our soul then lacks the forces necessary to sustain its vigour. In order to maintain our consciousness and keep it alert, we have been continually damaging our bodily sheaths. With the forces that are still available at the end of one incarnation, we could do nothing in the next. It is necessary for us to reacquire the forces that are able to restore freshness and health within certain limits to the astral, etheric, and physical bodies, and to make them useful for a new incarnation. In earthly existence—as is evident even to external observation—it is possible for us to damage these bodies, but not to restore them to health. Esoteric investigation reveals that in the life between death and a new birth we acquire from the extra-terrestrial conditions in which we are then living the forces that are able to restore our worn-out sheaths. Between death and a new birth, we expand into the universe, the cosmos, and we have to acquire the forces which cannot be drawn from the sphere of the Earth from the heavenly bodies connected with the Earth. These heavenly bodies are the reservoirs of forces needed for our bodily sheaths. On the Earth, we can acquire only the forces needed for the constant restoration of the 'I'. For the other members of our being, the forces must be drawn from other worlds.

Let us consider the astral body first. After death, the human being expands—quite literally expands—into all the planetary spheres. During Kamaloka, as a being of soul and spirit, we expand to the boundary demarcated by the orbit of the Moon around the Earth. Beings of various ranks are involved in the process. Afterwards we expand until the sphere of Mercury is attained—Mercury as understood in esotericism. Thence we expand into the spheres of Venus, Sun, Mars, Jupiter, and finally Saturn. Humans expand themselves ever more and more. The being who has passed through the gate of death becomes in a real sense a dweller on Mercury, a dweller on Venus, and so on, and in a certain sense we must have the faculty of becoming thoroughly acclimated to these other planetary worlds. How do we succeed or fail in this respect?

In the first place, when our time in Kamaloka is over, we ourselves must possess some quality that will enable us to establish a definite relationship with the forces in the sphere of Mercury into which we then pass. If the lives of various human beings between death and a new birth are investigated, it will be found that they differ greatly in the sphere of Mercury. A clear difference is evident according to whether an individual passes into the sphere of Mercury with a moral disposition of soul, with the outcome of a moral or an immoral life. There are of course nuances of every possible degree. People with the moral quality of soul, who bear within them the fruits of a moral life, are what may be called a spiritually 'social' being in the sphere of Mercury; it is easy for them to establish relationships with other beings—either with people who died before them, or with beings who also inhabit the sphere of Mercury—and to share experiences with them. An immoral person becomes a hermit, and feels excluded from the community of the other inhabitants of this sphere. Such is the consequence in the life between death and a new birth of a moral or immoral disposition of one's soul. It is important to understand that morality forges our connection and relationship with the beings living in this sphere, and an immoral disposition of soul encloses us, as it were, in a prison. We know that the other beings are there, but we seem to be within a shell, and make no contact with them. This self-isolation is an outcome of an earthly life that was unsociable and lacking in morality.

In the next sphere, which we will call the sphere of Venus—in esotericism it is always so named—our contact with it is mainly dependent upon a religious attitude of soul. Contact with the beings of this sphere can be established by individuals who, during their life on Earth, came to realize that everything transitory in physical things and in humans themselves is after all related in some way to immortality; thus they had a feeling that the attitude of soul in every individual should incline to divine and spiritual reality. On the other hand, people who are materialists and cannot direct their souls to the eternal, the divine, the immortal, are condemned in the sphere of Venus to be imprisoned within their own being, in isolation. Particularly in connection with this sphere, we can learn from esoteric investigations how in our astral body during life on Earth we create the conditions of existence as they will be in the sphere of Venus.[24] On the Earth, we must already develop understanding of and inclination for what we hope to contact and experience in that sphere. Let us consider for a moment the fact that human beings living on the Earth during entirely different epochs—as was both inevitable and right—were connected with divine and spiritual life through the various religions and prevailing conceptions of the world. The only way in which human evolution could progress was that out of the one source—for example the religious life—at different times and for very different peoples, according to their natural traits and climatic and other conditions of existence, the varying religious principles were imparted by those destined for this mission. These religious principles stem from one source, but are graduated according to the conditions prevailing among particular peoples. Humanity today is still divided into groups determined by their religious tenets and views of the world. But it is through what is thereby formed in our souls that we prepare our understanding of and possibility for contacts in the sphere of Venus. Hindu, Chinese, Islamic, or Christian religions prepare the soul in such a way that in the sphere of Venus it will understand and be attracted to those individuals whose souls have been moulded by the same religious tenets. Esoteric investigation shows clearly that whereas today, humans on Earth are divided by race, descent, and so forth, and can be distinguished by these factors—although this will change in the future and has already begun to do so—in the sphere of Venus, in which we live together with other human beings, there are no such divisions. The only division there depends upon our religious principles and conceptions of the world while we were on Earth. It is true that to some extent a classification according to race is possible, because this classification on Earth—even according to religion—is still, in a certain respect, a matter of racial relationships. All the same, it is not the element of race that is decisive, but what the soul experiences through its adherence to the principles of a particular religion.

We spend certain periods after each death within these spheres; then our being expands, and we pass on from the sphere of Venus to the sphere of the Sun. In very truth, we become, as souls, Sun-dwellers between death and a new birth. Something more than was necessary in the sphere of Venus is required for the sphere of the Sun. If we are to fare well in the solar sphere between death and a new birth, it is essential to be able to understand not merely one particular group of human beings, but to understand and find points of contact with all human souls. In the solar sphere, we feel isolated, like hermits, if the prejudices of one particular faith render us incapable of understanding a human being whose soul has been filled with the principles of a different faith. An individual who on the Earth regarded only one particular religion as valuable is incapable in the solar sphere of understanding adherents of other religions. But the consequences of this lack of understanding are not the same as they are on Earth. On Earth, we may live side-by-side without any inner understanding of each other, and then separate into different faiths and systems of thought. In the solar sphere, however, since we interpenetrate one another, we are together, and yet at the same time separated in our inner being; and in that sphere, every separation and every lack of understanding are at once sources of terrible suffering. Every contact with an adherent of a different faith becomes a reproach which weighs upon us unceasingly, and which we cannot escape because on Earth we did not educate ourselves in this respect.

Taking the life between death and a new birth as a starting point, what is now to be said will in a certain sense be easier to understand if reference is made to initiation. What the initiate experiences in the spiritual worlds is in a certain respect closely akin to experiences undergone in the life between death and rebirth. Initiates have to make their way into the same spheres, and were they to maintain the prejudices resulting from a biased, one-sided view of the world, they would undergo similar suffering in the solar sphere. It is therefore essential that initiation should be preceded by a thorough understanding of every religious faith spread over the Earth, and also an understanding of what is taking place in every individual soul, regardless of the creed or system of thought to which they adhere. Otherwise, whatever has not been met with understanding becomes a source of suffering, as if towering mountains were threatening to crash down upon us; as if explosions were discharging their whole force upon us. Whatever lack of understanding has been shown to human beings on Earth due to our own narrow prejudices has this effect in the spiritual worlds.

It was not always so. In pre-Christian times, the process of evolution did not require us to acquire unconditionally this understanding of every human soul. Humanity was obliged to pass through the phase of one-sided attitude. But those who were trained for some kind of leadership in the world were obliged to acquire, either consciously or less consciously, an understanding for every human being without distinction. Even when some individual was to be the leader of a particular people, he would be required to develop a measure of understanding for every human soul. This is indicated magnificently in the Tanakh or Old Testament in the passage describing the meeting between Abraham and Melchizedek,[25] the priest of the Most High. Those who understand this passage know that Abraham, who was destined to become the leader of his people, underwent an initiation at this time—even if not in full consciousness, as is the case in later initiations. Abraham's initiation was connected with a realization of the divine element that can flow into all human souls. The passage which tells of the meeting of Abraham and Melchizedek contains a deep secret connected with the evolution of humanity. But we had to be gradually prepared to become more and more qualified for fruitful existence in the solar sphere. How did that occur?

The first impulse[26] in the evolution of our Earth towards a fruitful existence in the sphere of the Sun was given by the Mystery of Golgotha, after preparation for it had been made by the people of the Tanakh or Old Testament—about which there will be more to say.

It is not essential at the moment to deal with the question as to whether Christianity in its development hitherto has achieved all its goals and possible fruits. Needless to say, in its various sects and denominations, Christianity has [historically] produced only one-sided aspects of its essential principle; and certain of its historical tenets are, on the whole, not on the level of certain other faiths. What really matters, however, is its potential for development, is the enrichment it can give to us when we penetrate more and more deeply into its essential truth.

We have already tried to indicate these possibilities for development. There is infinitely much to be said, but one matter only shall now be mentioned, because it can throw light upon the point under consideration at the moment. If we have a genuine understanding of the different faiths, we find one outstanding characteristic, namely that in the earlier periods of Earth's evolution, the individual religions were adapted to the particular races, tribes, or peoples. There's still evidence of this. Only one who has been born a Hindu can be an orthodox adherent of the Hindu religion today.[27] In a certain respect, the earlier religions are cultural religions, popular religions. Do not take this as disparagement, but simply as a characterization. The different religions, although deriving from the primal source of the universal religion of the world, were given to the peoples by initiates and adapted to the specific tribes and races; hence in that sense there is something egoistic about them. Peoples have always loved the religion that has been determined by their own flesh and blood. In ancient times, when a religion stemming from a Mystery centre had been established among a particular people, a person with different bodily features who wanted to start another religion among them did not do so, but instead founded a second Mystery centre. People were always given a leader from their own tribe or clan.

In this respect, true Christianity is very different. Christ Jesus, the Individuality to whom Christians turn, was least active among the people and in the area on the Earth where He was born. In respect of religion, can conditions in the Western world be equated with those existing in India or China, where popular religions still survive? No, they cannot! The regions where we ourselves are living could be equated with India and China only if here, in Central Europe, we were, for example, faithful followers of Wotan. We should then be at the same stage and the element of religious egotism would be in evidence here, too. But in the West, this aspect has disappeared, for the West accepted a religion that was not confined to any particular community of peoples. This fact must be remembered. The influences that bound blood to blood and were a determining factor in the founding of the old religious communities played no part in the spread of Christianity. The life of *soul* was the essential factor, and in the West, a religion unconnected with the single people or community of peoples was adopted. Why has it been so? It is because in its deepest roots and from the very beginning, Christianity was meant to be a religion for all people without distinction of belief, nationality, descent, race, and whatever separates human beings from one another. Christianity is rightly understood only when it is realized that it is concerned solely with the essentially human elements and all peoples. The fact that in its early phases, and also in our own times, sects have arisen from Christianity should be no cause for apprehension; for Christianity makes possible the evolution of the 'universally human'. It is also true that a great transformation will have to take place within the Christian world if the roots of Christianity are to be rightly understood. A distinction will have to be made between *knowledge* of Christian tenets and the *reality* of Christianity.

St Paul did in fact begin to make this distinction, and those who understand his words can realize something of what they mean, although up to now understanding has been rare. When St Paul made it clear the belief in Jesus Christ was not the prerogative of Judaism, and spoke the words [tantamount to] 'Christ died not only for the Jews but also for the Gentiles',[28] this was an enormous contribution to the true conception of Christianity. It would be quite false to maintain that the Mystery of Golgotha was fulfilled only for those who call themselves Christians. The Mystery of Golgotha was fulfilled for *all* of humanity! This is indeed what St Paul meant in the words I just quoted. What passed over from the Mystery of Golgotha into earthly life has meaning and significance for *all* that life. Grotesque as it may still seem today to those who do not distinguish between knowledge and reality, it must nevertheless be said that they alone understand the roots of Christianity who can view adherence of a different religion—no matter whether they call themselves Indian, or Chinese, or anything else—in such a way that they ask themselves: To what extent are they Christ-like? The fact of knowing this is not what really matters. What *does* matter is that such a person knows the reality of Christianity—in the sense that it is not essential to know physiology for digestion to occur. People whose religion has failed to bring about in them a conscious relationship to the Mystery of Golgotha have no understanding of it, but that does not entitle others to deny them the reality of Christianity. Not until Christians become so truly Christian that they seek for the Christ-like principle in all souls on Earth—not when they have implanted it in the souls of others by attempts at conversion—not until then will the root principles of Christianity have been understood. All this belongs to Christianity when rightly understood. We have to make a distinction between the *reality* of Christianity and an *understanding* of it. To understand what has been present on the Earth since the Mystery of Golgotha is a great ideal, an ideal of supremely important knowledge for the Earth—knowledge that we will gradually acquire. But the *reality* itself has come to pass; the Mystery of Golgotha was fulfilled.

Our life in the sphere of the Sun after death depends upon the relationship we have established with the Mystery of Golgotha. The contact with all human souls that can be experienced in the sphere of the Sun is possible only if a relationship with the Mystery of Golgotha has been established in the way described. It is a relationship that ensures freedom from any still imperfect form of Christianity as practised in this or that sect. If we have no such relationship with the Mystery of Golgotha, we condemn ourselves to becoming solitary individuals in the solar sphere, unable to make contact with other human souls. There is a certain utterance that retains its power even in the solar sphere. When we encounter in the sphere of the Sun another human soul, we can become companions and not be thrust away from that soul, if these words have been preserved in our inner being: 'For where two or three are gathered together in My name, there I am in the midst of them'.[29] In the sphere of the Sun, all human souls can be united with one another in a true recognition of

Christ. And this union is of tremendous significance. For in the solar sphere, we must make a decision; we must acquire a certain understanding. And what this means can best be explained by referring to an extraordinarily important fact which every human soul should be able to realize, but does not always do so. One of the most beautiful sayings in the New Testament occurs when Christ Jesus is endeavouring to make us conscious of the divine and spiritual core of being within us; of the truth that God is present as the divine spark in every human soul; that all human beings have divinity within them. Christ Jesus emphasizes this, declaring with all power and intensity: 'Ye are gods!'[30] The emphasis laid upon the words shows that He recognized this as a rightful claim when we apply its implications to ourselves. But this utterance was also made by another being. The Tanakh or Old Testament tells us in symbolic words when in evolution it was made. At the very beginning of human evolution, Lucifer proclaimed: 'Ye shall be as gods!'[31] This is something that must be noticed. A saying in identical terms is uttered by two beings: by Lucifer and by Christ: 'Ye shall be as gods'! What does the Bible imply by emphasizing these two utterances? It implies that from Lucifer, this utterance leads to a curse, but from Christ, to the highest blessing. Is there not a wondrous mystery here? The words hurled into humanity by Lucifer, the tempter—when uttered by Christ to humanity are supreme wisdom. What is really important is not the content of an utterance, but from whom it comes—this fact is inscribed with incisive letters into the biblical record. From an instance such as this, let us feel that it behoves us to understand things in adequate depth, and that we can learn a very great deal from what may lie openly before us.

In the sphere of the Sun between death and a new birth we hear the words spoken to our soul again and again with all their force: Thou art a god, be as a god! We know with all certainty when we arrive in the solar sphere that Lucifer meets us again and impresses the meaning of this utterance forcibly upon us. From then onwards we can understand Lucifer very well, but Christ only if on Earth we have prepared ourselves to understand Him. Christ's utterance will have no meaning for us in the sphere of the Sun if we have not gained some understanding of it by our relationship on Earth to the Mystery of Golgotha. Trivial as the following words may be, let me say this: In the solar sphere we find two thrones. From the throne of Lucifer—which is always occupied—there sound the words of temptation, asserting our divinity. The second throne seems to us— or rather to many human beings—to be still empty, for on this other throne in the solar sphere between death and a new birth, we have to discover what can be called the Akashic[32] picture of Christ. If we can find the Akashic picture of Christ in the life between death and rebirth, it will be for us a blessing—this will become evident in later lectures. But it has become possible to find that picture only because Christ came down from the Sun and has united Himself with the Earth, and because we have been able to open our eyes of spirit here on Earth through understanding in some measure the Mystery of Golgotha. This will ensure that the throne of Christ in the sphere of the Sun does not appear empty to us, but that the deeds He enacted while His dwelling-place was still the sphere of the Sun become visible. As I said, I have to use trivial words in speaking of these two thrones; this sublime fact can only be spoken of figuratively. But anyone who acquires more and more understanding will realize that words coined on Earth are inadequate, and that one is obliged to resort to imagery in order to be intelligible.

Now we shall understand and find support for what we need in the solar sphere only if on the Earth we have acquired something that plays not only into the astral forces, but into the etheric forces as well. You will know from what I have previously said that the religions influence the etheric forces and the human etheric body. A considerable spiritual inheritance is available for all of us inasmuch as forces from the solar sphere are instilled into us if we have acquired understanding of the Mystery of Golgotha. For it is from the solar sphere that we must draw the forces necessary for the renewal of our etheric body for the next incarnation, whereas the forces necessary for our astral body in the next incarnation have to be drawn from the other planetary spheres.

Let nobody believe that what I've been saying is unconnected with the whole course of evolution. I've told you that already in pre-Christian times a leader of humanity such as Abraham was able at his meeting with Melchizedek (or Malekzadik) to acquire the forces needed for the sphere of the Sun. I'm making no intolerant statement implying that we can acquire the forces necessary for establishing a right relationship to the beings of the solar sphere through orthodox Christianity alone. I'm stating a fact of evolution. Another fact is that the time when it was still possible, as in ancient days, to behold the Akashic picture of Christ through other means is drawing nearer and nearer to a close as evolution proceeds. Abraham's spiritual eyes were fully open to the Akashic picture of Christ in the sphere of the Sun. You must not argue that the Mystery of Golgotha had not yet taken place, and that Christ was still in the solar sphere, for during that period, Christ in His reality was united with the other planetary spheres. It is indeed a fact that back then and even down to our own epoch, human beings were able to perceive what was perceptible in those spheres. And if we go still further back to those primeval ages when the Holy Rishis[33] were the first teachers of the people of Ancient India, those teachers certainly had knowledge of Christ, who at that time was still in the sphere of the Sun, and they imparted this knowledge and understanding to their followers, although of course not using the later nomenclature. Although in those ancient times the Mystery of Golgotha was not yet within their ken, individualities were able, by drawing intimate truths from the depths of their being, to acquire from the sphere of the Sun what was needed for the renewal of their etheric bodies. But these possibilities ceased as evolution proceeded, and this was necessary because new forces must perpetually be instilled into humanity.

What has been said is meant to indicate a fact of evolution. We are moving towards a future when it will be less and less possible for us during the period between death and a new birth to live through our existence in the solar sphere in the right way if we alienate ourselves from the Christ-Event. It is true that we must look for the Christ-like quality in each soul. If we are to understand the root of Christianity, we must ask ourselves in the case of everyone we meet, how much in that individual's nature is Christ-like? But it is also true that we can sever ourselves from Christianity if we fail to become conscious of what it is in reality. And when we remind ourselves again of St Paul's words, that Christ died not only for the Jews, but also for the Gentiles, we must also add that if in the course of further progress we were to deny more and more the reality of the Mystery of Golgotha, we would prevent what was done for our sake from reaching us. The Mystery of Golgotha was a deed of blessing for all humanity. All humans are free to allow that event to influence them or not; but the effect of the influence will depend in the future more and more upon the extent to which we are able to draw from the solar sphere the forces required to ensure that our etheric bodies will be rightly formed in our next incarnation. The immeasurable consequences of this for the whole future of the human race on Earth will be considered in the forthcoming lectures.

Christianity, which—admittedly with little understanding—is nevertheless connected with the Mystery of Golgotha, is the first preparation if humanity is to regain the relationship to the sphere of the Sun. The second impulse would be a genuine anthroposophical understanding of the Mystery of Golgotha. We can gain a proper relationship to the sphere of the Sun when we learn ever more and more to penetrate the Mystery of Golgotha. After we have lived into the solar sphere, our life expands further outwards, into the sphere of Mars, for example. What is essential is that we not only establish the right relationship to the forces of the solar sphere, but that we maintain this relationship when our life expands into the sphere of Mars. For in order that our consciousness will not become dim, will not fade away altogether after the solar sphere, but that we can carry it over into the sphere of Mars and the sphere of Jupiter, in the present cycle of human evolution it is necessary that spiritual understanding of the gist of our religions and conceptions of the world should take root in human souls. Hence our endeavours to understand the essence of religions and systems of thought. Anthroposophical understanding will eventually be replaced by another, quite different understanding, of which people today cannot even dream. For certain as it is that the truth is right when an epoch is possessed of a genuine sense of truth, it is also a fact that continually new impulses will make their way into the evolution of humanity. It is true indeed that what anthroposophy has to give is right for a particular epoch, and humanity, having assimilated anthroposophy, may bear it into later times as an inner impulse, and through these forces also acquire the forces of the later epoch.

Thus it has been possible to show the relationship of human life on Earth to the life between death and a new birth. Nobody can fail to realize that it is just as necessary for a human being to have knowledge, feeling, and sensation of the life between death and a new birth as of earthly life itself. For when we enter earthly life at birth, the confidence, strength, and hopefulness connected with that life depend upon what forces we bring with us from the life between the last death and the present birth. But again, the forces we are able to acquire during that life depend upon our conduct in the earlier incarnation, upon our moral and religious disposition, or the quality of our attitude of soul. We must realize that whether the future evolution of the human race will be furthered or impeded depends upon our active and creative co-operation with the supra-sensible world in which we live between death and a new birth. If we failed to acquire the forces able to provide ourselves with healthy astral bodies, the forces in our astral bodies would become ineffective and sterile, and humanity would sink into moral and religious turpitude. Similarly, if we failed to acquire the forces needed for our etheric bodies, as members of the human race we would wither away on the Earth. Every individual can ask themselves the question: In what measure must I co-operate with the spiritual world in order that the Earth will not be peopled only by sickly bodies? Anthroposophy is not mere knowledge. Rather, it is a responsibility that brings us into connection with the whole nature of the Earth, and sustains that connection.

LECTURE 3

BERLIN, 3 DECEMBER 1912

From what has already been indicated about the life between death and a new birth, you will recall that during that period we continue, to begin with, to live in conditions and with relationships we ourselves prepared during our existence on Earth. It was said that when we again encounter some personality in the spiritual world after death, the relationship between us is, at first, the same as was formed during our existence on Earth and we cannot, for the time being, change it at all. Thus if in the spiritual world we come into contact with a friend or an individual who has predeceased us, and to whom we owed a debt of love, but during life withheld that love from them, we shall now have to experience again the relationship that existed before death because of the lack of love of which we were guilty. We confront the person in question in the way described in the last lecture, beholding and experiencing over and over again the circumstances created during the life before our death. For instance, if at some particular time, say ten years before the death of the person in question, or before our own death, we allowed the relationship caused by our self-incurred debt of love to be established, we shall have to live through the relationship for a corresponding length of time after death and only after that period has elapsed shall we be able to experience once again, during our life after death, the happier relationship previously existing between us. It is important to realize that after death we are not in a position to expunge or change relationships for which we had been responsible on Earth. To a certain extent change has become impossible.

It might easily be believed that this is inevitably a painful experience and can only be regarded as suffering. But that would be judging from the standpoint of our limited earthly circumstances. Viewed from the spiritual world things look different in many respects. It is true that in the life between death and a new birth, the individual concerned must undergo all the suffering resulting from the admission: I am now in the spiritual world and realize the wrong I committed, but I cannot rectify it and must rely upon [external] conditions to bring about a change. Individuals who are aware of this undergo the pain connected with the experience, but they also know that it must be so and that it would be detrimental for their further development if it were otherwise, if they could not learn from the experience resulting from such suffering. For through experiencing such conditions and recognizing that they cannot be changed, we acquire the power to change them in our later karma. The technique of karma enables these conditions to be changed during another physical incarnation. There is only the remotest possibility that the dead themselves can change them. Above all during the first period after death, during the time in Kamaloka, we see what has been determined by our lives before death, but to begin with we must leave it as it is; we are unable to bring about any change in what we experience.

Those who have remained behind on Earth have a far greater influence on the dead than the dead have on themselves, or others who have also died have upon the deceased. And this is tremendously important. It is really only an individual who has remained on the physical plane, who had established some relationship with the dead, who through human free will is able to bring about certain changes in the conditions of souls between death and rebirth.

We will now take an example that can be instructive in many respects. Here we can also consider the life in Kamaloka, for the existing relationships do not change when the transition takes place into the period of Devachan.[34] Let us think of two friends living on Earth, one of whom comes into contact with anthroposophy at a certain time and becomes an anthroposophist. It may happen that because of this, the friend rages against anthroposophy. You may have known such a case. If the friend had been the first to find anthroposophy, they might themselves have become a very good adherent! Such things certainly happen, but we must realize that they are very often clothed in maya.[35] Consequently, it may happen that the one who rages against anthroposophy because the friend has become an adherent is raging in their surface consciousness only, in their ego-consciousness. In their astral consciousness, in their sub-consciousness, they may very likely not share in the antipathy. Without realizing it, they may even be longing for anthroposophy. In many cases it happens that aversion in the upper consciousness takes the form of longing in the sub-consciousness. It does not necessarily follow that an individual feels exactly what they express in their upper consciousness. After death we do not experience only the effects of the contents of our upper consciousness, our ego-consciousness. To believe that would be to misunderstand entirely the conditions prevailing after death. It has often been said that although we cast off the physical body and etheric body at death, our longings and desires remain. Nor need these longings and desires be only those of which we were actually aware. The longings and desires that were in our sub-consciousness also remain, including those of which we have no conscious knowledge or may even have resisted. They are often much stronger and more intense after death than they were in life. During life a certain disharmony between the astral body and the 'I' expresses itself as a feeling of depression, dissatisfaction with oneself. After death, the astral consciousness is an indication of the whole character of the soul, the whole stamp of the individual concerned. So what we experience in our upper consciousness is less significant than all those hidden wishes, desires and passions which are present in the soul's depths and of which the 'I' knows nothing.

In the case mentioned, let us suppose that someone denounces anthroposophy because their friend who has become an adherent passes through the gate of death. The longing for anthroposophy, which may have developed precisely because of their violent opposition, now asserts itself and becomes an intense wish for anthroposophy. This wish would have to remain unfulfilled, for it could hardly happen that after death they themselves would have an opportunity of satisfying it. But through a particular concatenation of circumstances in such a case, someone who is on Earth may be able to help the other and change something in their conditions. This is the kind of case that may frequently be observed in our own ranks.

We can, for instance, read to the one who has died. The way to do this is to picture the individual vividly there in front of us; we picture their features and go through with him in thought the content, for example, of an anthroposophical book. This need only be done in thought and it has a direct effect upon the one who has died. As long as they are in the stage of Kamaloka, language is no hindrance; it becomes a hindrance only when they have passed into Devachan. Hence the question as to whether the dead understands language need not be raised. During the period of Kamaloka a feeling for language is certainly present. In this practical way very active help can be given to one who has passed through the gate of death. What streams up from the physical plane is something that can be a factor in bringing about a change in the conditions of life between death and the new birth; but such help can only be given to the dead from the physical world, not directly from the spiritual world.

We realize from this that when anthroposophy actually finds its way into human hearts, it will in very truth bridge the gap between the physical and the spiritual worlds, and that will constitute its infinite value in life. Only a very elementary stage in anthroposophical development has been reached when it is thought that what is of main importance is to acquire certain concepts and ideas about the members of our nature or about what can come to us from the spiritual world. The bridge between the physical world and the spiritual world cannot be built until we realize that anthroposophy takes hold of our very life. We shall then no longer adopt a merely passive attitude towards those who have passed through the gate of death, but shall establish active contact with them and be able to help them. To this end, anthroposophy must make us conscious of the fact that our world consists of physical existence and supra-physical, spiritual existence; furthermore that we are on Earth not only to gather for ourselves the fruits of physical existence between birth and death, but that we are on Earth in order to send up into the supra-physical world what can be gained and can exist only on the physical plane. If for some justifiable reason or, let us say, for the sake of comfort, someone has kept aloof from anthroposophical ideas, we can bring them to them after death in the way described. Maybe someone will ask: Is it possible that this will annoy the dead, that they do not want it? This question is not entirely justifiable because individuals in the present age are by no means particularly opposed to anthroposophy in their sub-conscious. If the sub-conscious of those who denounce anthroposophy could have a voice in their upper consciousness, there would be hardly any opposition to it. For people are prejudiced and biased against the spiritual world only in their ego-consciousness, only in what expresses itself as ego-consciousness on the physical plane.

This is one aspect of mediation between the physical world and the spiritual world. But we can also ask: Is mediation also possible in the other direction, from the spiritual to the physical world? That is to say, can the one who has passed through the gate of death communicate in some way with those who have remained on the physical plane? At the present time the possibility of this is very slight because on the physical plane human beings live for the most part only in their ego-consciousness, and not in the consciousness connected with the astral body. It is not so easy to convey an idea of how we will gradually develop consciousness of what surrounds us as an astral or devachanic or other spiritual world. But if anthroposophy acquires greater influence in the evolution of humanity, this will eventually come about. Simply through paying attention to the teachings of anthroposophy, we will find the ways and means to break through the boundaries of the physical world and direct attention to the spiritual world that is round about us and eludes us only because we pay no heed to it.

How can we become aware of this spiritual world?

Today I want to make you aware of how little we really know about the things of the world surrounding us. We know very little indeed of what is of essential importance in that world. Through our senses and intellect, we get to know and recognize the ordinary facts of life in which we are involved. We get to know what is going on both in the world and in ourselves, establish some kind of association between these happenings, call the one 'cause' and the other 'effect' and then, having ascertained some connection based either upon cause and effect or some other concept, think we understand the processes that are in operation. To take an example. We leave our home at eight o'clock in the morning, walk along the street, reach our place of work, have a meal during the day, do this or that to amuse ourselves. This goes on until the time comes for sleep. We then connect our various experiences; one makes a strong impression upon us, another a weaker impression. Impressions are also produced in our soul, either of sympathy or antipathy. Even trifling reflection can teach us that we are living, as it were, on the surface of a sea without the faintest idea of what is down below on the seabed. As we pass through life we get to know external reality only. But an example will show that a very great deal is implicit in this external reality. Suppose one day we leave home three minutes later than usual and arrive at work three minutes late; after that we carry on just as if we had left home at the usual time. Nevertheless it may be possible to verify that had we been in the street punctually at eight o'clock we might have been run over by a car and killed; if we had left home punctually we should no longer be alive. Or on another occasion we may hear of an accident to a train in which we should have been travelling and thus have been injured. This is an even more radical example of what I just said. We pay attention only to what actually happens, not to what *may* be continually happening and which we have escaped. The range of such possibilities is infinitely greater than that of actual happenings.

It may be said that this happening had no significance for our outer life. For our inner life, however, it is certainly of importance! Suppose, for instance, you had bought a ticket for a voyage on the Titanic,[36] but were dissuaded by a friend from travelling. You sold the ticket and then heard of the disaster. Would your experience have been the same as if you had never been involved? Would it not far rather have made a most striking impression upon you? If we knew from how many things we are protected in the world, how many things are possible for good or for ill, things which are converging and only through slight displacement do not meet, we should have a sensitive perception of experiences of happiness or unhappiness, of bodily experiences which are possible for us but simply do not come our way. Who among all of you sitting here can know what you would have experienced if, for example, the lecture this evening had been cancelled and you had been somewhere else. If you had known about the cancellation your attitude of mind would be quite different from what it now is, because you have no idea of what might conceivably have happened.

All these possibilities that do not become reality on the physical plane exist as forces and effects behind the physical world in the spiritual world, and reverberate through it. It is not only the forces which actually determine our life on the physical plane that stream down upon us, but also the measureless abundance of forces which exist only as possibilities, some of which seldom make their way into our physical consciousness. But when they do, this usually occasions a significant psychic experience. Do not say that what has been stated, namely that numberless possibilities exist, that for example this lecture might have been cancelled, in which case those sitting here would have had different experiences—do not say that this invalidates karma. It does nothing of the kind. If such a thing were said it would imply ignorance of the fact that the idea of karma just presented holds good only for the world of realities within physical life. The truth is that spiritual life permeates our physical life and there is a world of possibilities where the laws operating as karmic are quite different. If we could feel what a tiny part of what we might have experienced is represented by the physical realities, and that our actual experiences are only a fractional part of the possibilities, the infinite wealth and exuberance of the spiritual life behind our physical life would be obvious to us.

Now the following may happen. We may take serious account in our thoughts of this world of possibilities, or perhaps not in our thoughts but only in our feelings. We may realize that we probably would have been killed in an accident to a train that we happened to miss. This may make a deep impression upon us, and such happenings are able, as it were, to open the soul to the spiritual world. Moments such as this with which we are in some way connected may actually reveal to us wishes or thoughts of souls living between death and the new birth.

When anthroposophy wakens in us a feeling for possibilities in life, for occurrences or catastrophes which did not take place simply because something that might have happened did not do so, and when the soul abides firmly by this feeling, experiences conveyed by individuals with whom there had been a connection in the physical world may be received from the spiritual world.

Although during the hurry and bustle of daily life people are for the most part disinclined to give rein to feelings of what might have happened, nevertheless there are times in life when events that might have happened have a decisive influence upon the soul. If you were to observe your dream-life more closely, or the strange moments of transition from waking life to sleep or from sleep to waking life, if you were to observe with greater exactitude certain dreams which are often quite inexplicable, in which certain things that happen to you appear in a dream-picture or vision, you would find that these inexplicable pictures indicate something that might have happened and was prevented only because other conditions, or hindrances, intervened. A person who through meditation or some other means makes their thinking more mobile, will have moments in their waking life during which they will feel that they are living in a world of possibilities; this may not be in the form of definite ideas, but of feelings. If they develop such feelings, they are preparing themselves to receive from the spiritual world impressions from people who were connected with them in the physical world. Such influences then manifest as genuine experiences of dreams, which have meaning and point to some reality in the spiritual world. In teaching us that in the life between birth and death karma holds sway, anthroposophy makes it quite clear that wherever we are placed in life we are faced perpetually with an infinite number of possibilities. One of these possibilities is selected in accordance with the law of karma; the others remain in the background, surrounding us like a cosmic aura. The more deeply we believe in karma, the more firmly we shall also believe in the existence of this cosmic aura which surrounds us and is produced by forces which converge but have been displaced in a certain way, so that they do not manifest on the physical plane.

If we allow our hearts and minds to be influenced by anthroposophy, this will be a means of educating humanity to be receptive to impressions coming from the spiritual world. If, therefore, anthroposophy succeeds in having a real effect upon culture, upon spiritual life, influences will not only rise up from physical life into the spiritual world, but the experiences undergone by the dead during their life between death and the new birth will flow back. Thus here again the gulf between the physical and the spiritual worlds will be bridged. The consequence will be a tremendous widening of human life, and we shall see the purpose of anthroposophy fulfilled in the creation of an actual link between the two worlds, not merely a theoretical conception of the existence of a spiritual world. It is essential to realize that anthroposophy fulfils its task in the real sense only when it permeates our souls as a living force and when by its means we not only comprehend something intellectually, but our whole attitude and relationship to the world around us is changed.

Because of the preconceptions current in our times, our thinking is far too materialistic, even if we often believe in the existence of a spiritual world. Hence it is extremely difficult for us in the present age to picture the right relationship between soul and body. The habits of thought peculiar to the times tend to make us picture the life of soul as being connected too closely with the bodily constitution. An analogy may be the only means of helping to clarify what must be understood here.

If we examine a watch we see that it consists of wheels and other little metal parts. But do we look at our watch in the course of everyday life in order to study the works or the interplay of the wheels? No, we look at our watch in order to find out the time; but time has nothing whatever to do with any of the metal parts or wheels. We look at the watch and do not trouble about what there is to be seen inside the watch itself. Or let us take another example. When somebody speaks of telegraphing today, they have the electric apparatus in mind. But even before electric telegraphy was invented, telegraphing went on. Provided the right signs, etc. are known it would be possible for people to speak from one town to another without any electric telegraph—and perhaps the process would not be very much slower. Suppose, for instance, pillars or poles were erected along the highway between Berlin and Paris and someone posted on the top of each pole to pass on the appropriate signs. If that were done quickly enough there would be no difference between this method and what is done by means of the electric telegraph. Certainly the latter is the simpler and much quicker method, but the actual process of telegraphing has as little to do with the mechanism of the electric telegraph as time has to do with the works in a watch.

Now the human soul has just as much and just as little to do with the processes of the human body as the communication from Berlin to Paris has to do with the mechanism of the electric telegraph. It is only when we think in this way that we can have a true conception of the independence of the soul. For it would be perfectly possible for this human soul with all its content to make use of a differently formed body, just as the message from Berlin to Paris could be sent by means other than the electric telegraph. The electric telegraph merely happens to be the most convenient way of sending messages, given the conditions of our present existence, and in the same sense the body with its possibility of movement and the head above provides the most convenient means, in the conditions of our existence on Earth, for the soul to express itself. But it is simply not the case that the body as such has anything more directly to do with the life of the soul than the electric telegraph with its mechanism has directly to do with the transmission of a communication from Berlin to Paris, or a watch with time. It would be possible to devise an instrument quite different from our watches for measuring time. Similarly it is possible to conceive of a body—quite different from the one we use in the conditions prevailing on Earth—that would enable the soul to express itself.

How are we to picture the relation of the human soul to the body? A saying of Schiller,[37] applied to humans, is particularly relevant here: 'If you are seeking for the highest and the best, the plant can teach it to you.' We look at the plant which spreads out its leaves and opens its blossoms during the day and draws them in when the light fades. That which streams to the plant from the Sun and the stars has been withdrawn. But it is what comes from the Sun that enables the leaves to open again and the blossom to unfold. Out yonder in cosmic space, therefore, are the forces which cause the organs of the plant to fold up limply when they withdraw or unfold when they are active. What is brought about in the plant by cosmic forces is brought about in humans by our own ego and astral body. When do humans allow their limbs to relax and their eyelids to close like the plant when it draws in its leaves and blossoms? When our ego and astral body leave our bodily organism. What the Sun does to the plant, the ego and astral body do to the organs of the human being. Hence we can say: the plant's body must turn to the Sun, just as our body must turn to the ego and astral body, and we must think of these members of our being as having the same effect upon us as the Sun has upon the plant.

Even externally considered, will it still surprise you to know what occult investigation reveals, namely that the ego and astral body orig-inate from the cosmic sphere to which the Sun belongs and do not belong to the Earth at all? Nor will you be surprised, after what has been said in previous lectures, to realize that when human beings leave the Earth, either in sleep or at death, they live their way into the great conditions prevailing in the cosmos. The plant is still depen-dent upon the Sun and the forces operating in space. The human ego and astral body have made themselves independent of the forces in space, and they go their own way. A plant is bound to sleep when the sunlight withdraws; in respect of our ego and astral body, how-ever, we are independent of the sun and planets, which are our real home, and for this reason we are able to sleep by day, even when the sun is shining. In our egos and astral bodies, we have emancipated ourselves from that with which we are really united—namely the forces of the Sun and stars. Therefore it is not grotesque to say that what remains of the human being on the Earth and in its elements after death belongs to the Earth and to its forces, but the ego and astral body belong to the forces of the cosmos. After the death of the human being, the ego and astral body return to those cosmic forces and pass through the life between death and rebirth within their spheres. During the period on Earth between birth and death, while the soul is living in a physical body, the life of soul which strictly belongs to the Sun and the stars has no more to do with this physical body than time as such—which is in reality conditioned by the solar and stellar constellations—has to do with the watch and its mechanism of wheels. It is quite conceivable that if, instead of living on the Earth, we were born on some other planet, our soul would be adapted to quite a different planetary existence. The particular formation of our eyes and ears is not attributable to the soul but to the conditions prevailing on the Earth. All we do is to make use of these organs. If we make ourselves consciously aware of the fact that with our soul we belong to the world of the stars, we shall have taken a first step towards a real understanding of our relationships as human beings and our true human nature. This knowledge will help us to adopt the right attitude to our conditions of existence here on Earth. To establish even this more or less external relationship to our physical body or etheric body will give us a sense of security. We shall realize that we are not merely beings of the Earth but belong to the whole universe, to the macrocosm; that we live within the macrocosm. It is only because we here on Earth are bound to our bodies that we are not conscious of our connection with the forces of the great universe.

Wherever and whenever in the course of the ages a deepening of the spiritual life was achieved, efforts were made to bring this home to human souls. In point of fact, it is only during the last four centuries that we have lost this consciousness of our connection with the spiritual forces weaving and holding sway in cosmic space. Think of what has always been emphasized: that Christ is the great Sun-Being who through the Mystery of Golgotha has united Himself with the Earth and its forces and has thus made it possible for us to take into ourselves the Christ-force on Earth; permeation with the Christ-Impulse will include the impulses of the macrocosm and in every epoch of evolution it will be right to recognize in Christ the power that imparts feeling of kinship with the macrocosm.

In the twelfth century a story, a splendid allegory, became current in the West.[38] It was as follows: Once upon a time there was a girl who had several brothers, all of whom were as poor as church mice. One day the girl found a pearl, thereby becoming

the possessor of great treasure. All the brothers were determined
to share the wealth that had come her way. The first brother was
a painter and he said to the girl: 'I will paint for you the finest
picture ever known if you will let me share your wealth.' But the
girl would have nothing to do with him and sent him away. The
second brother was a musician. He promised the girl that he would
compose the most beautiful piece of music if she would let him
share her wealth. But she sent him away. The third brother was an
apothecary and, as was customary in the Middle Ages, dealt chiefly
in perfumes and other goods that were not remedial herbs but
quite useful in life. This brother promised to give the girl the most
fragrant scent in the world if she would let him share her wealth.
But she sent this brother away too. The fourth brother was a cook.
He promised the girl that he would cook such good dishes for her
that by eating them she would get a brain equal to that of Zeus
and would be able to enjoy the very tastiest food. But she rejected
him too. The fifth brother was an innkeeper, and he promised to
find the most desirable suitors for her if she would let him share
her wealth. She rejected him too. Finally, or so the story tells, came
one who was able to find his way to the girl's soul, and with him
she shared her treasure, the pearl she had found.

The story is graphically told and it has been narrated in greater
detail and even more beautifully by Jakob Balde.[39] There is also an
exposition dating from the thirteenth century by the poet himself,
so it cannot be called a mere interpretation. The poet says that he
had wanted to portray humans in their free will. The girl represents
the human soul endowed with free will. The five brothers are the
five senses: the painter is the sense of sight, the musician the sense
of hearing, the apothecary the sense of smell, the cook the sense of
taste, the innkeeper the sense of touch. The girl rejects them all, in
order, so the story tells, to share her treasure of free will with the
one with whom her soul has true affinity—with Christ. She rejects
the attractions of the senses in order to receive that to which the
Christ-impulse leads when it permeates the soul. The independence
of the life of the soul—the soul that is born of the Spirit and has
its home in the Spirit—is beautifully contrasted with what is born

of the Earth, namely the senses and all that exists solely in order to provide a habitation—an earthly body—for the soul.

In order that a beginning may be made in the matter of showing that right thinking can lead beyond the things of everyday life, we will now relate how reliable and well-founded the findings of esoteric investigation are when investigators know from their own direct vision of the spiritual world that the human ego and astral body belong to the world of the stars. When we consider how we are related to those members of our being which remain together during sleep, how this condition is independent of the world of the stars, as indicated by the fact that we can also sleep in the daytime, and if we then make a comparison with the plant and the sunlight, we can be convinced of the validity of occult investigations. It is a matter of recognizing the confirmations which can actually be found in the world. When someone asserts that the findings of esoteric research lack any real foundation, this is only a sign that he has not paid attention to everything that can be gathered from the external world and lead to knowledge. Admittedly this often calls for great energy and freedom from bias—qualities that are not always put into practice. But it may well be insisted that someone who genuinely investigates the spiritual world and then passes on the results of their investigation to the world, passes it on, presumably, to [an audience possessing] sound judgement. Genuine esoteric research is not afraid of intelligent criticism; it objects only to superficial criticism which is not, properly speaking, criticism at all.

If you now recall how the whole course of the evolution of humanity[40] has been described, from the Old Saturn period, through the periods of Old Sun and Old Moon up to our Earth period, you will remember that during the Old Moon period a separation took place; a second separation occurred again during the Earth period, one of the consequences being that the life of soul and the bodily life are more widely separated from each other than was the case during the Old Sun period. In the epoch of the Old Sun, they were still much more closely related. As a consequence of the separation of the Moon from the Sun already during the Old Moon period, our soul became more independent. At that time, in certain intervals between incarnations, the element of soul forced its way out into the macrocosm and made itself independent. This brought about those conditions in the evolution of the Earth which resulted in the separation of the Sun from the Earth and later of the Moon, during the Lemurian epoch. As a consequence, a host of individual human souls, as described in detail in the book *Esoteric Science*,[41] pressed outwards in order to undergo particular destinies while separated from the Earth, returning only at a later time. Now, however, it must be made clear that when we have passed through the gate of death into the spiritual world which is our real home, we—or rather what remains of us—live a life that is radically different from and fundamentally has very little relationship with the former earthly body.

In the next lecture we shall be able to learn what is necessary for more detailed knowledge of the life between death and the new birth.

Lecture 4

BERLIN, 10 DECEMBER 1912

In earlier lectures about the life between death and rebirth, we have heard that the imperishable part of the human being which leaves the physical body at death and, to a considerable extent, the etheric body also, passes through a life between death and the new birth, and that during this period its forces are drawn from the world of the stars. We have also heard how we are able to draw these forces from the world of stars to the extent to which we developed moral and religious qualities during our life on Earth. It was said that, for example, from the region which receives forces radiated from the planet known to esotericism as Mercury, we will be able to draw the requisite forces if, during our life on Earth before death, we developed a genuinely moral disposition. From the Venus region, we can draw the forces we need for our further life in the spiritual worlds, and for our subsequent life on Earth, if we have developed a truly religious attitude before our deaths. To sum up, we may say that as long as we are making use of our senses, as long as we let ourselves be guided and directed by the intellect that is bound to the brain as its instrument, we are connected with the forces of the Earth. But in the life between death and a new birth we are connected with the forces radiating from the worlds of the stars.

In the present age, however, there is a certain difference between our connection with the forces of the Earth during our physical life and our connection with the forces of the stars between death and the new birth. The forces that we draw into our consciousness during our earthly life—that is to say, the forces we experience consciously during earthly life—contribute nothing essential to what we need to build up and vitalize our own being, for they give rise to catabolic processes, processes of destruction. Evidence for this is the simple fact that during sleep we have no consciousness. Why not? The reason is that we are not meant to witness what happens to us during sleep. During sleep, the forces used up during waking life are restored, and we are not meant to witness this process, which is the antithesis of what is in operation during waking life and is concealed from human consciousness. The Bible uses profoundly significant words to express this fact. It is one of the passages in the Bible which, as is the case with all esoteric principles in religious records, is very little understood. In the story of the expulsion from Paradise, it is said that the divine spirit resolved that when we had acquired certain characteristics, for instance, the faculty of distinguishing between good and evil, insight into the forces of *life* should be withheld from us. That is the passage in the Bible where it is announced that we were not to witness the revivification of our members either during sleep or during our entire existence on Earth. We shall not witness it. While we are awake, the whole life-process is one of destruction, of wear and tear. During waking life, nothing in our nature is restored. In the very earliest years of childhood, when any actual inflow of life can still be observed, the child's consciousness is still dim, and the whole restorative process is concealed from us in our later years. The evidence for this is that we do not remember our earliest childhood. We can therefore say that the whole life-giving, restorative process is concealed from our conscious life on Earth. Processes of perception, of cognition, lie within the field of our consciousness, but the life-giving process does not.

This is different during the period of existence between death and a new birth. The purpose of the whole of that period is to draw into our nature the forces that can build up and fashion the next life, to draw these forces from the world of the stars. But this process is not as things are on Earth, when we do not really know our own being. What, after all, do we know about the processes working in our organism? We know nothing of them through direct perception, and what is learnt from anatomy or biology conveys no real knowledge of our being, but is rather something quite different. In the life between death and rebirth, however, we behold how forces from the world of stars work upon our being, how they gradually rebuild it. From this you can gather how greatly perception between death and rebirth differs from perception on Earth. On Earth, we stand at a particular point, direct our senses outwards, and then our sight and hearing expand into space; from the centre where we are standing we face the expanse of space. Exactly the opposite is the case during the life after death. There we feel as if our whole being were outspread, and what we perceive is really the centre. We look at a point. There comes a period between death and a new birth when we describe a circle which passes through the whole Zodiac. We look out, as it were, from every point of the Zodiac, that is to say from different viewpoints, upon our own being, and we feel as if we were gathering from each particular section of the Zodiac the forces which we pour upon our being for the needs of the next incarnation. We look from the circumference towards a centre. It is as if you could duplicate yourself, move around while leaving yourself at the centre, and could drink in the forces of the universe, the life-giving 'soma'[42] which, streaming as it does from different points of the Zodiac, assumes different characteristics as it pours into your being which you have left at the centre. Translated into terms of spiritual reality, this is actually how things are during the life between death and a new birth.

If we now think of the difference between a condition that is really very similar to life between death and rebirth, namely, the condition of sleep, this difference can be characterized very simply, although people who are not accustomed to these ideas will not be able to make much of it. Put simply, the condition of sleep can be characterized as follows.

When we sleep during our earthly existence, that is to say when we have left our physical and etheric body and are living in our ego and astral body, which are then in the world of stars, we too are actually in that world. And it is a fact that our condition in sleep is objectively far more similar to the condition between death and rebirth than is usually imagined. Objectively, the two conditions are very similar. The only difference is that during sleep in normal life we have no consciousness of the world in which we are living, whereas between death and the new birth we are conscious of what is happening to us. That is the essential difference. If we were to awake in our ego and astral body when these members are outside our physical body during sleep, we would be in the same condition as we are between death and a new birth. The difference is actually only a state of consciousness. This is a matter of importance because as long as we live on Earth, therefore also during sleep, we are bound to our physical body. Nor do we become free from the physical body until it passes into the lifeless condition and undergoes a change at death. As long as the physical body remains alive, the union is maintained between our spiritual nature—that is to say, ego and astral body—and the physical and etheric bodies.

Our conception of the state of sleep is, as a rule, too simple; and that is quite comprehensible because usually we describe things from one point of view only, whereas when a human being passes into the higher worlds, conditions are complicated. A complete picture becomes possible only as we progress patiently in anthroposophy and learn to view things from all sides. We generally characterize the state of sleep—and rightly so—by saying that the physical and etheric bodies remain in the bed, while the ego and astral body move outwards and unite with the forces of the stars. But correct as this is from one point of view, it nevertheless presents only one aspect of the matter, as we can realize if we consider from the standpoint of anthroposophy the sleep that occurs at a more or less normal time. Objectively speaking, an afternoon nap is a quite different matter from ordinary sleep at night. What I have now said is concerned not so much with our ordinary state of health, but rather with our whole relationship to the world. We will therefore not consider an afternoon nap, but the sleep of a healthy human being, let us say at midnight, regarded from the standpoint of clairvoyant consciousness.

During the waking life of day, there is a certain regulated connection between the four members of the human constitution: physical body, etheric body, astral body, and ego. This connection can be indicated if I make sketches to show how the so-called aura of the human being appears to clairvoyant consciousness—but of course the sketches are only very rough [Figures 1 and 2].

If we focus on the normal waking state, then we would draw the
auric constellation of the human
being in the following way: the
physical body is the sharper line;
within the punctuated line the
etheric body; what is shaded more
intensely is the astral body; and
the aura of the ego would have
to be drawn in such a way that it
penetrated the whole of human
nature. But I am drawing it as
streams that, without actual bor-
ders, surround it above and below
as though radiating out.

Now I shall juxtapose the difference in the auric composition
of someone sleeping around midnight, or rather the auric image of

Fig. 1

the same person [see Figure 2]. We have the physical and etheric bodies just as in the first drawing. The more darkly shaded area would
be the astral body, the continuation of which would stand out, but
yet would remain in a vertical position. I would then have to draw
the aura of the ego as streaming in the way that you see here. In the
vicinity of the throat, the aura of the ego is interrupted, and begins
again only in the region of the head, but in such a way that it radiates outwards, and proceeds upwards into the indefinite when we are
in a horizontal position. But it is oriented upwards, from the head
upwards. So that essentially our view of the aura of the sleeping
human being would be such that the astral body is substantially condensed and dark—in the drawing, the region that is shaded darkly—
and in the upper parts, it is thinner than during the day. In the region
of the neck, the aura of the ego is interrupted. Below, it radiates
again, and proceeds into the indeterminate.

The essential thing is that in such a sleeping state, what one can call
the auric image of the ego is in fact divided into two parts. During the

Fig. 2

waking state, the aura of the ego coheres like an oval, but during such a sleeping state it divides in the middle, and consists during sleep of two pieces. Through a kind of gravity, one piece is turned downwards and spreads itself out below, so that one has to do not with a closing, but rather with an aura of the ego that's opening up towards the bottom. This part of the aura of the ego is rendered in its appearance for clairvoyant consciousness as a substantially very dark part of the aura, which has dark threads, which however are strongly tinged, for example in dark reddish nuances. What separates itself off above is again such that it runs out slenderly early on from the region of the head, but then expands out into the indefinite, expands so to speak above into the world of stars. The astral aura is not divided in the same way in the middle, so that one cannot speak of an actual division of it, while the aura of the ego is, at least to appearances, divided in two.

Thus in this esoteric view we have a kind of pictorial expression showing that what permeates us as forces of the ego during the waking state goes out into cosmic space. There it finds connection with the world of stars, in order, as it were, to suck in forces out of the world of stars.

Now that part of the ego-aura which streams downwards and becomes dark and more or less opaque while the part streaming upwards is luminous and radiant—all this lower part is particularly exposed to the influence of ahrimanic powers. The adjacent part of the astral aura is, on the other hand, particularly exposed to the luciferic forces. The account that has been given—quite rightly from a certain standpoint—that the ego and astral body leave the human being during sleep is, however, strictly true only as regards the upper parts of the ego-aura and astral aura. It is not correct as regards the parts of the ego-aura and astral aura which correspond more to the lower areas of the human figure, particularly the lower parts of the trunk. Actually, during sleep, these parts of the astral aura and of the ego-aura are more closely bound up with the physical and etheric bodies than is the case during the waking state, and below they are denser, more compact. For we see also that upon awakening, what I have drawn so strongly once again withdraws from the lower portions of the human being. Just as the upper part escapes when we fall asleep, so the lower part of the ego-aura and the astral aura escapes after a certain fashion, and there remains only a kind of piece of both auras inside, as I have drawn in the first figure.

Now it is extremely important to know that in view of the evolution of our Earth and all the forces that have played their part in that evolution—which you will find described in the book *Esoteric Science*[43]—it was ordained that we should not participate in this more lively activity of the lower aura during sleep—that is to say, we were not to witness this activity. The reason for this was that the revitalizing forces we need for the restoration of what has been used up during the waking hours, are kindled by the lower ego-aura and lower astral aura. The vitalizing forces must be drawn from these parts of the aura. That they work upwards and revitalize us depends upon the upper aura developing powers of attraction drawn from the world of stars; it can therefore attract the forces, which, rising from below, act restoratively. That is the objective process.

Understanding of this fact is the best preparation for understanding certain information available to whoever studies ancient records or records based on esotericism. You have always heard—and from a certain standpoint the statement is quite correct—that we leave our physical and etheric bodies in the bed and go forth with our astral body and ego; this is absolutely correct regarding the upper parts of the ego-aura and astral aura, especially of the ego-aura. But if you study Eastern writings, you will find a statement that is exactly the opposite. It is stated there that during sleep what is otherwise present in our consciousness penetrates more deeply into the body. This is the opposite description of sleep. And especially in certain Vedanta writings you will find it stated that the part of us of which we say that during sleep it leaves the physical and etheric bodies, sinks more deeply into those bodies, and that what gives us the power of sight withdraws into deeper regions of the eye so that sight is no longer possible. Why is the process described in this way in Eastern writings? It is because Orientals still have a different standpoint. With their kind of clairvoyance they pay more attention to what goes on *within* the human being; they pay less attention to the emergence of the upper aura and more to the permeation by the lower aura during sleep. Hence from their particular point of view they are right.

The processes which take place in humans during the course of our evolution are very complicated, and as evolution progresses it will become more and more possible for us to envision the whole range of these processes. But evolution consists in our having gradually acquired knowledge of particular processes; hence the differing statements in the different epochs. Although the statements seem to differ, they are not for that reason false; rather, they relate to the particular condition prevailing at the time. But the process of evolution as a whole becomes clear only when all the various processes are taken into account. That is what it depends on.

We ourselves have now reached the point when it is possible to survey quite well a certain portion of the process of evolution. There is a most significant difference in the whole attitude and disposition of our soul when we observe its development during incarnations, let us say in the Egypto-Chaldean[44] period, then in the Greco-Roman period and then again in our own. Even externally it is not difficult to discover what the soul is experiencing. I think that even in this enlightened audience there will be quite a number of individuals who, when they look at a star-strewn sky, cannot locate the particular constellations or perceive how their positions change in the heavens during the night. Speaking generally, it can be said that the number of individuals who are still well-informed about the starry sky will steadily decrease. There will even be people, among town-dwellers for example, whom one might ask in vain: Is there now a Full Moon or a New Moon? This does not in any way imply reproach, for it lies in the natural course of development. What holds good for the soul now would have been utterly impossible during the Egypto-Chaldean epoch, particularly during its earlier periods. In those days our insight into the heavens was very great. Our present age, however, has a definite advantage over the Egypto-Chaldean epoch, inasmuch as logical thinking—of which most people would be capable today if they were to make efforts—was quite beyond the people of that earlier epoch. They lived their lives and carried out their daily tasks more instinctively than we do today. It would be quite erroneous to imagine that when a building or, say, an aqueduct was to be constructed, engineers would sit in their offices and work out the project with the help of plans and the other methods employed nowadays. Engineers in those times no more worked from plans than beavers do today when with such skill and accuracy they set about building their den.

In those early times there was no logical, scientific thinking such as is general today; then our activities during waking life were instinctive. They had acquired their knowledge—and stupendous knowledge has been preserved from the Egypto-Chaldean epoch—in a quite different way. They knew about the secrets of the stars in the night, about the heavens, although they had no astronomy of the kind that is available to us in the present age. They watched the spectacle presented by the stars in the heavens on successive nights and the whole power of the astral forces in space worked upon them, and not merely the sensory impressions made by what they observed. They participated in it. For example, the passage of the Great Bear or of the Pleiades was an actual experience within them. The experience continued while they were asleep, for they were sensitive to the spiritual reality connected with the passage of a constellation such as the Great Bear across the heavens. Together with the spectacle perceived by the senses they were inwardly aware of the living spiritual reality in cosmic space. Something came into their consciousness which ours today is quite unable to experience. Nowadays we have eyes only for the material picture of the stars in the sky. And being very clever, we look at a chart of the heavens into which figures of animals are inscribed, and say: The ancients inscribed symbols here and there to represent their idea of the grouping of the stars, but we have now progressed sufficiently to be cognisant of the reality. We of the modern age do not know that the ancients had actually seen what they inscribed into their charts; they drew something of which they had a direct vision. Some of them were more skilful drawers than others, but they drew what they had actually perceived. They did not, however, perceive in the way that is customary in physical life. When they experienced, for example, the passage of the Great Bear across the heavens at night they saw the physical stars implanted in a mighty spiritual Being whom they could actually perceive. But it would be childish to imagine that they saw an animal moving across the heavens in the way we should see a physical animal on the Earth. This experience of the passage of the constellation of the Pleiades, for example, across the heavens affected them intimately. They felt that the experience had an effect upon their astral bodies and caused changes there.

You can form an idea of this experience by picturing that there is a rose in front of you, but you are not looking at it; you are merely holding it and what you experience is your own contact with it. You then form an idea of the rose. It was in this way that the ancients 'contacted' as it were with their astral bodies what they experienced about the constellation of the Great Bear; they 'felt' the astral reality and experienced their own contact with it. This brought about changes in their very being, changes which are still brought about today but are unnoticed.

Evolution leading into our modern scientific age with its power of rationalistic judgement consists in the fact that direct experience of spiritual processes has ceased and that we are left with the world of the senses and the brain-bound intellect. Thus when people living in the Egypto-Chaldean epoch spoke of the spiritual beings in space and drew figures of these beings, inscribing physical stars as focal points, this was in keeping with the reality—which was an actual experience. Hence people living in the Egypto-Chaldean epoch had a faculty of perception far more in line with the life between death and rebirth than is our present physical consciousness. When we actually realize how the astral body and the ego experience what is happening in the heavens, it is also obvious that we are then living outside our physical and etheric bodies. There is not the slightest reason for believing that a life in which such experiences occur is impossible when the physical and etheric bodies are actually laid aside at death. Thus in the people of old it was a matter of direct knowledge that between death and the new birth they would experience the happenings in the world of stars. A person living in the Egypto-Chaldean epoch would have thought it ridiculous if anyone set out to prove to him the immortality of the soul. He would have said: 'But that needs no proof!' He would not even have understood what a proof is in our meaning of the word, for logical thinking did not yet exist. If they had learnt in an esoteric school what in the future would be meant by 'proof', they would still have insisted that it is unnecessary to prove the immortality of the soul, because in experiencing the nocturnal, starry heavens one is already experiencing something that is independent of the body. Immortality was thus an actual experience, and the people of those times knew a great deal about what we today describe in connection with perception in the disembodied state. They knew it intimately.

And now, turning from the more remote worlds of stars to the planets, these people of old experienced the spiritual sphere that is connected, for instance, with Saturn. They were able to perceive— this is true especially of the earlier periods of the Egypto-Chaldean epoch—what remains of a human being during their life in the Saturn sphere between death and the new birth. People would have thought it very strange if it had been suggested to them that they should try to establish connection with Mars as is sometimes hinted at today, for they were quite conscious of being related to these worlds. If someone has knowledge of Saturn or Mars or another planetary state and can follow its functions in our planetary system, this leads to knowledge of the pre-earthly conditions of Old Saturn, Old Sun and Old Moon described in the book *Esoteric Science*.[45] This was once a matter of actual experience. There would have been no need to lecture about it. All that was necessary would have been to make us conscious that it was simply a matter of inducing in those no longer capable of perceiving such things conditions which made perception possible. This could not have been achieved otherwise.

By the time of the Greco-Latin epoch this state of things had already changed. We had lost our sensitivity for everything I have been describing, and only *remembrance* of it remained. In the Greco-Latin epoch, among the leading cultures, for example of Southern Europe, there was no longer any equal possibility of direct vision of the spiritual beings of the heavens, but remembrance of that vision remained. Thus a soul who was born within Greco-Latin culture no longer had the possibility of seeing into the world of stars in order to intuit the spiritual. They no longer saw to the same degree as in the Egypto-Chaldean epoch the spiritual beings that belonged to the world of stars. Just as we remember today what we experienced yesterday, so did souls in the Greco-Latin epoch still remember what they had experienced of the universe in earlier incarnations. This radiated into human souls and was a living experience. Plato[46] speaks of it as 'recollection', but we do not always call it so. Progress in evolution consisted in the suppression of this direct experience and the development during the Greco-Latin epoch of the faculty of judgement and the formation of concepts. Hence the earlier vision was bound to recede and could survive only as recollection, remembrance. This is exemplified most clearly of all in Aristotle,[47] who lived in the fourth century BCE and was the founder of logic, of the art of judging. He was himself no longer able to perceive anything of the spiritual realities in the worlds of the stars, but in his writings he brings all the old theories back again. He does not speak of the physical heavenly bodies as we know them today, but rather of the 'Spirits of the Spheres', of spiritual beings. And a great many of his utterances were an enumeration of the individual planetary spirits and of the fixed stars, finally leading to the one universal Godhead. The Spirits of the Spheres still play an important role in the works of Aristotle.

But even the remembrance in Greco-Latin times of the spiritual beings in the universe was gradually lost to humanity, and it is interesting to watch how the ancient knowledge disappears piece by piece as later epochs approach. The more spiritually-minded individualities still drew from their remembrance the consciousness that spiritual beings are connected with all physical bodies existing in space—as anthroposophy describes today. A great deal in this connection was presented magnificently by Kepler.[48] The nearer we come to modern times, however, the more the possibility fades of even a remembrance of what the soul experienced in the Egypto-Chaldean epoch from contemplation of the heavens. As the age of Copernicanism[49] approached, even the memory that still survived in the Greco-Latin epoch faded, and astronomers had eyes only for the physical globes rushing through space. Only occasionally something plays into the consciousness of more modern thinkers that there is still a possibility of gleaning from the constellations in the heavens genuine knowledge of spiritual events. Kepler, for example, set out independently to calculate from the stars the date of the birth of Jesus of Nazareth.[50] Such a calculation was possible because Kepler's whole being was still permeated through and through with spirituality. The same applies to his realization that a certain constellation of stars in the year 1604[51] would be followed by further suppression of the ancient remembrances.

The nearer we come to the modern age, the more is humanity dependent upon the physical senses and the brain-bound intellect, because what our souls had experienced in ancient times has been thrust down into the deeper strata of consciousness. All of you once harboured in your souls the experience of still being aware of the spiritual life pervading cosmic spheres. This is everywhere present in the depths of your own souls. But it is not possible today to lead souls during the hours of darkness and guide their vision, let us say, to the constellation of the Great Bear and enable them to experience as realities the spiritual forces emanating from that group of stars. It is not possible because the powers of vision and perception lie in such depths of the soul. During sleep at night we experience the heavens with the radiating upper part of the aura, but we are not conscious of it. Hence, for souls of the present age the right procedure is to raise into consciousness by valid methods the forgotten impressions received in olden times. And how is this done? As we do it in anthroposophy! Nothing

recapitulation

new is imposed upon souls; rather, what they experienced in earlier epochs is drawn forth. What souls could no longer actually
experience in the Greco-Latin epoch but had not yet entirely forgotten—today it is entirely forgotten, but it can be drawn forth
again. Anthroposophy is the stimulus for drawing forth the forces
of knowledge which lie deep within our souls. All human beings
who have partaken in evolution up to the time of Western culture
have in the depths of their souls the conceptions that should be
kindled to life through anthroposophy; and the methods used in
anthroposophy are the stimuli for achieving this.

We will now consider the difference between these two attitudes to the world, between that of a human soul incarnated in
the Greco-Latin epoch and one incarnated today. We have heard
that during the Greco-Latin epoch, in earthly life too, the soul had
a certain connection with and capacity for perception of what
is lived through in the period between death and the new birth.
These experiences had not yet withdrawn into such deep strata
of the soul. Hence in those very ancient times there was much
less difference between human consciousness on Earth and the
consciousness between death and rebirth than there is today. The
ancient Greeks had some remembrance of what they had once
experienced, but even so the difference was already great. Conditions today have reached the stage when between death and the
new birth, consciousness can still be kindled in a human being in
the Venus sphere if, on Earth, we have cultivated a moral and religious attitude of soul. But in and especially beyond the sphere of
the Sun, it is impossible for consciousness to be kindled if during
our life on Earth we have made no attempt to raise to the level
of waking consciousness the concepts lying in the depths of the
soul. Here, in earthly life, anthroposophy seems to be a kind of
theoretical world-conception which we master because it interests
us. After death, however, it is a torch which from a certain point
of time onwards between death and rebirth illumines the spiritual
world for us. If anthroposophy is disdained here in the physical
world, no torch is available in that other world and consciousness is dimmed. To pursue anthroposophy is not merely a matter

of imbibing so many theories; it is a living force, a torch which can illumine life. The contents of the spiritual teachings here on Earth are concepts and ideas, but after death they are living forces! This applies, however, only to consciousness. It will be clear to you from what I said at the beginning of the lecture that already in earthly existence, the spiritual ideas we acquire are life-giving forces. But we cannot witness the outcome of these life-giving forces because knowledge of the powers from which they originate is withheld from us. After death, however, we actually behold them. Here on Earth, anthroposophy seems to be so much theory, and the human being in the waking state has no consciousness of what is spiritually life-giving, but nevertheless objectively present. After death, we are a direct witness of how the forces we took into ourselves together with the spiritual teachings received during our life on Earth have an organizing, vitalizing, strengthening effect upon what is within our being when we are preparing for a new incarnation.

In this way spiritual teaching actually becomes part of the evolution of humanity. But if this spiritual teaching were to be rejected— at the present time it suffices if only a few accept it but in the future more and more individuals must do so—then, as they return to incarnations on Earth, human beings will gradually find that they lack the life-giving forces they need. Decadence and atrophy would set in during the subsequent incarnation. Human beings would quickly wither; they would be prematurely wrinkled. Decadence of physical humanity would set in if spiritual forces were not received. The forces that we once drew from the worlds of stars must now be drawn from the depths of our own souls and used for furthering the evolution of humanity.

If you reflect about these matters you will be filled through and through with the thought that existence on Earth is of immense significance. It was necessary that we should be so inwardly deepened by our union with the worlds of stars that the forces we had otherwise always drawn from those worlds would become the inmost forces of our soul and be drawn up again from its depths. But that can be done only on Earth. One could say: In primeval times the soma-juice rained down from the heavens into individual souls, was preserved there and must now be drawn forth again from those souls. In this way we acquire a conception of the mission of the Earth. And having presented this conception today we will proceed to study the life between death and the new birth in even greater detail.

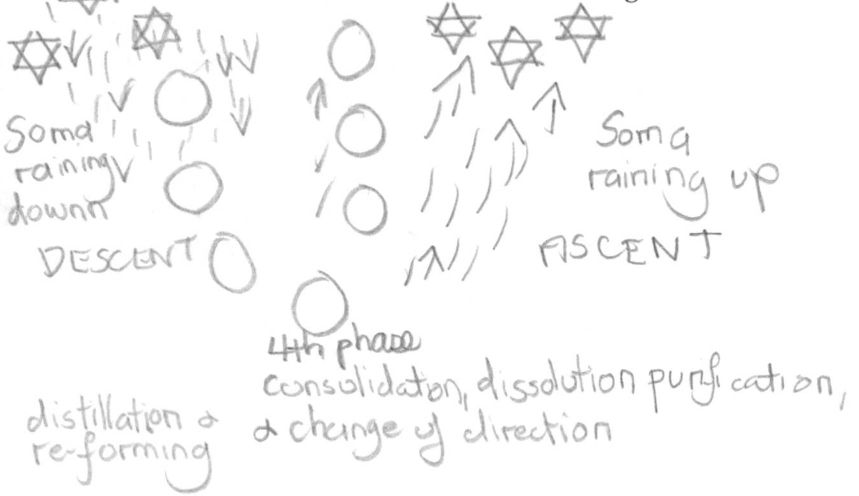

Handwritten annotations:
Ascent
Soma raining down
DESCENT
Soma raining up
ASCENT
4th phase
Consolidation, dissolution purification, & change of direction
distillation & re-forming

LECTURE 5

BERLIN, 22 DECEMBER 1912

I SHALL not be speaking today about the Christmas Festival in general as in previous years, for I propose to do that on Tuesday. I would ask you to think of what I shall say as a gift placed under the Christmas tree in the form of an anthroposophical Christmas study—a study which, because of the significant knowledge it contains, may well be the subject of lengthy reflection and meditation. At this Christmas season we may very properly think of an individual considered by many people to be a mythological or mystical figure, but with whose name we ourselves connect the spiritual impulses of Western cultural life. I refer to Christian Rosenkreutz.[52]

With this individuality and his activity since the thirteenth century we associate everything that has to do with the propagation of the impulse given by Christ's appearance on the Earth and the fulfilment of the Mystery of Golgotha. On one occasion, I also spoke of what may be called the last initiation of Christian Rosenkreutz in the thirteenth century. Today I shall speak of a deed he performed towards the end of the sixteenth century. This deed is of particular significance because it linked with the Christ-Impulse an achievement of supreme importance in the history of human evolution—an achievement before the time of the Mystery of Golgotha.

One of the innumerable factors which enable us to grasp the supreme significance of the Mystery of Golgotha in the history of humanity is the deed of Gautama Buddha, the founder of a different religion. Eastern tradition tells us that in the life usually spoken of as Buddha's, Gautama Buddha rose in his twenty-ninth year from the rank of Bodhisattva to that of Buddhahood. We are

aware of what that ascent means, and also of the world-wide significance of the Sermon at Benares,[53] the first great accomplish-
ment of the Buddha who had previously been a Bodhisattva. Of
all this we are deeply conscious. Today we will think especially of
one aspect only, namely, what it signifies in the history of worlds
when a Bodhisattva rises to the rank of Buddhahood. The Eastern
teaching—which does not differ from that of Western esotericism
in regard to this event—is that when a human being rises from
the rank of Bodhisattva to that of Buddhahood, they need not
henceforward incarnate on the Earth in a physical body, but rather
they can continue their work in purely spiritual worlds. And so
we recognize as a valid truth that the individuality who lived on
Earth for the last time as Gautama Buddha has since then been
present in lofty spiritual worlds continuing to influence evolution
and sending impulses and forces from those spheres to further the
development and stature of humanity.

We have also spoken of a significant deed of the Buddha, a deed
that was his contribution to the Mystery of Golgotha. We have been
reminded of the beautiful narrative in the Gospel of St Luke concerning the shepherds who had gathered together at the time of the
birth of the Jesus Child described in that Gospel.[54] The narrative tells
of a song which rang out from Angels and resounded in the devout,
expectant souls of the shepherds: 'And suddenly there was with the
angel a multitude of the heavenly host praising God, and saying,
Glory to God in the highest, and on earth peace, good will toward
men.'[55] It is the song which tells of the revelation of the divine-spir-
itual forces in the spiritual worlds and the reflection of these forces
in the hearts of people who are of good will. We have heard that the
song of peace which then rang out was the contribution of the Buddha from spiritual heights to the Mystery of Golgotha. The Buddha
united with the astral body of the Jesus Child of whom we are told
in St Luke's Gospel, and the song of the Angels announced in that
Gospel is to be understood as the influx of the Gospel of peace into
the deed subsequently to be wrought by Christ Jesus. The Buddha
spoke at the time of the birth of Jesus, and the song of the Angels
heard by the shepherds was the message from ancient, pre-Christian

times, of peace and all-embracing human love, which were also to be integrated into the mission of Christ Jesus.

Thereafter the Buddha continued to be active in the advancing stream of Christian evolution in the West, and special mention must be made of his further activity. The Buddha was no longer working in a human body, but rather in the spiritual body in which he had revealed himself at the time of the birth of Jesus. He continued to work, perceptible to those who through some form of initiation are able to establish a relationship not only with physical human beings, but also with those sublime leaders and teachers who come to us in purely spiritual bodies.

A few centuries after the Mystery of Golgotha, in a Mystery school situated in the region of the Black Sea in the South of Russia, there were teachers of great significance. What actually took place there can be no more than indicated—and even then only half-met-aphorically. Among the physically incarnated teachers present in the School there was one who did not work in a physical body and could therefore be contacted only by pupils and neophytes able to establish relations with leaders and teachers who appeared in this Mystery Centre in spiritual bodies. One such teacher was the being spoken of as Gautama Buddha. In the seventh and eighth century after the Mystery of Golgotha, this being had a notable pupil. At that time the Buddha, in his true nature, was in no way concerned with propagating Buddhism in its old form, for he too had advanced with evolution. He had taken the Christ-Impulse into the very depths of his being; he had actually co-operated in its inception. What had still to be transmitted of the old form of Buddhism came to expression in the general tone and character of what the Buddha imparted in the Mystery Centre referred to above; but everything was clothed in a Christian form. It may truly be said that when the Buddha had become a being who no longer needed to incarnate in a human body, he co-operated from the spiritual world in the development of Christianity. A faithful pupil of his had absorbed into the depths of his soul the teaching which the Buddha gave at that time, but which could not become the common possession of all humanity. It was a teaching which represented a union of Buddhism and Christianity.

It implied absolute surrender to what is supra-sensible in human nature, the abandonment of any direct bond with the physical and earthly, complete dedication in heart and soul, not merely in mind and intellect, to what is of the nature of soul and spirit in the world. It meant withdrawal from all the externalities of life and absolute devotion in the inner life to the mysteries of the Spirit. And when that being who had been a pupil of the Buddha and Christ, who had learnt of the Christ through the Buddha, appeared again on Earth, he was incarnated as the person known in history as Francis of Assisi.[56] Those who desire to understand from esoteric knowledge the absolutely unique quality of soul and manner of life of Francis of Assisi, especially what is so impressive about him because of its remoteness from the world and everyday experience—let them realize that in his previous incarnation he was a Christian pupil in the Mystery Centre of which I have spoken.

In this way the Buddha continued to work, invisibly and supersensibly, in the stream that had become part of the process of evolution since the Mystery of Golgotha took place. The figure of Francis of Assisi is a clear indication of what the effect of the Buddha's activity would have been in all subsequent times if nothing else had happened and he had continued to work as he had done while preparing Francis of Assisi for his mission in the world. Many, many human beings would have developed from the character and disposition of Francis of Assisi. They would have become, within Christianity, disciples and followers of Buddha. But this Buddha-like quality in those who became followers of Francis of Assisi would have been quite unable to cope with the demands that would be made of humanity in modern civilization.

Let us remind ourselves of what has been said about the passage of the human soul through the various regions of the cosmos between death and a new birth. We have heard how during that period of existence the human soul has to pass through the planetary spheres, to traverse the expanse of cosmic space. Between death and the new birth, we actually become inhabitants, in succession, of the Moon, Mercury, Venus, Sun, Mars, Jupiter, and Saturn. We then draw our life together again in order to incarnate through a parental pair and undergo the experiences that are possible on Earth, but not in other planetary spheres. Since the last death, every soul incarnated on the Earth has undergone the experiences that belong to the heavens. Through birth, we bring into our existence on Earth the forces we have acquired in the various heavenly spheres.

Now let us remind ourselves of how life flows by on Earth, how at each new incarnation the human being finds that the Earth has changed and that our experiences are quite different. In the course of our incarnations, an individual will have lived in pre-Christian times and have been incarnated again after the impulse of the Mystery of Golgotha had been given to evolution. Let us picture with the greatest possible clarity how the Earth evolves, descending from divine and spiritual heights to a certain nadir. The impulse of the Mystery of Golgotha then made an ascent possible in the evolutionary process. The ascent is presently only beginning, but it will continue if human souls receive the impulse of this Mystery and then, later on, rise again to the stage they had reached before the temptation of Lucifer. Let us realize that, in accordance with the fundamental laws of evolution, whenever we return to the Earth through birth we find quite different conditions of existence.

The same applies to the heavenly spheres into which we pass between death and a new birth. Like our Earth, these heavenly bodies also pass through descending and ascending phases of evolution. Whenever we pass into a planetary sphere after death—let us say of Mars, or Venus, or Mercury—we enter different conditions, have different experiences, and receive different impulses, which we bring back again into physical existence through birth. And because the heavenly bodies are also undergoing evolution, our souls bring back different forces into each incarnation.

Today, because of the profound significance of the Christmas Festival, our thoughts are directed to the spiritual realities of cosmic space itself, and we will consider a particular example of evolution. This example is revealed to esoteric investigation if that investigation is able to penetrate deeply enough into the spiritual nature of other planets and planetary systems as well as into that of the Earth. In the spiritual life of the Earth, there was a descending phase of evolution until the time of the Mystery of Golgotha and thereafter a phase of ascent—now latent for the sole reason that a deeper understanding of the Christ Impulse is necessary. Similarly, there were phases of descent and ascent in the evolution of Mars, into whose sphere we pass between death and rebirth. Until the fifteenth and sixteenth century, the evolution of Mars was such that what had always been bestowed upon it from the spiritual worlds was undergoing a phase of descent, just as was the case in the evolution of the Earth until the beginning of the Christian era. By the time of the fifteenth and sixteenth century, it was necessary that the evolution of Mars should become a process of ascent, for the consequences of the phase of descent had become all too evident in that sphere. As already said, when we pass again into earthly existence through birth, we bring with us the impulses and forces gathered from the worlds of stars, among them the forces of Mars. The example of a certain individuality is clear evidence of the change that had come about in the forces brought by human beings from Mars to the Earth.

It is known to all esotericists that the same soul which appeared on Earth in Nicolaus Copernicus, the inaugurator of the dawn of the modern age, had been previously incarnated from 1401 to 1464 in Cardinal Nicholas of Cusa, Nicholas Cusanus.[57] But how utterly different were these two personalities who harboured the same soul within them! Nicholas of Cusa in the fifteenth century was dedicated in mind and heart to the spiritual worlds; all his study was rooted in the spiritual worlds, and when he appeared again as Copernicus he was responsible for the great transformation which could have been achieved only by eliminating from the conception of space and the planetary system every iota of spirituality, and thinking only of the external movements and interrelationships of the heavenly bodies. How was it possible that the same soul which had been on the Earth in Nicholas of Cusa and was wholly dedicated to the spiritual worlds, could appear in the next incarnation in an individual who conceived of the heavenly bodies purely in terms of their mathematical, spatial and geometric aspects? This was possible because a soul who passed through the Mars sphere during the interval between the time of Nicholas of Cusa and that of Copernicus had entered into a phase of decline. It was therefore not possible to bring from the Mars sphere any forces that would have inspired souls during physical life to soar into the spiritual worlds. The souls who passed through the Mars sphere at that particular time could grasp only the physical and material nature of things. If these conditions on Mars had continued without change, if the phase of decline had been prolonged, souls would have brought with them from the Mars sphere forces that would have rendered them incapable of anything except a purely materialistic conception of the world. Nevertheless the results of the decline of Mars were responsible for bringing modern natural science into existence; these forces poured with such strength into human souls that they led to triumph after triumph in the domain of materialistic knowledge of the world; and in the further course of evolution this influence would have worked exclusively for the promotion of materialistic science, for the interests of trade and industry only, of external forms of culture on the Earth.

It would have been possible for a class of human beings to be formed entirely under the influence of a lack of certain old Mars-forces, and to be interested in external culture only; these human beings would have confronted another class of individuals, composed of followers of Francis of Assisi, in other words, of Buddhism transported into Christianity. A being such as the Buddha, having continued to work as previously indicated until the time of Francis of Assisi, would have been able to produce on the Earth a counterweight to the purely materialistic conception of the world by pouring strong forces into human souls. But this would have led to the formation of a class of individuals capable only of leading a monastic life patterned on that of Francis of Assisi; and these individuals alone would have been able to scale the heights of spiritual life.

If this state of things had remained, humanity would have divided more and more sharply into two classes: the one composed of those who were devoted entirely to the interests of material existence on the Earth and the advancement of external culture, and the other class, due to the continuing influence of Buddha, would have consisted of those who fostered and preserved spiritual culture. But the souls belonging to the latter class would, like Francis of Assisi, have been incapable of participating in external, material forms of civilization. These two categories of human beings would have become more and more sharply separated. As the inevitability of this state of things could be prophetically foreseen, it became the task of the individual whom we revere under the name of Christian Rosenkreutz to prevent such a separation taking place in the further evolution of humanity on the Earth. Christian Rosenkreutz felt it to be his mission to offer to every human soul, living no matter where, the possibility of rising to the heights of spiritual life. It has always been emphasized among us, and it is clearly set forth in my book *How to Know Higher Worlds: A Modern Path of Initiation*,[58] that our goal in the sphere of esoteric development in the West is not to rise into spiritual worlds as the result of ascetic isolation from life, but rather to make it possible for every human soul to discover for itself the path into the spiritual world; that the ascent into spiritual worlds should be compatible with every status in life; that humanity should not divide into two categories, one composed of people devoted entirely to external, industrial and commercial interests, becoming increasingly ingenious, materialized, and animalized, whereas those in the other category would hold themselves aloof in a life patterned on that of Francis of Assisi—all this was the concern of Christian Rosenkreutz at the time when the approaching modern age was to inaugurate the epoch of materialistic culture during which all souls would bring with them the Mars-forces in their state of decline. And because there could not be within human souls the power to prevent the separation, it has to be ensured that from the Mars-forces themselves there would come to us the impulse to work with our whole being for spiritual aims. For example, it was necessary that human beings should be educated to think in terms of sound scientific principles, to formulate ideas and concepts in line with those principles; but at the same time the soul must have the capacity to deepen and develop the ideas spiritually, in order that the way can be found from a scientific view of the world to lofty heights of spiritual life.

This possibility had to be created! And it was created by Christian Rosenkreutz, who towards the end of the sixteenth century gathered

around him his faithful followers from all over the Earth, enabling
them to participate in what takes place outwardly in space from one
heavenly body to another, but is prepared in the sacred Mystery
Centres, where aims are pursued leading beyond those of planetary
spiritual life to the spiritual life of cosmic worlds. Christian Rosenkreutz gathered around him those who had also been with him at
the time of his initiation in the thirteenth century. Among them was
one who for long years had been his pupil and friend, who had at
one time been incarnated on the Earth, but now no longer needed
to appear in a physical incarnation: this was Gautama Buddha, now a
spiritual being after having risen to the rank of Buddhahood. He was
the pupil of Christian Rosenkreutz. And in order that what could
be achieved through the Buddha should become part of the mission of Christian Rosenkreutz at that time, a joint deed resulted in
the transference of the Buddha from a sphere of earthly activity to
one of cosmic activity. The impulse given by Christian Rosenkreutz
made this possible. We will speak on another occasion in greater
detail of the relationship between Gautama Buddha and Christian
Rosenkreutz; at the moment it is simply a matter of stating that this
relationship led to the individuality of the Buddha ceasing to work
in the sphere of the Earth as he had formerly worked in the Mystery
Centre near the Black Sea, and transferring his activity to Mars. And
so at the beginning of the seventeenth century there took place in
the evolution of Mars something similar to what had come about at
the beginning of the ascending phase of Earth evolution through
the Mystery of Golgotha. What may be called the advent of the Buddha on Mars was brought about through Christian Rosenkreutz and
the ascending phase of Mars evolution began from then onwards
just as on Earth the ascending phase of culture began with the Mystery of Golgotha.

Thus the Buddha became a Redeemer and Saviour for Mars as
Christ Jesus had become for the Earth. The Buddha had been prepared for this by his teaching of Nirvana, lack of satisfaction with
earthly existence, liberation from physical incarnation. This teaching had been prepared in a sphere outside the Earth, but with the
Earth's goal in view. If we can look into the soul of the Buddha and

grasp the import of the Sermon at Benares, we shall witness the preparation of activity that was not to be confined to the Earth. And then we shall realize how infinitely wise was the contract between Christian Rosenkreutz and the Buddha, as the result of which, at the beginning of the seventeenth century, the Buddha relinquished his activity on the Earth through which he would have been able, from the spiritual world, to influence human souls between birth and death, in order henceforward to work in the Mars sphere for souls between death and rebirth.

This is the momentous outcome of what might be called the transference of the essence of the Christmas Festival from the Earth to Mars. As a result, all human souls, in a certain sense, pass through a phase of being followers of Francis of Assisi and thereby, indirectly, of the Buddha. But they do not pass through this phase on the Earth; they pass through their monasticism—to use a paradoxical expression—their adherence to Francis of Assisi, on Mars, and bring forces from there to the Earth. As a result, what they have thus acquired remains in the form of forces slumbering in their souls, and they need not adopt a strictly monastic life in order to undergo the experiences undergone by intimate pupils of Francis of Assisi. This necessity was avoided by the transference of the Buddha to cosmic worlds by agreement with Christian Rosenkreutz, whose work on Earth now continued without the collaboration of the Buddha. If the Buddha had continued his activity on the Earth, all that he could have achieved would have been to make us into Buddhist or Franciscan monks, and the other souls would have been abandoned to materialistic civilization. But because what may be called a kind of 'Mystery of Golgotha' for Mars took place, during a period when human souls are not incarnated on Earth, these souls absorb, in a sphere outside the Earth, what they need for their further terrestrial existence, namely, an element of true Buddhism, which in the epoch after Christ's coming can be acquired only between death and a new birth.

We are now at the threshold of a great Mystery, a Mystery which has brought an impulse still operating in the evolution of humanity. Those who genuinely understand this evolution know that any truly effective influence in life on the Earth inevitably becomes part of the general stream of evolution. The event that may be called the Mystery of Golgotha on Mars was different from the Mystery of Golgotha on Earth—less powerful, less incisive, not culminating in death. But you can have some idea of it if you reflect that the Being who was the greatest Prince of Peace and Love, who was the Bringer of Compassion to the Earth, was transferred to Mars in order to work at the head of the evolution of that planet. It is no mythological fable that Mars received its name because it is the planet where the forces are involved in most bitter strife. The mission of the Buddha entailed his crucifixion in the arena of the planet where the most belligerent forces are present, although these forces are essentially of a psychic and spiritual nature.

Here, then, we face a deed of a Being whose destiny it was as a great servant of Christ Jesus, to receive and carry forward the Christ Impulse in the right way. We stand face to face with the Mystery of Christian Rosenkreutz, recognizing his wisdom to have been so great that, as far as lay within his power, he incorporated into the evolution of humanity as a whole the other impulses that had been decisive factors in preparation for the Mystery of Golgotha.

A subject such as this cannot be grasped merely in terms of words or intellect; in its depth and range it must be *felt*—with the whole heart and soul. We must grasp what it signifies to be aware that among the forces we bring with us in the present epoch when we pass into incarnation on the Earth there are also the forces of the Buddha. Those forces were transferred to a sphere through which we pass between death and a new birth in order to enter in the right way into earthly life; for in this earthly life between birth and death it is our task to establish the right relationship to the Christ Impulse, to the Mystery of Golgotha. And this is possible only if all the impulses work together in harmony. The Christ descended from other worlds and united with the Earth's evolution. His purpose is to give to everyone the greatest of all impulses with which the human soul can be endowed. But this is possible only if all the forces connected with the evolution of humanity take effect at the right point in the process of that evolution. The great Teacher of the doctrine of Nirvana, who exhorted us to liberate our souls from the urge for reincarnation, was not destined to work in the sphere of physical incarnation. But in accordance with the great Plan designed by the Gods—in which, however, we must participate because we are servants of the Gods—in accordance with this Plan, the work of that great Teacher was to continue in the life that lies in the realm beyond birth and death.

Try to feel the inner justification of this conception and in its light follow the course of evolution; then you will realize why the Buddha had necessarily to precede Christ Jesus, and how he worked after the Christ Impulse had been given. Think about this and you will understand in its true light the phase of evolution and of spiritual life which began in the seventeenth century and in which you yourselves are living; you will understand it because you will realize that before human souls pass into physical existence through birth they are imbued with the forces that bear them forward.

At the time of an important festival, instead of a seasonal lecture, I wanted to lay under the Christmas tree, as a kind of Christmas gift, certain information about Christian Rosenkreutz. Perhaps some or even many of you will receive it as was intended—as a means of strengthening the heart and the forces of the soul. We shall need this strengthening if we are to live with inner security amid the harmonies and disharmonies of existence.

If at Christmastide we can be strengthened and invigorated by consciousness of our connection with the forces of the great universe, we may well take with us from this centre of anthroposophical work something that was laid as a gift under the Christmas tree and as an encouragement can remain a living force throughout the year if we nurture it during our life from one Christmas season to the next.

LECTURE 6

W E have already considered certain aspects of our lives between death and rebirth, and a short time ago an account was given of the relationship between Christian Rosenkreutz and Buddha. This was done because since then, the Buddha has been connected with the planetary sphere of Mars. Humans, after experiencing the Christ Event in the sphere of the Sun between death and rebirth, pass into the sphere of Mars and there undergo an experience connected with Buddha in the form that is right for the present age—though not, of course, for the age when the individuality of whom we are now thinking lived on the Earth as Gautama Buddha. Genuine enlightenment about human nature and our connection with the evolution of worlds is possible only if our understanding keeps abreast of that evolution.

We know that in the post-Atlantean era there have so far been five main consecutive epochs during which the human soul has undergone significant experiences. These epochs are: the Ancient Indian, the Ancient Persian, the Egypto-Chaldean, the Greco-Latin, and our own. We also know that in each such epoch the next is prepared—as it were, in germ. In our present epoch, the sixth post-Atlantean period is already slowly being prepared in human souls, and this preparation must be of the following kind. The preparation consists in our being helped to understand what is now spreading in the world in the form of esoteric teachings, of anthroposophy. In this way, not only will a knowledge of human nature that is necessary for the future be promulgated, but there will also be an ever deepening understanding of the Christ-Impulse. Everything that contributes to this increasing understanding of the Christ-Impulse is comprised for the West in what may be called the Mystery of the Holy Grail.[59] This Mystery is also closely connected with matters such as the one spoken of recently—namely, the mission for Mars having been delegated by Christian Rosenkreutz to Buddha. This Mystery of the Holy Grail can impart to modern humanity knowledge that will help us to understand the life between death and rebirth in the way that is right for our time. This understanding depends upon resolute efforts to answer a question of vital importance, and unless we try to carry this question to greater depths than has hitherto been possible, we shall be unable to make further progress in our studies of human life between death and a new birth. The question is this: Why was it that even in areas where Christianity was proclaimed in its deeper aspect, certain teachings were left in the background—teachings that must be introduced today into the presentation of Christianity in its more advanced form?

You are aware that everything connected with the subject of reincarnation and karma was left in the background not only in the outer, exoteric presentations of Christianity, but also in the more esoteric expositions of past centuries. Many people who hear about the content of the anthroposophical worldview ask: How does it come about that although Rosicrucianism must, we are told, be included in everything that esotericism has to give—how does it come about that hitherto, indeed until our own time, Rosicrucianism did not contain the teachings of reincarnation and karma? Why must these teachings now be added to Rosicrucianism?

To understand this we must again consider our relationship to the world. The preconditions for the advanced study we hope to reach in these lectures is already to be found in my book *Esoteric Science*. But we must now consider closely how we are related to the world in our own time, in the epoch that was preceded by the planetary stages of Old Saturn, Old Sun, and Old Moon.

We know that the human being on Earth consists of physical body, etheric body, astral body, and the 'I' or ego, together with everything that belongs to these members. We know, too, that when individuals pass through the portal of death, they leave behind them, first of all, their physical body; then, after a certain time, most of the etheric body dissolves into the cosmic ether, and only a kind of extract of it remains with us. The astral body accompanies us for a considerable time, but again a kind of sheath of that body is cast off when the period of Kamaloka is over. After that, the extracts of the etheric and astral bodies are subject to the further transformations undergone by humans between death and rebirth. In its innermost nature, the human 'I' remains unchanged. Whether we are passing through the period between birth and death in the physical body, through the period of Kamaloka when we are still completely enveloped by the astral body, or through the period of Devachan, which lasts for the greater part of the time between death and rebirth—it is the 'I' or ego which, basically speaking, passes through all these periods. But this 'I', the real, true 'I', must not be confused with the 'I' that the human being on Earth recognizes as our own. Philosophers have a good deal to say about this human 'I' in the physical body, which they think they understand. They say, for instance, that the 'I' is the principle that remains intact, although everything else in the human being changes. The true 'I' does indeed remain, but whether this can be said of the 'I' of which the philosophers speak is another matter altogether. Anyone who insists on referring to the persistence of that 'I' of which the philosophers speak is refuted by the simple fact that during the night we sleep, for then the 'I' of the philosophers is extinguished; it is simply not there. And if during the whole period between death and rebirth conditions were the same as they are during sleep at night, to speak of the permanence of our soul during that period would be meaningless. Fundamentally speaking, there would be no difference between the 'I' not being there at all or merely continuing to live knowing nothing of itself, as if it were something external. The question of immortality cannot be a matter of the 'I' simply being there; it must also have some knowledge of itself. Thus the immortality of the 'I' of which human consciousness is first aware is refuted by every sleep at night, for then this 'I' is simply extinguished. The real, true 'I' lies much deeper—much, much deeper! How can we form an idea of this real 'I', even if we cannot yet claim to have any knowledge of esotericism?

We can form a valid idea if we say to ourselves: The 'I' must be present in the human being even when we cannot yet say 'I', when we are still crawling on the floor. The real 'I'—not the 'I' of which the philosophers speak—is already present and manifests itself in a very striking way.

Our observation of humans during the first months or even first years of their lives will seem to external science to be quite without significance. But for one who is intent upon acquiring knowledge of human nature, this observation is of supreme importance.

To begin with, humans crawl about on all fours, and extraordinary effort is required on their part to lift themselves out of this crawling position, out of this subjection to gravity, into the vertical position and to maintain this. That is one thing. The second is the following: We know that in the first period of our lives we are not yet able to speak, and have to learn how to do so. Try to remember how you first learnt to speak, how you learnt to utter the first word of which you were capable and to formulate the first sentence. Try to remember this, although without clairvoyance you will be as little able to remember it as you can remember how you made the first effort to lift yourself from the crawling into the vertical position. And a third capacity is thinking. Remembrance does indeed go back to the time when you were first able to think, but not before that time.

Who, then, is the actor in this process of learning to walk, to speak and to think? The actor is the real, true 'I'! Now let us observe what this real 'I' does.

We were ordained from the very beginning to walk upright, to speak and to think. But we are not immediately capable of this. We are not immediately the being we are intended to become as humans on Earth. We do not immediately possess the capacities that enable us to participate in the evolving culture of humanity; we have to acquire these capacities gradually. In the earliest period of our lives, there is a conflict between the spirit living within us when we stand permanently upright and the spirit living within us while we are still under the sway of gravity and crawl on all fours, while our faculties of speaking and thinking are still undeveloped. When humans reach the level ordained for them, when they can stand upright, walk, speak, and think, they are an expression of the form proper to humanity. There is, in fact, a natural correspondence between the true human form and the faculties of standing and walking upright, speaking, and thinking. It is impossible to conceive of any other being who can walk as we do, that is to say with a vertical spine, and who can speak and think. Even a parrot is able to talk only because its form is upright. The fact that it is able to talk is connected fundamentally with the vertical position. Animals with an intelligence much greater than that of a parrot will never learn to talk because their backbone is horizontal, not vertical. Other factors too, of course, play their part. The human being is not immediately able to adopt the posture ultimately ordained for him. The reason for this is that after the exertions made by our real 'I' or ego which have enabled us to think, to speak, and to adopt the upright posture, we are ultimately embedded, as it were, in the spheres of the Spirits of Form, the Exusiai.[60] These Spirits of Form, known in the Bible as the Elohim, are the beings from whom the human form actually stems; it is the form in which the human 'I' has its natural habitation and asserts itself during the first months and years of life.

But there is opposition from other Spirits who cast us down to a level below that of these Spirits of Form. To what category do these other Spirits belong?

The Spirits of Form are the beings who enable us to learn to speak, to think, and to walk upright. The Spirits who cast us down, causing us to move about on all fours and to be incapable in our earliest years of speaking and thinking in the real sense, are Spirits whom we have to overcome in the course of our lives, who give us, to begin with, a perverted form. These spirits ought really to have become Dynamis, Spirits of Movement, but fell behind in their evolution and have still not reached the level of the Spirits of Form. They are luciferic spirits who have come to a standstill in their evolution, who work upon us from outside, consigning us to the sway of gravity out of which we must lift ourselves with the help of the true Spirits of Form.

Observing how human beings come into existence through birth, in the efforts we make to acquire capacities which we will need later on in life, we can perceive the true Spirits of Form battling with those other Spirits who ought already to have become Spirits of Movement, but have remained at an earlier stage. We see the Spirits of Form battling with luciferic spirits who in this sphere are so strong and forceful that they suppress the consciousness belonging to the ego. Otherwise, if luciferic spirits did not suppress this consciousness, humans at this stage of their lives would realize: You are a warrior; you are aware of your horizontal position and consciously desire to stand upright, to learn to speak and to think! All this is beyond our power because we are enveloped by the luciferic spirits. There we have a dim inkling of what we shall gradually come to recognize as the true 'I', in contrast to an 'I' which merely appears in the field of our consciousness.

At the beginning of this series of lectures, it was said that we should endeavour to vindicate to healthy human reason what esotericism and seership have to say about human nature. But this healthy human reason must be willing to recognize how during the earliest periods of our life, we humans are only gradually finding our bearings in the physical world. Which part of us is most completely formed? Our stature as a whole is still not particularly noticeable because there is inconsistency between humans themselves and their outer form. By our own efforts, we have to make our way into the form destined for us. Which part is most completely finished—not only after, but also before birth? The head! The head is the most fully developed of all the physical organs, even in the embryo. Why is this? The reason is that the beings of the higher Hierarchies, the Spirits of Form, pervade and weave through all the organs of the human being quite differently in each case—the head in one way, the trunk to which the legs and arms are attached, in another. There is an essential difference between the head and the rest of the human physical body. If we observe the human head with clairvoyance, a remarkable difference is revealed between the head and, for example, the hand. When we move a hand, the physical hand and the etheric hand move together. But when a certain stage in the development of clairvoyance has been reached, the clairvoyant can hold the physical hands still and move the etheric hands only. To hold mobile parts of the body still and move only the corresponding etheric parts is an especially important exercise. If this is achieved, the clairvoyance of the future will develop to further and further stages, while to indulge in any way in unconscious, wriggling movements is a resurgence of Dervish[61] practices which are already obsolete. Repose of the physical body is the requirement of modern clairvoyance; wriggling movements of every kind were characteristic of epochs now past. It would be a very noteworthy achievement if clairvoyants were, for example, to hold their hands quite still in a certain position—perhaps crossed over the breast—and yet maintain complete mobility of their etheric hands. They would be keeping their physical hands still while engaging in all kinds of supra-sensible activities with their etheric hands. This would be an indication of very marked development, coming to expression in conscious control of the hands.

Now there is one human organ in which, even if we are not clairvoyant, the etheric part moves freely while the corresponding physical part remains immobile. This organ is the brain, around which the cosmic powers have placed the hard skull; the lobes of the brain would certainly like to move, but they cannot. Thus the brain of an average human being is permanently in the condition of clairvoyants, who, while they hold their physical hands still, move their etheric hands only. The brain is seen by a clairvoyant to be something that comes out of the head like writhing snakes. Every head is, in fact, a Medusa head. This is a very real phenomenon. The essential difference between the human head and the rest of the body is that in respect of the rest of the body, humans will need to undergo a lengthy process of evolution to achieve what has already been achieved by the head in the way of ordinary thinking. In a certain respect, the strength of thinking lies in our ability, while we are thinking, to bring the brain to rest even down to the finer, invisible movements of the nerves. The more thoroughly we can keep the brain at rest while we are thinking, including the more delicate movements of the nerves, the subtler, more deliberate, and more logical our thoughts will be.

So we can say that when humans pass into physical existence through birth, it is their head that is the most perfect, because in the head there has already been achieved what in the case of the hands—the part of our nature which expresses itself through gestures—can be achieved only in the future. In the evolutionary period of Old Moon the brain was still at the stage of the hands at the present time. On the Old Moon, the head was still exposed in several places and not yet enclosed by the skull. Whereas it is now fixed and static in a kind of prison, it could then expand outwards on all sides. All this applies, of course, to the conditions of existence in the Old Moon epoch, when we were still living in the fluid or watery element that had not yet condensed into the solid state. Even in a certain period of the ancient Lemurian epoch, when we had reached the stage of evolution recapitulating the Old Moon period—even then it was still the case that at the top of the brain there appeared not only the organ we have often mentioned, but a kind of efflux of thoughts. A formation like a fiery cloud was still to be seen over our heads even as late as the Atlantean epoch. Without supra-normal clairvoyance, simply with the clairvoyant faculty possessed by every single human being at that time, an Atlantean could see whether someone was or was not a thinker in the sense of that ancient epoch. Over the head of one who was a thinker, there was a luminous, fiery cloud, but no such phenomenon was present in the case of one who was not.

These are matters of which we must have knowledge if we are to understand the transformation that takes place in human nature when, after living in a physical body, we die and pass into the other period of existence between death and a new birth. All the forces that have been at work to enable a human being to come into existence disappear when we are already in the physical world; but they become all-important when we have laid aside our physical body. During our life between birth and death, we are quite unaware of the forces that moulded the physical brain. But everything of which we *are* aware between birth and death vanishes and is of no significance when we pass through the gate of death. We live then within the forces of which we are unconscious during our physical life on Earth. Whereas during this physical life we experience our 'representation-I'[62] as pictured during the waking state, in the period between death and the new birth we experience that higher 'I' of which we can have a dim inkling when we contemplate how a human being learns to walk, to speak and to think. While we are on Earth, we remain unaware of this 'I'; it does not penetrate into our consciousness. What thus remains entirely concealed we can follow back as far as birth and before birth, even still further back, when we contemplate the life that takes its course after death. What is most completely hidden because it has built us up and vanishes while we are living on Earth is most fully in evidence when we are no longer on Earth, namely during the period of our existence after death. The forces of which we can have a faint inkling only, the forces which, working from within, enable the human being to walk, which launch the sounds of speech, which make him into a thinker and mould the brain into becoming the organ of thinking—these are the forces of supreme importance during our existence between death and a new birth. It is then that our true 'I' comes to life. Of this we will speak in the next lecture.

LECTURE 7

DURING this winter we have prepared the ground in various ways in order to understand with greater exactitude than has hitherto been possible our whole life between birth and death in the physical world on the one side, and on the other between death and rebirth in the spiritual world. And there will be still more to say about this subject in the coming months.

We will need to make an effort to draw together a number of details that will contribute towards a thorough understanding of this subject and throw new light upon many topics we have already studied from a different point of view. Today, then, I will ask you to think, above all, of the course of our physical life—about which something has also been said in my book, *The Education of the Child.*[63] Think of how physical life progresses in cycles: one from birth until about the seventh year, or until the change of teeth; a second cycle from the change of teeth until puberty at about the fourteenth year; then a third cycle, and so on in periods of seven years. Even to ordinary observation, it will be clear that this systematic arrangement into periods of seven years is well founded, but on the other hand, it will also be evident that in our actual lives other facts of incisive significance cut across these seven-year periods. We ourselves have repeatedly considered a crucial occurrence in our lives which eludes this division into cyclic periods. It is the point of time back to which our memory extends in later life, the moment when we begin to feel and know ourselves as an 'I', when ego-consciousness dawns in us. This experience does not by any means occur at exactly the same point of time, but in most cases it may be said that ego-consciousness flashes up in the human being at some point between birth and the seventh year. And something similar can be said to hold good in the later period of our lives. Although with less abruptness than the sudden flashing-up of ego-consciousness, there are other occurrences which, as it were, invalidate the regular seven-year cycle. We shall, however, always discover that whatever comes in this way into our lives and cuts across the cyclic periods, occurs much more irregularly than the experiences connected with the actual seven-year cycles. You will hardly find two human beings whose memories go back to exactly the same point of time, that is to say who experienced the flashing-up of consciousness of 'I' at the same age. Nor does the change of teeth occur at precisely the same age in different individuals. But why this is so in the latter case, we shall still have to consider.

When we study the cyclic periods already referred to and mentioned in my little book, *The Education of the Child,* we shall notice the peculiar circumstance that they begin in connection with the most physical, the most external member of human nature, and are then concerned with the other, more inward members of our constitution. From birth until the seventh year, development is connected primarily with the physical body, then for seven years with the etheric body, then for seven years with the astral body, the sentient soul, and so on. The evolutionary factors pass over more and more decisively from our external nature into our inner nature. That is the essential characteristic of the seven-year periods.

What, then, is there to be said about occurrences which cut across these seven-year periods? The flashing-up of 'I'-consciousness during the first cycle is emphatically an inner event. For the sake of clarity, here let us consider something that seems to be in contrast with this flashing-up of ego-consciousness. If we observe human life with discernment, we shall find that we may compare the cessation of growth with some happening that cuts across the seven-year cycles of evolution. We will therefore think about the cessation of growth, which after all occurs comparatively late in life, and study its implications. What is the relationship of this fact to human life?

The first seven-year period ends with the change of teeth. The appearance of the second teeth is, as it were, the final act of what

we can call the formative principle. The last contribution made by
the forces that give us our form is the moment they drive out the
second teeth. That is the culmination of the formative process,
for the principle that builds up the human form is no longer at
work. With the seventh year, the formative principle ceases to be
active. What comes about later on is only an expansion of what
has already been laid down as form. After the seventh year, there
is no more particular remodelling of the brain. All that happens is
growth of what is already established as basic form. Therefore we
can say that the principle of form unfolds its activity specifically in
the first seven years of the life of a human being. The principle of
form stems from the Spirits of Form; thus these Spirits of Form
are active in us during the first seven years of our life. Therefore we
can say that when humans enter into life through birth, their actual
form is not complete. What happens is that the form-giving principle, the Spirits of Form, continue their active intervention during
the first seven years of life; we have then reached the point in life
where our form merely needs to grow. We have established the basis
for the form by the seventh year, and the second teeth are what the
formative principle still produces out of the human being. The formative principle has now come to its conclusion. Were its activity to
continue, the second teeth would inevitably make their appearance
later than is now the case.

Here we may ask: When these Spirits of Form have worked upon
us until the seventh year of our life, does everything they do for us
come to an end?

The answer is 'No', for the human being goes on growing and the
dispositions of our form develop still further. If nothing else intervened, growth could continue without interruption. If we think only
of the principles of form that are active in the human being until the
seventh year, there is no more reason in the case of humans than in
that of other beings why these forms should not continue to grow if
nothing were to intervene. But something does intervene. When we
humans stop growing, certain principles of form still have an effect
upon us. They have already been creeping up on us, but now they
unite in the fullest sense with our organism, lay hold of it, but in such

a way that they now act as a hindrance, and prevent further growth. The formative principles that are active until the seventh year of life allow the human being a certain elasticity. But at that point other formative principles approach him; their nature is such that they capture and confine what is elastic in the demarcated form, thus preventing any further growth. That is why growth stops at some point. When growth stops, this means that formative forces approaching from outside are at work. Whenever formative forces are active, whenever forms grow larger, provision must be made for the stoppage of growth by the appearance of counter-formative forces, which oppose the first category as its polar antithesis. And thus it is with humans. When our form has developed until about the seventh year of life [indicated in the shaded portion of Figure 3] this form can continue to grow.

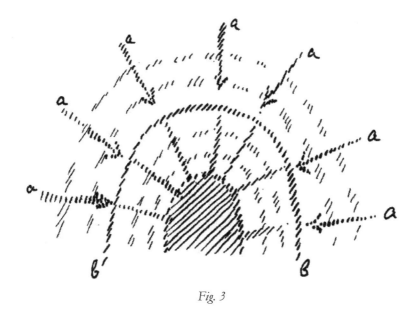

Fig. 3

The formative forces have been at work until the seventh year; these forces work from within. Then different formative forces work in opposition from outside, so that the human being can grow only to the limit indicated by the line b–b. It is really as if until the seventh year of our lives we were given an elastic garment that we can constantly stretch and enlarge. But at a specific point of time, we are given one that is not elastic; we are obliged to put it on, and thenceforth cannot grow beyond its limits.

We can therefore say that within the human nature a confrontation takes place between two kinds of formative principles, one working from within and the other from without. The formative principles belonging to the first category come from the Spirits of Form, from those Spirits of Form who have passed through a perfectly normal process of evolution in the Cosmos. The formative forces working from without are not of the same kind. They come from Spirits of Form whose development has been retarded, and who have acquired a luciferic character. They are the factor that works in the purely spiritual domain, whereas the forces working in the material sphere have had a normal development. Having evolved through the stages of Old Saturn, Old Sun, and Old Moon, they then pass to the Earth in the regular way and shape the human form from within. The 'irregular' Spirits of Form take what is presented to them and hold back its further development. Thus the human process of growth is brought to a halt by these backward Spirits of Form. The beings of the higher Hierarchies have the most varied tasks, among them the one that has been characterized today.

We have now been able to consider many different aspects of the work of the 'regular' Hierarchies, and also of the work of the backward spiritual beings belonging to the different Hierarchies. In my book, *Esoteric Science* you can read how humans reached the stage where, through the Spirits of Form, they could be endowed with the germinal foundation for the 'I', the ego. We know that we received the germ of our physical body from the Thrones, of our etheric body from the Spirits of Wisdom, of our astral body from the Spirits of Movement, and the germinal foundation for the 'I' in our physical body from the Spirits of Form. Bearing this in mind, we can say that humans, in their outer stature, have been organized by the regular Spirits of Form into an ego-bearing being, and that this comes into manifestation in the first seven-year cycle of our lives. But then the backward Spirits of Form who are the opponents of the regular Spirits of Form put a stop to this growth. This is actually the antithesis of the first, most deeply inward experience we have as humans, namely, the kindling of the consciousness of 'I'—the ego. This happens in the early years of life, in the innermost realm of being. The outermost manifestation, the form, is checked at a later age, as a final act. Thus we perceive two evolutionary—but antithetical—processes in the human being. Of the one I have said that it comes from without and moves inward, taking hold of the sentient soul and so on, in the twenty-first year of life. Then there is another evolution proceeding from within outwards until the growth of the physical form is checked. The one evolution, the regular evolution, proceeds from the spiritual to the corporeal, from within outwards, and is of interest especially for education. The other evolution—which is a much less regular and also more individual process—proceeds from without inwards and, when we have reached a certain age, it comes to expression in the completion of the outermost principle—the physical body.

It is very important that teachers should have knowledge of these two antithetical lines of evolution. Hence in my book, *The Education of the Child* it was right to call attention to the first process of evolution, which proceeds from within outwards, because it is only there that education is possible. On the other line of evolution—from without inwards—which is the line of individual development, it is impossible to make any actual impression. This is something which we can take into account, but it cannot be halted; neither can much be achieved in the way of education. And to be able to distinguish between where education is possible, and where it is not, is of fundamental importance.

Just as the backward Spirits of Form cause the cessation of growth, the first actual manifestation of the 'I' in the human being that flashes up during early childhood is the work of the backward Spirits of Will (Thrones). Between these two extremes there are other happenings which are to be attributed to backward Spirits of Wisdom and backward Spirits of Movement.

No adequate characterization of our life as a whole, including the existence between death and a new birth, is possible unless we take account of all the factors that have an effect upon us, and recognize that even in everyday life the influences of luciferic beings exert their effects in many different ways. This influence is evident in other spheres as well. Since our endeavour in these lectures is to acquire a really fundamental understanding of human life as a whole, we will not hesitate to think about matters which seem to be somewhat remote.

We shall first draw attention to a phenomenon from which it is evident that on the physical plane too, between birth and death, human life has undergone essential changes in the course of evolution. If we realize this, it will become evident that the life between death and rebirth has also changed. Those who think intellectually, but superficially, about life today may readily believe that, in essentials, things were always the same as they are at present. By no means was it so! And in certain cases we need go back only a few hundred years to find that conditions were very different. Thus at the present time there is something that has a very great influence upon human psychic life between birth and death, but that simply did not exist in its present form only a few centuries ago. It is what we today mean by the expression 'public opinion'. Even as recently as the thirteenth century, it would have been nonsense to speak of public opinion as we do today. A great deal is said nowadays against belief in authority, although in actual fact it exists in a much more oppressive form in our time than it did in these earlier, often despised centuries. In earlier centuries there were, of course, defects, but there was no blind belief in authority such as exists at present. This blind belief in authority is usually revealed in that the authority in question cannot be specified. A person today will readily be floored when they are told that science has proved this or that. In earlier centuries, however, people attached more weight to authorities whom they encountered physically. Reference to an intangible 'something' is implied when it is said: 'There is scientific proof of it'. Such a saying urges belief in authority when confronted with something incomprehensible. Such belief did not exist in earlier centuries. People belonging to our civilization usually concern themselves very little with matters about which the simplest, most, primitive human being in earlier centuries endeavoured to have some knowledge—matters relating, for example, to health and illness. Why, it is asked today, should anyone need to know about health and illness? The doctors know about these matters and the problems concerned can be left to them. This is also an example of what comes into the category of intangible but sovereign authority. But countless other influences make their way into life; from earliest youth we become dependent on them, and our tendencies of judgement and feeling force themselves into our life! These living currents swirling around among human beings are usually referred to as 'public opinion'—and prompted the philosophers to say: 'Public opinions are mostly private errors'. To realize this, however, is not as important as it is to be aware that public opinion exerts tremendous power upon the life of an individual. It would be a complete misconception of history to speak about the influence of public opinion upon the life of an individual living in the thirteenth century. In those days, there were single personalities who admittedly exerted a great deal of authority either in affairs of government or in practical life, and in these spheres they were obeyed. But at this time there was nothing resembling what impersonal public opinion has become today. Anyone who is unwilling to believe this on the basis of the esoteric facts should study the history of Florence during those centuries and in later times too—when the government of the city passed into the control of the Medici. The tremendous power of individual authorities will then be apparent, but there was no such thing as public opinion. It first arose in an epoch preceding our own by four or five centuries and one can speak of its actual beginning. Such things must be regarded as realities, for a world of swirling thoughts does indeed exist.

What is the origin of this public opinion which we often accept as something that cannot be verified? What *is* public opinion in reality? You may remember that I have spoken of certain spiritual beings belonging to the Hierarchy immediately above humans—beings who participate in various ways in the guidance and leadership of humanity. In my little book, *The Spiritual Guidance of the Individual and Humanity*,[64] you will find a great deal on the subject of spiritual beings belonging to the higher Hierarchies. Now we know that the mightiest incision into the evolution of humanity was made by the Mystery of Golgotha.

In that event, there came to pass something that was most wonderfully expressed in the esoteric teaching of St Paul. Paul spoke in simple language, but the actual way in which he spoke was rooted in profound esotericism. It was not possible for him always to give out openly what he, as an initiate, knew; for in the first place he wanted to speak to a wider circle of people and, secondly, it was not possible in his day to give out everything he knew in a way of which he would have been capable. Nevertheless his very presentation was based upon profound esoteric knowledge. We find, for example, that there is a deeply significant truth in the distinction he makes between the 'first Adam' and the 'higher Adam'—the Christ.[65] According to Paul, the various generations of human beings are to be traced back to Adam, that is to say, the bodies of humans descend from Adam. Hence it can be said that the physical increase of humanity over the Earth during the different periods, leads back finally to the physical body of Adam—Adam and Eve, naturally. We can then ask: What lies at the basis of the physical evolution of humanity from Adam onwards? Naturally, the evolution of souls! The physical bodies which have descended from Adam are the habitations of living souls. These souls had descended from cosmic worlds and had brought with them to the Earth a certain spiritual heritage, a spiritual endowment. But in the course of time this spiritual endowment had undergone decline. Individuals who lived, say, six or seven thousand years before the founding of Christianity had within them much stronger, more extensive spiritual forces than those who lived a mere thousand years before the Mystery of Golgotha. The spiritual heritage which once came to the Earth with human beings had gradually withered away in the soul. Now the life between death and rebirth is of particular significance for this spiritual heritage. If we go back to the epoch long before the Mystery of Golgotha, we find that after death, we had an active, inwardly illumined life of soul; but then this life of soul became dimmer and dimmer, darker and darker. An ever-fading life of soul came with human beings when they passed through death. This was particularly the case among the Greeks, although they were the most advanced peoples then on the Earth, and their sages had every reason to say, in view of the stage reached in evolution: 'Better it is to be a beggar in the upper world than a king in the realm of the shades'. We know that this saying was true when applied to the Greeks who lived a fully satisfying life on the physical plane; but as soon as they had passed through the gate of death, their life became dim and shadowy.

In the fullest sense, it is true that the spiritual life which they had brought with them to the Earth and which manifested after death as a somewhat dim clairvoyant consciousness, had become even dimmer. And especially in the fourth Atlantean epoch, the Greco-Latin epoch, during which the Mystery of Golgotha took place, the spiritual life had reached the stage of its greatest darkness.

The all-important purpose of the Baptism by John the Baptist was that some of those who sought to be baptized should be made conscious of the conditions just described. The individuals baptized by John were completely submerged in the water. As a result, the etheric body of these individuals was liberated from them and for a short time, while under the water, they became clairvoyant. John was able to reveal to them that there had been such deterioration in the life of soul over the course of time that humans now possessed very little of the spiritual treasure that they had once been able to take with them through the gate of death and that could give them clairvoyant consciousness. Individuals whom John baptized in this way became aware that a revitalization of the life of soul was essential, that something new must radiate into human souls in order that after death there might be a life in the real sense. This new impulse streamed into human souls through the Mystery of Golgotha. You need only read my course of lectures entitled *From Jesus to Christ* [66] and you will realize that a rich and abundant spiritual life streams from the Mystery of Golgotha into the souls of individuals who develop a relationship to that Mystery.

Hence Paul could say: Just as human physical bodies descend from Adam, so will the content of their souls in greater and greater measure 'descend' from the Christ who is the second Adam, the spiritual Adam. It is a profound truth that Paul uttered here, clothed in his simple words. If the Mystery of Golgotha had not taken place, we would have become progressively empty in soul, and would either have developed a longing only to live outside the physical body, or to live on Earth with no other wishes or desires than for a purely physical life, and so would have become more and more materialistic. Because all development is a slow and gradual process, there are still some peoples on the Earth who have not yet wholly lost the original spiritual treasure, who still retain some measure of it in spite of having failed to establish any relationship to the Mystery of Golgotha. Individuals belonging to the most advanced peoples, however, can become conscious after death only to the extent to which they have learnt 'to die in Christ', as the second line of the Rosicrucian formula expresses it. And so in actual fact the Mystery of Golgotha has acted as illumination in human souls.

With this clearly in mind, we shall understand the gist of a question relating to human evolution. It is the question: How did it come about that understanding of the Mystery of Golgotha enabled the content of our souls to be carried into the sphere of our 'I', our ego? How did this psychic content differ from what existed before the Mystery of Golgotha as an ancient heritage? The difference is that, before the Mystery of Golgotha, in respect of the content of their souls, humans were far less independent. They were under the direct guidance of the beings we know as the Angeloi, Archangeloi and so on. Before the Mystery of Golgotha, humans were under the leadership of the beings of the nearest higher Hierarchies to a far greater extent than was the case after that event. Indeed the progress of these beings themselves—Angeloi, Archangeloi, Archai—consists in the fact that they have learnt to lead human beings in a way that respects their independence. Humans were intended to live on the Earth in a state of greater and greater independence. The leading spiritual beings of the higher Hierarchies have recognized this, and therein consists their progress.

But it is possible for these Spirits also to remain behind in their evolution. Not all the Spirits who participated in the leadership of humanity have acquired through the Mystery of Golgotha the power to guide and lead us while ensuring our freedom. Among these beings of the higher Hierarchies there are some who remained backward and have become luciferic spirits. What we call 'public opinion' is an example of the way in which some of them are active. Public opinion is not created by human beings alone, but also by a certain category of luciferic spirits of the lowest rank—retarded Angeloi and Archangeloi. These spirits are only beginning their luciferic career and have not yet risen very high in the ranks of the luciferic spirits, but they are definitely luciferic in character. With a clairvoyant eye one can perceive how certain spirits of the higher Hierarchies did not keep pace with evolution after the Mystery of Golgotha, how they adhere rigidly to the old kind of leadership and therefore cannot make any direct approach to humanity. Those who have kept pace with evolution can make regular and direct contact with humanity; the other spirits are incapable of this and they manifest their activity in the muddled, turbulent thinking that comes to expression as public opinion. The function of public opinion is intelligible only when we realize that this is how it entered human life.

Thus we have among us beings who abandon the regular course of evolution and become luciferic in character. It is important that this should be known. The work of the luciferic beings of whom we have already spoken, and who now have great power, also began on a small scale. Indeed, this is true in the case of the whole host of luciferic beings. Admittedly, on the Old Moon there was no public opinion as we know it, but something that can be compared with it—a kind of guidance of humanity. Some among this host of luciferic spirits of whom we have spoken are powerful and important beings, for example backward Spirits of Form who surge in upon us with such violence that they stop our growth. The others are merely the recruits; nevertheless this is the beginning of the career of the luciferic spirits, a career which later on will assume a quite different dimension because the spirits become more and more powerful. Public opinion, which under the guidance and direction of certain luciferic spirits of the lowest order, influences human beings because they absorb it between birth and death, must necessarily have its counterweight during the life between death and rebirth. That is to say, because humans in our lives between birth and death have been caught up into the current of public opinion described, they must experience the counterweight in their life between death and rebirth. Otherwise the following would ensue.

The backward spirits who are responsible for the creation of public opinion have no significance or power whatever in human life between death and rebirth. They have relinquished all possibility of working in that sphere because they are active here, on the physical plane, in a spiritual way—indeed in a way that is only possible in the form of public opinion. We cannot take even an iota of anything like public opinion with us into the spiritual world, and whatever element of it we might want to accompany us into the life after death would be entirely out of place. It must be said, although it will seem strange to many people, that life in Kamaloka becomes very difficult for anyone who clings to public opinion or has been caught in the coils of their own judgement very early in life. This applies particularly to persons who believe that within the world of public opinion there can still be independent judgement—which is an utter impossibility. For such people, Kamaloka is admittedly difficult. But when the period of Kamaloka is over, public opinion has no weight or significance whatever, and after death it is irrelevant whether people adhered to nuances of it, such as liberal or conservative, radical or reactionary. This has no significance whatever in the different groupings of human beings and moreover exists on Earth solely for the purpose of hindering us from making progress towards illumination of consciousness after death. The beings behind public opinion resolved to forgo the progress made possible by the Mystery of Golgotha. But the Mystery of Golgotha will become of greater and greater importance for the Earth's evolution. We must clearly understand that the future of the Earth's evolution cannot be assured simply by rectifying phenomena such as public opinion and the like, which are inevitable in the course of evolution. We can, however, become better in our own inner nature. Therefore, the process of evolution must take root more and more deeply in our inner life. In the future, humans will be still more exposed to the pressure of public opinion, but inwardly they will have developed greater strength. This is possible only through anthroposophy. But if we are gradually to become a match for those spirits who are now exerting their influence in public opinion as recruits of the luciferic beings, this will be possible only if, between death and rebirth too, we undergo something that strengthens us inwardly, strengthens the principle in us that is *independent* of life on Earth. Whereas through the influence of public opinion we become more and more dependent upon earthly life, in the life between death and rebirth we must receive into our very self something that in the next life on Earth will make us ever freer from the influence of public opinion.

Connected with this is the fact that at the time when public opinion began to assume importance, the realm of Buddha was established in the Mars sphere—as we heard in the lecture at Christmas. Consequently, between death and rebirth, we pass through this realm of Buddha on Mars. Christian Rosenkreutz had entrusted to Buddha a special mission in the Mars sphere. And what would be futile on Earth, namely the desire to flee from the conditions of terrestrial existence—this is an experience which we must undergo between death and rebirth during our passage through the Mars sphere. Among other things, we strip off the incubus of public opinion that takes effect only on Earth. Many, even more overbearing influences will come in the future and it will be more than ever necessary to undergo the experience that is possible for us as pupils of Buddha in the sphere of Mars. Here on Earth, we can now be pupils of the Buddha in the orthodox sense only if we refuse to participate in the progress made by the most advanced people on Earth. But between death and rebirth, Buddha unfolds what has developed from the teaching he gave on Earth, which was that we should free ourselves from the need for further incarnations. This has been developed into a doctrine that is inapplicable to the Earth, where life must progress from incarnation to incarnation. Thus the doctrine preached by Buddha on Earth contained the seed of what we must acquire in the disembodied state of existence. In this advanced form, Buddha's teaching is right for the period between death and rebirth. The Buddha himself appeared in the astral body of the child Jesus of St Luke's Gospel,[67] and Christ Himself leads us between death and rebirth through the sphere of Mars, enabling us there to receive the Buddha's advanced teaching. Thus in the sphere of Mars, we can be emancipated from the tendency to uniformity resulting from the effects of public opinion, which are detrimental for our further progress on Earth. Whereas in earlier times Mars was said to be the planet of warlike traits, it is now the Buddha's task gradually to transform these warlike traits in such a way that they become the foundation of the sense for freedom and independence needed in the present age. Whereas nowadays we have the tendency to surrender our sense of freedom and succumb to the fetters of public opinion, on Mars between death and rebirth we will strive to throw off these fetters and not bring them again into the life on Earth when we return to new incarnations.

It seems to me that here we have something that characterizes most wonderfully how wisdom holds sway in the world, how everything that progresses or remains backward is manipulated in such a way that the final outcome is harmony in the evolution of worlds. We cannot achieve progress by keeping, as it were, to the middle line, although there are many who realize the uselessness of adopting a one-sided standpoint. Admittedly, we come across idealists, materialists and other '-ists' who swear by their own standpoint, but truly great individuals such as Goethe[68] do no such thing. They try to grasp material conditions by means of material thinking, and spiritual conditions through idealism. When people of less eminence imagine that they have understood this, they say: Truth lies in the middle, between two different standpoints. But that would be the same as if someone in practical life wanted to sit between two chairs! The truth cannot be found by a one-sided adoption of this or that standpoint, but rather by applying the modes of knowledge appropriate either for materialism or idealism. The world does not progress by undeviating adherence to a middle course: a middle course is appropriate when the opposing sides are also present and are recognized as forces. If something has to be weighed, the two scale pans are needed as well as the beam. Thus, there must be a counterbalance to public opinion; and this is provided by Buddha's teaching in the sphere of Mars—which would not be necessary if public opinion had never existed. Life needs antithesis; life progresses in and through polarity. Somebody might think that as the North and South Poles are antitheses, it would be better if neither existed! They are not, of course, antithetic in the sense implied by a certain Professor of whom it was said that because he had written his books in such haste he could not think about their contents, and stated that civilization could develop only in the middle zone of the Earth because at the North Pole people would freeze through cold and at the South Pole melt through heat! In another connection, of course, North and South Poles are genuine opposites and are necessary because progress is not achieved by adopting a neutral course, but by the maintenance and harmonizing of opposites. Thus what develops on Earth had to undergo a process that lies below the level of progress. Public opinion is of less value than the judgements that an individual can reach on a path of progress. Public opinion is sub-human, and it is this sub-human influence that is counteracted by the stream of Buddha through which we pass between death and rebirth. Both influences are necessary, and it is extremely important to bear this in mind in connection with evolution.

It can therefore be said with truth: Yes, there are indeed backward spirits, but everything that remains behind on the one side and on the other outstrips the evolutionary process, is manipulated by the wisdom of the universe in such a way that harmony is the final result. The backward spirits are utilized to constitute the opposite pole to the spirits who have progressed to further stages.

If we look at life in this way it will be clear to us that in the future course of Earth evolution humans will bring into life more and more qualities which will have greater weight and influence than the purely physical qualities. And it will be increasingly apparent that qualities other than the purely physical will have to be taken into account. Physical qualities will be evident, which—although they become manifest only gradually—can be traced back to infancy; but there will be other qualities to which this does not apply and which show themselves in a marked form only comparatively late in life. A characteristic feature of evolution in the future will be the existence of an increasing number of individuals about whom it will inevitably be asked: What can have happened to them at a certain age in their life? They have completely changed; it is as though they have become a different being! Qualities that were completely absent in earlier life, that appear only when a certain age has been reached, will reveal themselves. This will happen in the case of souls who are the most highly developed, and in whom a certain break in their life becomes evident. For the fact that an individual was a pupil of Buddha in the life between death and rebirth reveals itself only at a certain age. This would apply to persons of whom it can be said: Up to a particular point in their lives, their individual qualities were in evidence; but then entirely new trends appeared and they were able to understand matters altogether different from those for which they had previously shown understanding. These will be individuals who in the future will be the vehicles of true spiritual progress, although they may simply be regarded as late developers, manifesting these qualities only late in life. In truth, however, the reason why these individuals display these qualities only in later life is that in previous incarnations on the Earth they had established the causes which enabled them to experience the spiritual life in the sphere of Mars with particular intensity, and so to acquire qualities which enabled them to bring a new impulse into the evolution of humanity. True spiritual culture will more and more be in the hands of individuals of this kind, who in their youth showed little aptitude for the spiritual standpoint they adopt in later life.

We now see that this is the reason why a certain fact has always been stressed in the Rosicrucian line of thought of which we ourselves have heard in the past, although it could not then be substantiated because our studies were not as advanced as they now are. Representatives of the Rosicrucian principle of initiation in the West have always emphasized that it is impossible to discover in their childhood those who are to become leading figures, because these are individuals who give evidence of that fundamental change in later life of which I have spoken. When a seer speaks of Buddha today, they know that Buddha has faithfully adhered to what his teaching promised; he has continued to work for that in human nature which has no direct urge for physical embodiment and therefore does not appear at the beginning of life in a physical body, but only when the physical body has undergone a certain development, when a certain stage towards spirituality has been reached. Then, at a later stage of life the gift of the Buddha to humanity becomes an effective influence.

All this must be borne in mind if we are to understand the whole process of human development. What it signifies for each individual in their life between birth and death—of this we shall hear later.

Lecture 8

BERLIN, 11 FEBRUARY 1913

W HEN we study human life in its relation to life in the rest of the universe with the normal perception belonging to outer existence, we are observing only the smallest part of the world that is connected with ourselves. In other words, what we can observe if we are not prepared to penetrate behind the mysteries of existence, can throw no real light upon our essential nature and being. For when we look around us with the ordinary organs of perception, with the organ of thinking, we have before us only what does not in any way contain the deepest and most significant secrets of existence. This fact will strike us most strongly of all if we succeed in developing, even to a comparatively small extent, the capacity to view life and the world from the other side, namely, from the side of sleep. What can be seen during sleep is for the most part concealed from our present faculty of perception. As soon as a person goes to sleep, from then until the moment of waking they actually see nothing at all. But if and when in the course of development the time comes when observation is also possible during sleep, most of what we see to begin with is connected with us as humans, but remains entirely hidden from ordinary observation. It is easy to understand why this is so, for the brain is an instrument of judgement, of thinking. Hence, we must use or at least activate the brain when in everyday life we want to think or form judgements, but for that very reason, we cannot see it. After all, the eye cannot see itself while it is actually observing something, and the same holds good of the whole organism. We bear it about with us, but we cannot observe it in the real sense; we cannot penetrate it to any depth. We direct our gaze out into the world, but in modern life we cannot direct this gaze into our own being.

Now the greatest mysteries of existence are not to be found in the outside world, but within ourselves. Let us recall what we know from anthroposophy, namely that the three kingdoms of nature around us owe their existence to a certain retardation in evolution. Mineral kingdom, plant kingdom, animal kingdom are, fundamentally speaking, entities attributable to the fact that something remained backward in the evolutionary process. Normal progress in evolution has in fact been achieved only by beings who have reached the stage of human existence during the period of Earth. When we look at the mineral, plant, or animal kingdoms, we are really observing in the world what amounts in our own existence to what we 'remember', to the content of our memory of our actual experiences; we are in fact contemplating what has taken place in the past and still enjoys a certain existence. But we are not experiencing the living, invisible psychic life of the immediate present when we concern ourselves only with our memory. Memory with all its mental pictures represents something that has been deposited in our living psychic existence, is fixed there. All this is, of course, to be taken metaphorically, but the memories embedded in the soul are not the direct, basic elements of its life. The same applies to the mineral, plant, and animal kingdoms in outer nature. The thoughts conceived by divine and spiritual beings in the past live on in these kingdoms, and they continue into present existence, just as our memories continue into our present life of soul. Hence we have in the world around us, not the thoughts of the immediately present, living, divine and spiritual beings, but the memories, the preserved thoughts of the Gods.

As to the content of our memory, this may well be of interest because with our memory we grasp a tiny corner of the created world; we grasp what has passed over from creation into existence. Our memories are the first, the lowest, the most fugitive stage of created existence. But when we waken spiritually during sleep, we see something quite different. We see nothing of what is outside in space, nothing of the processes manifesting in the mineral, plant, and animal kingdoms or in the external aspects of the human kingdom. But then we know that the essential realities which we are there beholding are the creative, life-giving principles working on us ourselves. It is actually as if everything else were blotted out and as if the Earth, observed from the viewpoint of sleep, contained nothing except the human being. What would never be seen by day, in the waking state, is revealed when contemplated from the viewpoint of sleep. And it is then, for the first time, that knowledge dawns in us of the thoughts which the spiritual beings kept in reserve in order to work at the creation of humans, at a level above that of mineral, plant, and animal existence.

Whereas through physical perception of the world we see everything except the real human nature, through the spiritual perception exercised from the viewpoint of sleep, we see nothing except humans—as a creation, together with happenings in the human kingdom—that is to say, from the viewpoint of sleep we see everything that is hidden from the ordinary perception of waking life. This accounts for the element of strangeness that is present in our vision when we are contemplating the world from the viewpoint of sleep—in other words, when we become clairvoyant, having wakened spiritually during sleep.

Now the human body—and here I mean the physical and etheric bodies together—which lies in the bed during sleep—this human body itself has a singular appearance, which can be characterized in words somewhat as follows. Only in the very first years of a child's life does this human body as seen during sleep show a certain similarity with the weaving life and activity in the other kingdoms of nature. The body of a grown-up person, however, or of a child from a certain age onwards, when seen from the viewpoint of sleep, reveals a constant process of decay, of destruction. Every night during sleep the forces of destruction are subjugated repeatedly by the forces of growth; what is destroyed by day is repaired during the night, but the forces of destruction are always in excess. And the consequence of this fact is that we die. The forces that are renewed during the night are never the equal of those that have been used up during the waking life of day, so that in the normal life of the human being a certain surplus of destructive forces is always present. This surplus

accumulates and the natural death of old age ensues when the catabolic forces eclipse the anabolic forces.

Thus when we observe the human being from the viewpoint of
sleep we are actually witnessing a process of destruction—but without sadness. For the feelings we might have in our waking life about
this process of destruction are absent when we see it from the viewpoint of sleep, because then we know that it is the precondition of
our true spiritual development. No being who did not destroy their
body in some measure would be capable of thinking or of developing an inner life of soul. No life of soul as experienced by us would
be possible if the process of growth were not opposed by processes
of destruction. We therefore regard these processes of destruction
in the human organism as the precondition of our life of soul, and
feel the whole development to be beneficial. Looked at from the
other side of life, the fact that our body can gradually be dissolved is
felt to be a blessing. Not only do things look different when viewed
from the other side of life, but all our feelings and ideas are different;
consciousness during sleep has always before it the spectacle of the
body in decline—and rightly in decline.

Study of the life between death and rebirth, however, affords a
different spectacle. A certain connection with the preceding life is
experienced for a time after death. All of you are aware that this
is the case during the period of Kamaloka. Even after that period,
however, the experience of connection with the previous life continues for a time. But then, at a certain point during the life between
death and rebirth, a reversal of all ordinary vision and perception
takes place, a reversal far more radical than takes place during the
consciousness of sleep. During existence on Earth we look out from
our body into the world that is not our body; from the point of
time to which I have just referred, between death and the new birth,
we direct hardly a gaze to the universe around us but look with all
the great intensity at what may now be called the human body; we
discern all its secrets. Thus between death and rebirth there comes a
moment when we begin to take special interest in the human body.
It is extremely difficult to describe these conditions and it can really
only be done with halting words. There comes a time between death

and a new birth when we feel as if the whole universe were within us and outside us is only the human body. We feel that the stars and other heavenly worlds are within our being, just as here on Earth we feel that the stomach, the liver, and the spleen are within us. Everything that here, in life on Earth, is outside us becomes in that other life an inner world, and just as here we look outwards to the stars, clouds and so forth, in that other life we gaze at the human body. But at which human body?

To understand this we must be clear that the new human being who at our next birth is to enter into existence has for a long time previously been preparing our essential characteristics. Preparation for a return to the Earth begins a long time before birth or conception. The conditions of central importance here are quite different from those accepted by modern statistical biology, which assumes that when human beings come into existence through birth, they simply inherit certain traits from their father, mother, grandparents, and the whole line of ancestors. An otherwise attractive little book about Goethe has recently been published,[69] in which his characteristic qualities are traced back to his ancestors. Outwardly speaking, that is absolutely correct in the sense I have often indicated, namely, that there is no contradiction between a scientific fact that is correctly presented and the facts brought forward by anthroposophy. It is just as if someone were to say: Here is a person; how does it come about that they are alive? It is because they have lungs inside them and there is air outside. Needless to say, that is quite correct. But someone else may turn up and say: This person is alive for an entirely different reason. A fortnight ago, they fell into the water and I jumped in after them and pulled them out; but for that they would not be alive today! Both these assertions are correct. In the same way, science is quite correct when it says that a person bears within themselves characteristics inherited from their ancestors; but it is equally correct to attribute them to their karma and other factors. In principle, therefore, anthroposophy cannot be intolerant; it is external science alone that can be intolerant—for example, in rejecting anthroposophy. Someone may insist that they have preserved the characteristics of their own ancestors. But there is also the fact that from a certain point of time between death and rebirth human beings themselves begin to develop forces which work down upon their ancestors. Long before individuals enter into physical existence there is a mysterious connection between themselves and the whole line of their ancestors. And the reason why specific characteristics appear in a line of ancestors is that perhaps only after hundreds of years a particular individual is to be born from that ancestral line. This human being who is to be born, perhaps centuries later, from a line of ancestors, regulates their characteristics from the spiritual world. Thus Goethe—to take this example once again—manifests the qualities of his ancestors because they worked continuously in the spiritual world with the aim of implanting into these ancestors qualities that were subsequently to be his. And what is true of Goethe is true of every human being.

From a specific point of time between death and rebirth, therefore, humans are already concerned with the preparation of their later earthly existence. The physical body which we have on Earth does not by any means derive in all details from the physical lives of our ancestors, nor indeed from processes that can operate on the Earth. The physical body we bear is in itself fourfold. It has evolved through the periods of Saturn, Sun, Moon, and Earth. Its very first foundation was laid during the Old Saturn period; during the Old Sun period the etheric body was woven into this foundation; during the Old Moon period the astral body was added and then, during the Earth period, the ego, the 'I'. Because of these processes, the physical body has undergone many changes. Thus, we have within us the transformed foundation of Saturn, the transformed conditions of Sun and Moon. Our physical human body is the product of transformed physical conditions. The only part of all this that is visible is what has come from the Earth; everything else is invisible. Our human physical body is visible because we take in the substances of the Earth, transform them into our blood, and permeate them with something that is invisible. In reality, we see only the blood and what has been transformed by the blood—that is to say, a quarter of the physical human body; the other three-quarters are invisible. In the first place, there is an invisible framework containing invisible currents—all this exists in the form of forces. Within these invisible currents there are also the influences exercised by one current upon another. All this is invisible. Now this threefold entity is filled out, permeated by the foodstuffs that have been transformed into blood. It is through this process that the physical body becomes visible. And it is only when we come to deal with the laws governing this visible structure that we are in the earthly realm itself. Everything else stems from cosmic, not from earthly conditions, and has already been prepared when, at the time of conception, the first physical atom of the human being comes into existence. Thus, what is later on to become the body of the human being has been prepared in past ages without any physical connection with the ultimate father and mother. It was then that the qualities transmitted by heredity were first worked into the process of development.

The human soul looks down upon what is thus being prepared from the aforementioned point of time onwards between death and a new birth. It is the spiritual embryo, the spiritual seed of life. This is what constitutes the soul's outer world. Notice the difference between what is seen when we wake spiritually during sleep and have clairvoyant perception of the human body undergoing a process of continual destruction, and what is seen when our own inner organism is perceived as outer world. The outer world is then our inwardness in process of coming into being! This means that we are then seeing the reverse of what is perceived clairvoyantly during sleep. During sleep, we feel that our inner organs are part of the outer world, but otherwise what we see is a process of destruction. From the above-mentioned time onwards between death and rebirth, our gaze is focused upon a human body in process of coming into being. We are unable to preserve any remembrance of what we have seen between death and rebirth, but the spectacle of the building of the wonderful structure of the human body is veritably more splendid than anything to be seen when we gaze at the starry heavens or at the physical world with vision dependent in any respect upon the physical body. The mysteries of existence are truly great, even when contemplated from the standpoint of our physical senses only, but far greater still is the spectacle before us when, instead of external perception of our inner organs, we gaze at the human body that is in process of coming into being with all its mysteries! We then see how everything is directed to the purpose of enabling humans to cope with existence when we enter the physical world through birth.

There is nothing that can truly be called bliss or blessedness except vision of the process of creation, of 'becoming'. Perception of anything already in existence is trivial compared with vision of what is in process of coming into being; and what is meant by speaking of the states of bliss or blessedness which we can experience between death and rebirth is that during this period we can behold what is in process of coming into being. Truths such as these, that have been revealed through the ages and grasped by minds adequately prepared, are indicated in words to be found in the 'Prologue in Heaven' in Goethe's *Faust*:

> *Das Werdende, das ewig wirkt und lebt,*
> *Umfaß' euch mit der Liebe holden Schranken,*
> *Und was in schwankender Erscheinung schwebt,*
> *Befestiget mit dauernden Gedanken.*

> May that which works and lives, the ever-growing,
> In bonds of love enfold you, mercy-fraught,
> And Seeming's changeful forms, around you flowing,
> Do ye arrest, in ever-during thought![70]

The difference between vision in the world between birth and death and vision in the world between death and rebirth is that in the former we behold what is already in existence, and in the latter what is coming into being.

The thought might occur: Are we, then, concerned only with the vision of our own being? No, that is not the case. For at the stage of coming into being, this body is actually part of the outer world; it is the manifest expression of divine mysteries. And it is then that we realize for the first time why the physical body—which after all is only maltreated between birth and death—may be seen as the temple of cosmic mysteries, for it contains more of the outer world than is seen when we are within it during earthly existence. At that stage between death and rebirth what is otherwise outer world is our inner world; what is otherwise called universe is now that of which we can say 'I'— and what we then behold is outer world. We must not allow ourselves to be shocked by the fact that when we are looking at our body— or rather the body that will subsequently be ours—all other bodies which are coming into being must naturally also be there. This is of no significance because here it is simply a matter of number. In point of fact, differentiation between human bodies that can be of interest and importance to us has little significance until shortly before human beings enter into physical existence. For the greater part of the period between death and the new birth, when we are looking down upon the body that is coming into being, it is actually the case that the single bodies are differentiated only according to their number. If we want to study the essential properties of a grain of wheat, it will not make much difference whether we pick an ear from a grain of wheat in a particular field or go fifty paces farther on and pick one there. As far as the essential properties are concerned, one grain is as good as another. Something similar applies when between death and rebirth we are gazing at our own body; the fact that it is our own has significance only for the future because later on we are to inhabit it on the Earth. At the moment it interests us only as the bearer of sublime cosmic mysteries, and its blessedness consists in the fact that it can be contemplated just like any other human body. Here we stand before the mystery of number which will not be further considered now, but among many other relevant aspects there is this, namely, that number—that is to say, multiple existence—cannot be regarded from the spiritual standpoint exactly as it is from the physical. What is seen in countless examples will again be seen as a unity.

Through the body we feel ourselves to be in the universe, and through what in physical life is called the universe, we feel that we are living within our own selves. Such is the difference when the world is contemplated at one time from this world and at another from yonder.

For the seer, the most significant moment between death and a new birth is when we cease to concern ourselves only with our previous lives and begin to direct our attention to what is in process of coming into existence. The shattering impression received by clair-voyants when, as they follow a soul between death and the new birth, this soul begins to be concerned with what is coming into being—this shattering impression is caused by the soul itself at this moment receiving a severe shock. The only experience comparable with this is the coming of death in physical existence, when the human being passes over from *life into being*. In the other case—although it is impossible to describe it quite exactly—the transition is from some-thing connected with a life that ended in death to experience of the process of 'becoming', of resurrection. The soul encounters what bears a new life germinally within it. This is the moment of death in reverse. That is why it is so immensely significant.

In connection with these matters, we must turn our minds to the course of human evolution on Earth. Let us look back to an age, for example the ancient Egypto-Chaldean epoch, when our souls, looking out through physical bodies, did not see the stars merely as material bodies in the heavens. Rather, spiritual beings were con-nected with the stars—although this experience occurred only in certain intermediate states during the life between birth and death. Human souls were deeply affected by this vista, and in those times impressions from the spiritual world crowded in upon them. It was inevitable that in the course of evolution the possibility of behold-ing the spiritual should gradually cease and the human gaze be limited to the material world. This came about in the Greco-Latin epoch, when the human gaze was diverted to an ever greater extent from the spiritual world and limited to the world of the senses. And now we ourselves are living in an era when it is becoming more and more impossible for the soul to see or detect spiritual reality in the life of the physical environment. The Earth is now dying, withering away, and we are deeply involved in this process. Thus, whereas in the Egypto-Chaldean epoch we still beheld the spiritual around us, we now see only what is material, and actually boast of having established a science which deals only with what is physical and material. This process will go to further and further lengths. A time will come when we will lose interest in the direct impres-sions of the world of the senses and we will concentrate attention on what is sub-material, sub-sensory. Today, in fact, we can already detect the approach of the time when we will be interested only in what is sub-sensory, below the level of the sense-world. This often becomes obvious, for example when modern physics no longer concerns itself with colours as such. In reality, it takes no account of the actual quality of colour, but concerns itself only with the vibrations and oscillations below colour. In many books today, you can read the nonsensical statement that a yellow colour, for example, is merely a matter of oscillations, wavelengths. Observation here is already diverted from the quality of the colour and directed to something that is not in the yellow colour at all, but yet is considered to be the reality. You can find books on physics and even on physiology today in which it is emphasized that attention should no longer be fettered to the direct sense-impression, but rather that everything resolves itself into vibrations and wavelengths. This kind of observation will go to further and further extremes. We will pay no attention to material existence as such; we will take account only of the working of forces. Historically, one example suffices in order to provide empirical evidence of this. If you refer to du Bois-Reymond's[71] lecture 'On the Boundaries of Natural Knowledge', given on 14 August, 1872, you will find a peculiar expression for something that Laplace[72] already described, the expression 'astronomical knowledge of a material system'—that is to say when what lies behind a light- or colour-process is presented as something brought about only by mathematical-physical forces. A time will come when human souls—and some of those who are being educated in certain schools today will have the best possible foundations for this attitude in their next incarnation—will have lost real interest in the world of light and radiant colour and enquire only into the working of forces. People will no longer have any interest in violet or red but will be concerned only with wavelengths.

This withering of our inner spirituality is something that is approaching, and anthroposophy is there to counter it in every detail. It is not only our present form of education that helps to bring about this withering; the trend is there in every domain of life. In contrast to everyday life, with our anthroposophy we want to give again to human souls something that fertilizes them, that is not only a maya of the senses, but springs forth as spirit. And this we can do when we impart to human souls knowledge that will enable them to live in the true world in their following incarnations. We have to speak of these things in a world which, with its indifference to form and colour, is in such contrast to what we ourselves desire. For it is particularly in regard to colours that the world of today is preparing souls to thwart what we want to achieve. We must work not only according to the concepts and ideas of everyday existence, but also with cosmological ideas. Hence it is not a mere liking on our part when we arrange surroundings such as those to be seen in this room, but it is connected with the very nature of anthroposophy. Immediate response to what is presented to the senses must again be generated in the soul in order that active life in the spirit may begin. Now, in this incarnation, each one of us can assimilate anthroposophy in the life of soul; and what is now assimilated is transformed into faculties for a new incarnation. Then, during our life between death and the next birth, individuals send their souls from their bodies that are coming into being influences which prepare their future bodily faculties to adopt a more spiritual view of the world. This is impossible for us without anthroposophy. If we reject anthroposophy, we prepare our bodies to see nothing but barren forces and to be blind to the revelations of the senses.

And now something shall be said that enables a seer to form a judgement of the mission of anthroposophy.

When clairvoyants today direct their gaze to the life between death and the new birth of souls who have already passed beyond the above-mentioned point of time and are contemplating the body that is coming into being for a further existence, they may realize that this body will afford the soul no possibility of developing faculties for the comprehension of spiritual truths. For if such faculties are to be part of life in the physical body, they must have been implanted before birth. Hence in the immediate future more and more human beings will be born devoid of the faculties needed for the acceptance of spiritual knowledge—a state of things that has existed for some time already. Before the seer there

will be a vista of souls who in previous lives deprived themselves
of the possibility of accepting any knowledge of a spiritual kind.
In their life between death and rebirth, such souls can indeed gaze
at a process of development, but it is a development in which
something is inevitably lacking. These vistas lead to a grasp of
the mission of anthroposophy. It is a shattering experience to see
a soul whose gaze is directed towards its future incarnation, its
future body, beholding a budding, burgeoning process of becoming and yet being obliged to realize: something will be lacking in
that body, but I cannot provide it because my previous incarnation
is responsible! In a more trivial sense, this experience may be compared with being obliged to work at something knowing from the
outset that ultimately it is bound to be imperfect. Try to be vividly
aware of the difference: either you can do the work perfectly and
be happy in the prospect, or you are condemned from the outset
to leave it imperfect.

This is the great question: Are human souls in the spiritual world
to be condemned in increasing numbers to look down upon bodies
which must remain imperfect, or can this be avoided? If this fate is
to be avoided, souls must accept during their life in physical bodies
the proclamations and tidings of the spiritual worlds.

What those who make known these tidings regard as their task is
verily not derived from earthly ideals, but from the vista of the entire
span of life, that is to say, when to life on Earth is added the period
of existence between death and the new birth. Herein is revealed
the possibility of a fruitful future for humanity, the possibility too
of militating against the withering of human souls. The feeling can
then be born in us that anthroposophy *must* be there, *must* exist in the
world. Anthroposophy is a *sine qua non* for the life of humanity in the
future but not in the sense that is applicable to some other kind of
knowledge. Anthroposophy imparts *life*, not concepts and ideas only.
But the concepts of anthroposophy, accepted in one incarnation,
bring life, inner vitality, and inner forcefulness. What anthroposophy gives is an elixir of life, a vital force of life. Hence, anyone who
regards himself as belonging to a movement for the promulgation of
anthroposophy should feel anthroposophy to be a dire necessity in

life, unlike anything that originates from other unions and societies. The realization of being vitally involved in the necessities of existence is the right feeling to have in regard to anthroposophy.

We have embarked upon these studies of the life between death and rebirth in order that by turning our minds to the other side of existence we may receive from there the impulse that can kindle in us enthusiasm for anthroposophy.

LECTURE 9

BERLIN, 4 MARCH 1913

At the time when materialism—mainly theoretical materialism—was in its prime, in the middle and still to some extent during the last decades of the nineteenth century, when the writings of Büchner[73] and Vogt[74] ('bulky Vogt' as he used to be called) had made a deep impression upon people who considered themselves enlightened, one could often hear a way of speaking that is occasionally also heard today, because stragglers from that epoch of theoretical materialism are still to be found in certain circles. When people do not flatly deny the possibility of a life after death, or even here and there admit it, they are likely to say: Well, there may be a life after death, but why should we trouble about it during life on Earth? When death has taken place, we shall discover whether there is indeed a future life, and meanwhile if here on Earth we concern ourselves only with the affairs of earthly existence, and take no account of what is alleged to come afterwards, we cannot miss anything of importance. For if the life after death has anything to offer, we shall then discover what it is!

As I said, this way of speaking could be heard time and time again, and this is still the case in wide circles today; in the way the subject is expressed it may often, in a certain respect, almost seem acceptable. And yet it is utterly at variance with what is disclosed to spiritual investigation when the facts connected with the life between death and rebirth are considered in their spiritual aspect. When we have passed through the portal of death, we come into contact with many and infinitely varied forces and beings. We do not only find ourselves living amid a multitude of supra-sensible facts, but we come into contact with definite forces and beings—namely, the beings of the several higher Hierarchies. Let us ask ourselves what this contact signifies for one who is passing through the period of existence between death and the new birth.

We know that when we have spent this period of life in the supra-sensible world and have entered into physical existence again through birth, we become in a certain way the moulder of our own bodily constitution, indeed of our whole destiny in the life on Earth. Within certain limits, human beings build and fashion their bodies, even the very convolutions of their brains, by means of the forces brought with us from the spiritual worlds when we enter again into physical existence through birth. Our whole earthly existence depends upon our physical body possessing organs that enable us to come in touch with the outer physical world, to act, and moreover to think in that world.

If, here in the physical world, we do not possess the appropriately formed brain which, on passing through birth we formed for ourselves out of the forces of the supra-sensible world, we remain unable to cope with life in this physical world. In a real sense, we are fitted for life in the physical world only when we bring with us from the spiritual world forces by means of which we have been able to build a body able to cope with this world and all its demands. The supra-sensible forces which we need in order to fashion our body and also our destiny are received by us from the beings of the higher Hierarchies with whom we have made contact between death and a new birth. What we need for the shaping of our life must be acquired during the time that has preceded our birth since the last death. Between death and the next birth, we must approach, stage by stage, the beings who can endow us with the forces we need for our physical existence.

In the life between death and rebirth, we can pass before the beings of the higher Hierarchies in two ways. We may recognize them, understand their nature and essential characteristics, be able to receive what they can give us, and what we shall need in the following life. We must be able to understand or at least to perceive what is being offered us and what we shall subsequently need. But we might also pass before these beings in such a way that, figuratively speaking, their hands are offering gifts which we do not receive because it is dark in the higher world in which we then live. Thus we may pass through that world with understanding, with awareness of what these beings are offering us, or we may pass through it without understanding, unaware of what they wish to bestow. Now the way in which we pass through this spiritual world, which of the two ways we necessarily choose in our life between death and the new birth, is predetermined by the after-effects of the previous life and of earlier lives on Earth. People whose attitude in their last life on Earth was unresponsive and antagonistic to all thoughts and ideas that may enlighten them about the supra-sensible world—such people pass through the life between death and rebirth as if through a world of darkness. For the light, the spiritual light we need in order to realize how these different beings approach us and what gifts we may receive from them for our next life on Earth—the light of understanding for what is here coming to pass cannot be acquired in the supra-sensible world itself; it must be acquired here, during physical incarnation on Earth. If, at death, we bear with us into the spiritual life no relevant ideas and concepts, we shall pass unknowingly through our supra-sensible existence until the next birth, receiving none of the forces needed for the next life. From this we realize how impossible it is to say that we can wait until death itself occurs, because we shall then discover what the facts are—whether indeed we shall encounter any reality at all after death. Our relationship to that reality depends upon whether in earthly life we have been receptive or antagonistic in our souls to concepts or ideas of the supra-sensible world that have been accessible to us and will be the light through which we must ourselves illumine the path between death and rebirth.

Something further can be gathered from what has been said. The belief that we have, so to say, only to die in order to receive everything that the supra-sensible world can give us, even if we have made no preparation for it—this belief is utterly false. Every world has its own special mission. And what we can acquire during an incarnation on Earth we can acquire in no single one of the other worlds. Between death and a new birth, we are able, in all circumstances, to enter into communion with the beings of the higher Hierarchies. But in order to receive their gifts, to avoid having to grope in darkness through life there or in fearful loneliness, in order to establish contact with those beings and receive their forces, the ideas and concepts which are the light enabling the higher Hierarchies to be visible to the soul must be acquired in earthly life. Therefore, individuals who in earthly life during the present cycle of time have rejected all spiritual ideas, pass through the life between death and rebirth in fearful loneliness, groping in darkness. In the next incarnation, they will fail to bring with them the forces wherewith to build their body efficiently and mould their organs; they can fashion them in an imperfect form only, and consequently they will be an inadequate human being in their next life.

We realize from this how karma works over from one life to the next. In one life someone deliberately scorns to develop in their soul any relationship with the spiritual worlds; in the next life, they have no forces wherewith to create even the organs enabling them to think, feel, or will the truths of spiritual life. They remain dull and indifferent to spiritual things, and spiritual life passes them by as though in dream—as is so frequently the case today. On the Earth, such an individual can take no interest in spiritual worlds; and their soul, after passing through the gate of death, is an easy prey for the luciferic powers. Lucifer makes straight for such souls. Here we have the strange situation that in the next life in the spiritual world, the life that follows the dull, unreceptive one, the deeds and the beings of the higher Hierarchies are indeed illumined for such an individual, but in this case *not* as a result of what they acquired in earthly life, but rather by the light which Lucifer sends into their soul. It is Lucifer who illumines the higher worlds for them when they pass into the life between death and rebirth. Now, they can, it is true, perceive the higher Hierarchies, recognize when they are offering their gifts to them. But the fact that Lucifer has tainted the light means that all the gifts have a particular colouring and character. The forces of the higher Hierarchies are then not exactly as the human being could otherwise have received from them. Their nature then is such that when the human being passes into their next life on Earth they can certainly form and mould their body, but they mould it then in such a way that although they become individuals who are, admittedly, able to cope with the outer world and its demands, in a certain respect they are inwardly inadequate, because their soul is tinged with Lucifer's gifts, or at least by gifts that have a luciferic tendency.

When we come across individuals who have worked on their bodies in such a way that they are able to make effective use of their intellect and acquire certain skills that will help them to raise their status in the world, although to their own advantage only, snatching at what is in their own interest, dryly calculating what is beneficial to themselves without any consideration for others—and there are many such people nowadays—in these cases the seer will very often find that their previous history was what has been described. Before they began to display their dry, intellectual, sharp-witted character in life, they had been led through their existence between death and rebirth by luciferic beings who were able to approach them because in the preceding incarnation they had lived an apathetic, dreamy existence. But these traits themselves had been acquired because such individuals had passed through an earlier existence between death and rebirth groping in darkness. The spirits of the higher Hierarchies would have bestowed upon them the forces needed for fashioning a new life, but they were unable to receive these forces; and that in turn was because they had deliberately refused to concern themselves with ideas and concepts relating to a spiritual world. That is the karmic connection! Such examples do certainly occur; they appear before the eyes of spirit only too frequently when with the help of powers of spiritual investigation and knowing the conditions of human life, we penetrate into higher worlds.

It is therefore wrong to say that here on Earth we need concern ourselves only with what is around us in earthly existence, because what comes later will be revealed in good time. But the form in which it will be revealed depends entirely upon how we have prepared ourselves for it here.

Another possibility may easily occur. I am saying these things in order that by understanding the life between death and rebirth, life between birth and death may become more and more intelligible.

When we study life on Earth with discernment, we see many human beings—and in our time they are very numerous—who can, as it were, only 'half think', whose logic invariably breaks down when faced with reality. Here is an example. A certain free-thinking cleric, an honourable man in all his endeavours, wrote in the first *Freethinkers' Calendar* as follows. Children ought not to be taught any ideas about religion, for that would be against nature. If children are allowed to grow up without having any ideas about religion pumped into them, we find that they do not of themselves arrive at ideas of God, immortality, and so forth. The inference to be drawn from this is that such ideas are unnatural to humans and should not be drummed into them; they should work only with what can be drawn from their own souls. As in many other cases, there are thousands and thousands of people nowadays to whom an utterance such as this seems very clever, very subtle. But if only genuine logic were applied, the following would be obvious. If we were to take a human being before they have learnt to speak, put them on a lonely island and take care that they can hear no single word of speech, they would never learn to speak. And so anyone who argues against children being taught any ideas about religion would logically have to say that human beings should not have to learn to speak, for speech does not come of itself. So our free-thinking cleric cannot propagate his ideas by means of his logic, for both he and his logic come to a halt when confronted by the facts. His logic can be applied to a small area only, and he does not notice that his idea, assuming one can get hold of it, cancels itself out.

Anyone who is alert to their surroundings will find that this inadequate pseudo-thinking is very widespread. If with the help of supra-sensible research we trace the path of such an individual backwards and come to the regions through which their soul passed between the last death and the last birth, when this illogical mentality was caused, the seer often finds that such human beings, in their last life between death and rebirth, passed through the spiritual world in such a way that they encountered the spiritual beings and forces while under the guidance of Ahriman; and that although those beings would have bestowed upon them what they needed in

life, they could not make it possible for them to develop the capacity
for sound thinking. Ahriman was the leader, and it was Ahriman who
contrived that the gifts of the beings of the higher Hierarchies could
only be received by them in a form that would finally result in their
thinking coming to a halt when confronting actual facts, and in their
inability to make their thinking exhaustive and valid. A large pro-
portion of those human beings—and their number is legion—who
are incapable of genuine thinking today owe this to the fact that in
their last life between death and rebirth they were obliged to submit
to Ahriman's guidance. They had somehow prepared themselves for
this in their last earthly life—that is to say, in the incarnation preceding the present one.

   And what was the course of that preceding life as viewed by a
seer? It is found that these were morose individuals, hypochondriacs who shied away from facts and people in the world and always
found it difficult to establish any relation with their environment.
Often they were intolerable hypochondriacs in their previous life;
on medical examination they would have been found to be suffering
from the type of illness occurring very frequently in hypochondriacs.
And if we were to go still further back, to the life between death
and rebirth that preceded the incarnation as a hypochondriac, we
would find that during that period such people were obliged again
to forego the right guidance, and could not become truly aware of
what the gifts of the higher Hierarchies would have been. And how
had they prepared themselves for this fate in the life preceding the
last two incarnations? We would find that they had developed what
it is certainly true to call a religious, pious attitude of soul, but an
attitude based on sheer egotism. They were people with a pious, even
mystical nature emanating from egotism. After all, mysticism very
often has its origin in egotism. An individual of this type might say:
I seek within myself in order that there I may recognize God. But
what they are seeking there is only their own self made into God!
In the case of many pious souls, it becomes evident that they are
pious only in order that after death one or another of their spiritual
inclinations may bear fruit. All that they have acquired is an egotistic
attitude of soul.

When in the course of spiritual research we trace the sequence of three such earthly lives, we find that in the first, the basic attitude of the soul was that of egotistic mysticism, egotistic religiosity. And when today we observe human beings with this attitude to life, we shall be able, by means of spiritual investigation, to trace them back to times when souls without number developed a religious frame of mind out of sheer egotism. They then passed through an existence between death and rebirth without being able to receive from the spiritual beings the gifts which would have enabled them to shape their next life rightly. In that life, they became morose hypochondriacs, finding everything distasteful. This life again prepared them for the ensuing one when, having passed through the gate of death, Ahriman and his hosts became their leaders and the forces with which they were imbued manifested in the following earthly life as defective logic, as an obtuse, undiscerning kind of thinking.

Here, then, we have another example of three successive incarnations. And we realize again and again what nonsense it is to believe that we can wait until death to establish connection with the supra-sensible world. For how this connection is established after death depends upon the inner psychic tendencies acquired here on Earth towards the supra-sensible world. Not only are successive earthly lives connected as causes and effects, but the lives between death and the new birth are also connected in a certain way as causes and effects. This can be seen from the following.

When seers direct their gaze into the supra-sensible world where souls are sojourning after death, they will find among them those who during part of this life between death and rebirth are servants of those powers whom we may call the lords of all healthy, budding, and burgeoning life on the Earth. (In the very lengthy period between death and rebirth, innumerable experiences are undergone, and in accounts of the present kind, parts only can be described.) Among the dead, we find souls who for a certain length of time in the supra-sensible world co-operate in the wonderful task—for wonderful it is—of pouring, infusing into the physical world everything that can further the health of beings on the Earth, can help them to thrive and blossom. Just as in certain circumstances we can become servants of the evil spirits of illness and misfortune, so too we can become the servants of those spiritual beings who promote health and growth, who send down from the spiritual world into our physical world forces that help life to flourish. It is nothing but a materialistic superstition to believe that physical hygiene and external regulations are the sole means of promoting health. Everything that happens in physical life is directed by the beings and powers of higher worlds who are all the time pouring into the physical world forces which in a certain way work freely, upon human or other beings, either promoting or harming health and growth. Certain specific spiritual powers and beings are responsible for these processes in health and illness. In the life between death and rebirth, we co-operate with these powers; and if we have prepared ourselves in the right way, we can experience the bliss of co-operating in the task of sending the forces which promote health and growth, from the higher worlds into this physical world. And when the seer enquires into why such souls have deserved this destiny, he becomes aware that in physical life on Earth there are two ways in which human beings can execute and think about what they want to achieve.

Let us take a general look at life. We see numbers of human beings who carry out the work prescribed for them by their profession or office. Even if there is no radical case of any one of these people regarding their work as if they were animals being led to the slaughterhouse, it is at least true to say that they work because they are obliged to. Of course they would never neglect their duty—although of course anything may happen! In a certain sense it cannot be otherwise in the present phase of human evolution; the only urge such people feel towards their work is that of duty. This does not by any means suggest that such work should be criticized root and branch. It should not be understood in this sense. Earthly evolution is such that this aspect of life will become more and more widespread; nor will things improve in the future. The tasks that we will have to carry out will become increasingly complicated in so far as we are connected with outer life, and we will be condemned more and more to think and do only that to which duty drives us. Already there are hosts of human beings who do their work only because duty forces them to it, but on the other hand there will be people who look for a society such as ours in which they can also achieve something, not simply from a sense of duty as in everyday life, but for which they feel enthusiasm and devotion. Thus there are two aspects of human work: has it been thought out or done as an outer achievement merely from a sense of duty, or has it been done with enthusiasm and inner devotion, solely out of an inner urge of our own soul? This attitude—to think and act not merely out of a sense of duty, but out of love, inclination and devotion—this prepared the soul to become a server of the beneficent powers of health and salutary forces sent down from the supra-sensible world into our physical world, to become a servant of everything that brings health and to experience the bliss that can accompany these circumstances.

To know this is extremely important for general human well-being, for only by acquiring during life the forces that will enable us to co-operate with the powers in question will we be able to work spiritually for an ever- intensifying process of healing and betterment of conditions on the Earth.

We will now consider still another case, of one who makes efforts to adapt himself to our environment and its demands. This by no means applies to everybody. There are some people who take no trouble to adjust themselves to the world and are never at home with the conditions either of spiritual or outer physical life. For example, there are individuals who notice an announcement that here or there an anthroposophical lecture will be given; they go to the place but almost as soon as they get seated, they are already asleep! In such cases the soul cannot adapt itself to the environment, is not attuned to it. I have known people who cannot even sew on a button to replace one that has been torn off; that again means that they cannot adapt themselves to physical conditions. Countless cases could be quoted of people who cannot or will not adapt themselves to life. These symptoms are very significant, as I have said. At the moment, however, we will think only of the effects upon the life between death and rebirth.

Everything becomes cause and everything produces effects. Someone who makes efforts to adapt himself to their environment, someone, that is to say, who can actually sew on a button or can listen to something with which they are unfamiliar without immediately falling asleep, is preparing himself to become, after death, a helper of those spirits who further the progress of humanity and send down to the Earth the spiritual forces which promote life as it advances from epoch to epoch. After death, we can experience the bliss of looking down upon earthly life and co-operating with the forces that are perpetually being sent to the Earth to further its progress, but this is possible only if we endeavour to adapt ourselves to our environment and its conditions. To be rightly and thoroughly understood, karma must be studied in details, in details which reveal the manifold ways in which causes and effects are connected here in the physical world, in the spiritual world and in existence as a whole.

Here again light is thrown upon the fact that our life in the spiritual worlds depends upon the mode of our life in the physical body. Each world has its own specific mission; no two worlds have an identical mission. The characteristic phenomena and experiences in one world are not the same in another. And if, for example, beings are meant to assimilate certain things on Earth, it is on Earth that they must do so; if they miss this opportunity, they cannot acquire them in some other world. This is particularly the case in a matter which we have already considered but of which it will be well to be thoroughly aware. The matter in question concerns the acceptance of certain concepts and ideas needed by us for our life as a whole. Let us take an example that is near at hand. Anthroposophy is a timely and active force in our epoch. People approach and accept anthroposophy during their life on Earth in the way known to you, but again the belief might arise that it is not necessary to cultivate anthroposophy on Earth, for one will be in a position after death to know how things are in the spiritual worlds; that moreover the higher Hierarchies will also be there and able to impart to the soul what is necessary.

Now it is a fact that, having passed through the phase of development leading to the present cycle of evolution, human beings, with their whole souls, have been prepared to contact on Earth the kind of anthroposophical life that is possible only while they are incarnated in a physical body. People are predestined for this, and if they fail they will be unable to establish a relationship with any of the spiritual beings who might have been their teachers. One cannot simply die and then, after death, find a teacher who might take the place of what here, during physical life on Earth, can come to souls in the form of anthroposophy. We need not, however, be dejected by the fact that many individuals reject anthroposophy and it is therefore to be assumed that they will not be able to acquire it between death and the new birth. We need not despair about them for they will be born in a new earthly life and by that time there will be a strong enough stimulus towards anthroposophy and enough anthroposophy on the Earth for them to acquire it. In the present age, despondency is still out of place, but that should not lead anyone to say: I can acquire anthroposophy in my next life and so can do without it now. No, what has been neglected here cannot be retrieved later on.

When our German theosophical movement was still very young I was once giving a lecture about Nietzsche, during which I said certain things about the spiritual worlds. At that time, it was customary to have discussions and on this occasion someone got up and said that such matters must always be put to the test of Kant's philosophy, from which it would be evident that we can have no knowledge of these things here on Earth, and can begin to know them only after death. That, quite literally, was what the man said. As I have repeatedly emphasized, it is not the case that one has only to die in order to acquire certain knowledge. When we pass through the gate of death we do not experience anything for which we have not prepared ourselves. Life between death and rebirth is throughout a continuation of the life here, as the examples already given have shown. Therefore as individuals we can acquire from the beings of the higher Hierarchies only that for which we have prepared ourselves on Earth—perhaps by having become anthroposophists. Our connection with the Earth and our passage through the life on Earth have a significance which nothing else can replace.

A certain form of mediation is, however, possible in this connection, and I have already spoken of it. A person may die and during their lifetime have had no knowledge at all of anthroposophy; but their brother or their wife or a close friend were anthroposophists.

The person who has died may have refused to have anything to do with anthroposophy during their life; perhaps they consistently abused it. Now they have passed through the gate of death and anthroposophy can be conveyed to them in some way by other personalities on Earth. But there must be someone on Earth who passes on the knowledge to them out of love. Connection with the Earth must be maintained. This is the basis of what I have called 'reading to the dead'. We can render them great benefit even if previously they would listen to nothing about the spiritual world. We can help them either by putting what we have to say into the form of thoughts, conveying knowledge in this way, or we may take an anthroposophical book, visualize the personality concerned, and read to them from it; then they will learn. We have had a number of striking and beautiful examples in our movement of how it has been possible in this way to benefit the dead. Many of our friends read to those who have died. I recently had an experience that others too may have had. Someone asked me about a friend who had died very recently and it seemed that he was trying to make himself noticed by means of all kinds of signs, especially at night, creating disturbance in the room, rapping and so on. Such happenings are often indications that the dead person wants something; and in this case it was quite evident. In his lifetime the man had been very erudite but had always rejected any knowledge of the spiritual world that might come his way. It became obvious that he would greatly benefit if a particular lecture course containing the subject-matter for which he was craving, were read to him. In this way, very effective help can be given beyond death for something left undone on Earth.

The fact that can convince us of the great and significant mission of anthroposophy is that anthroposophy can bridge the gulf between the living and the dead, that when human beings die they have not really gone away from us but we remain connected with them and can be active on their behalf. If it is asked whether one can always know whether the dead soul also hears us, it must be said that those who do what has been described with genuine devotion will eventually become aware from the way in which the thoughts which they are sending to the dead live in their own souls, that the dead person is hovering around them. But this is an experience, a feeling, of which sensitive souls alone are capable. The most distressing aspect is when something that might be a great service of love is not heeded; in that case, it has been done unnecessarily for the person concerned, but it may still have some effect in the general pattern of worlds. In any case, one should not grieve excessively about such lack of success. After all, it happens even here that something is read to people who do not listen!

These things may well give a true conception of the seriousness and worth of anthroposophy. But it must constantly be emphasized that the conditions of our life in the spiritual world after death will depend entirely upon the manner of our life here on Earth. Even our community with others in the spiritual world depends upon the nature of the relationship we sought to establish with them here. If there has been no relationship with a human being here on Earth, it cannot be taken for granted that any connection can be established in the other world between death and rebirth. The possibility of being led to him in the spiritual world is as a rule dependent upon the contact established here on Earth—not necessarily in the last incarnation only but in earlier lives as well.

In short, both objective and personal relationships established here on Earth are the decisive factor for the life between death and the new birth. Exceptions do occur, but must be recognized as such. What I said here at Christmastime [in Lecture Five] about the Buddha and his present mission on Mars is one such exception. There are a number of human souls on the Earth who were able to contact the Buddha—even in his previous existence as Bodhisattva—as a result of inspirations received from the Mysteries. But because the Buddha was incarnated for the last time as the son of Suddhodana, then worked in his etheric body as I have described[75] and has now transferred his sphere of activity to Mars, at the present time the possibility exists that even if we never previously came in contact with the Buddha, we can establish a relationship with him in the life between death and rebirth; and we can then bring the results of that contact with us into the next incarnation on Earth. But that remains an exceptional case. The general rule is that after death we find those individuals with whom we had actual contacts here on Earth and continue these relationships in that other state of existence.

What has now been said is closely related to the information given during this winter about the life between death and the new birth, and the aim has been to show that if anthroposophy remains simply a matter of theory and external science, it is only half of what it ought to be; it fulfils its true function only when it streams through souls as a veritable elixir of life and enables these souls to experience in depth the feelings that arise in us when we acquire some knowledge of the higher worlds. Death then ceases to appear as a destroyer of human and personal relationships. The gulf between life here on Earth and the life after death is bridged and many activities carried out with this in mind will develop. The dead will send their influences into life, the living their influences into the realm of the dead.

My wish is that your souls will feel more deeply that life is enriched, becomes fuller and more spiritual when everything is influenced by anthroposophy. Only those who feel this have the right attitude to anthroposophy. What is of prime importance is not the knowledge that we consist of physical body, etheric body, astral body and ego, that we pass through many incarnations, and that the Earth too has passed through the several incarnations of Old Saturn, Old Sun and Old Moon, and so forth. The most important and essential need is to allow anthroposophy to transform our lives in a way commensurate with the Earth's future. This feeling can never be experienced too deeply, nor can we bestir ourselves too often in this connection. The feelings we bear with us from these meetings and then move through life under the stimulus of the knowledge of the supra-sensible worlds acquired here—these feelings are the really important element in anthroposophical life. Merely to have knowledge of anthroposophy is not enough; knowledge and feeling must be combined. We must realize, however, how false it is to believe that without any understanding of the world we can do it justice. Leonardo da Vinci's[76] saying is true: 'Great love is the daughter of great understanding'. Whoever is not prepared to understand will not learn how to love.

It is in this sense that anthroposophy should find entry into our souls, in order that from this influence which proceeds from our own being a stream of spirituality may find its way into earthly evolution, creating harmony between spirit and matter. Life on the Earth will, it is true, continue to be materialistic—indeed outer life will become increasingly so—but as we move over the Earth we will bear within our souls the realization of our connection with the higher worlds. Outwardly, earthly life will become more and more materialistic—that is the Earth's karma—but in the same measure, if earthly evolution is to reach its goal, souls must become inwardly more and more spiritual. My purpose today was to make a small contribution towards understanding this task.

LECTURE 10

BERLIN, 1 APRIL 1913

WE have undertaken to study the life between death and rebirth from certain points of view, and the lectures given during the winter endeavoured to present many aspects of this life. Moreover, it has been possible to make important additions to the more general descriptions contained in the books *Theosophy*[77] and *Esoteric Science*. Today we shall occupy ourselves chiefly with the question: How is the information given, for example, in the book *Theosophy* on the subject of the life between death and rebirth related to what has been said in the course of the lectures given during the winter?

In the book *Theosophy* there is a description of the passage of the soul after death through the soul world.[78] This soul world is divided into a Region of Burning Desire, a Region of Mobile Sensitivity, a Region of Wishes, a Region of Liking and Disliking, and then into the higher Region of Soul Light, the Region of Active Soul Force, and finally the Region of Soul Force [pp. 85-86]. That was how the soul world through which the soul has to pass after death was described. Thereafter the soul has to pass through what is described as the spiritland, and this sphere, too, with its successive regions, is described in the book *Theosophy* by using certain earthly images: the 'continental' region of spiritland, the region like the sea, and so forth.

In the course of these lectures descriptions have been given of how the soul, having passed through the gate of death, lays aside the physical body, then the etheric body, and then expands and expands. It lives through regions which for reasons that were explained may be called the region of the Moon, then that of Mercury, of Venus, of

the Sun, of Mars, of Jupiter, of Saturn, and then of the starry firmament itself. The soul or, let us say, the actual spiritual individuality of
the human being concerned, continually expands, lives through these
regions which enclose ever more extensive cosmic spaces, and then
begins to contract, becoming smaller and smaller, in order finally to
unite with the seed which comes to it from the stream of heredity.
And through this union of the human seed which the individual
acquired through heredity with what has been absorbed from the
great macrocosmic spheres, there arises the human being who is to
embark on the course of earthly life, the being who is to live through
existence between birth and death.

Now as a matter of fact, what was said in the book *Theosophy*
and in the lectures was fundamentally the same, and your attention
has been called to this. In *Theosophy*, the description was given in
certain pictures more closely related to inner conditions of the
soul. In the lectures given here during the winter, the descriptions
dealt with the great cosmic relationships connected with the functions of the several planets. It is now a matter of harmonizing the
two descriptions.

During the first period after death, the soul has to look back
upon what was experienced on Earth. The period of Kamaloka,
or call it what you will, is a period during which the soul's life is
still concerned entirely with earthly conditions. Kamaloka is fundamentally a period during which the soul feels bound to disengage
itself gradually from any direct connections still persisting from the
last incarnation on Earth. Consider that in the physical body on
Earth, the soul has experiences that depend upon the bodily life,
indeed very largely upon sensory impressions. If you think away
everything that sensory impressions bring into the soul, and then
try to realize how much still remains in it, you will have a picture
of a very meagre content indeed! And yet, on final consideration,
you will be able to say: When the soul passes through the gate of
death, everything given by the senses comes to an end and whatever
is left can at most only be memories of earlier sensory impressions.
If, therefore, you think about how much of what is yielded by sensory impressions is left in the soul, it will be easy for you to form

an idea of what remains of these impressions after death. Recall any sensory impressions experienced, for example, yesterday, while they are still comparatively vivid, and you will realize how pale they have already become compared with their former vividness. That will give you some idea of how little of what the sensory impressions have conveyed is left to the soul as remembrance. This shows you that basically all the soul's life in the world of the senses is specifically earthly experience. When the sensory organs fall away at death, all significance of the sensory impressions falls away as well. But because we humans still cling to our sensory impressions and retain a longing for them, the first region through which we pass in the life after death is the Region of Burning Desire. We would like still to have sensory impressions for a long time after death, but this is impossible because we have discarded the sensory organs. The life spent in longing for sensory impressions and being unable to enjoy them is life in the Region of Burning Desire. It is a life that does actually burn within the soul and is part of the existence in Kamaloka. The soul longs for the sensory impressions to which it was accustomed on Earth and—because the sensory organs have been laid aside—cannot have them.

A second region of the life in Kamaloka is that of Mobile Sensitivity. When the soul lives through this region, it has already ceased to long for sensory impressions, but still longs for thoughts, for thoughts which in life on Earth are acquired through the instrumentality of the brain. In the Region of Burning Desire, the soul gradually realizes that it is nonsense to wish for sensory impressions in a world for the experience of which the necessary sensory organs have been discarded, a world in which no being can possibly have sensory organs formed entirely of substance of the Earth. The soul may long since have ceased to yearn for sensory impressions, but still longs to think in the way that is customary on Earth. This earthly thinking is discarded in the Region of Mobile Sensitivity. There the human being gradually recognizes that thoughts such as are formed on Earth have significance only in the life between birth and death.

At this stage, when we have weaned ourselves from fostering thoughts that are dependent upon the physical instrument of the brain, we are still aware of a certain connection with the Earth through what is contained in our wishes. After all, wishes are connected with the soul more intimately than thoughts. Wishes have their own distinctive colouring in every individual. Whereas thoughts differ in youth, in middle life, and in old age, a particular form of wishing continues throughout our earthly life. This form and colouring of wishes are only later discarded in the Region of Wishes. And then finally, in the Region of Liking and Disliking, we rid ourselves of all longing to be connected with a physical body, with the physical body which was ours in the last incarnation. While we are passing through these Regions, of Burning Desire, of Mobile Sensitivity, of Wishes, and of Liking and Disliking, a certain longing for the last earthly life is still present. First, in the Region of Burning Desire the soul still longs to be able to see through eyes, to hear through ears, although eyes and ears no longer exist. When the soul has finally cast off any such longing, it still yearns to be able to think by means of a brain such as was available on Earth. Having got rid of this longing, too, there still remains the desire to wish with a heart as on Earth. Finally, we cease to long for sensory impressions or for thoughts formed by our brain or for wishes of our heart, but a hankering for our last incarnation on Earth taken as a whole, still lingers. Gradually, however, we then rid ourselves of this longing, too.

You will find that all the experiences in these regions correspond exactly with the passage of the expanding soul into the region called the Mercury sphere, an expansion through the Moon sphere into the Mercury sphere. On approaching the Mercury sphere, however, the soul encounters conditions described in the book *Theosophy* as a kind of spiritual region of the soul world. Read the description of the passage of the soul through this region and you will see from what is said about the kind of experiences undergone there that what is generally called the unpleasant element of Kamaloka already comes to an end in the Region of Soul Light. This Region of Soul Light corresponds with what I have said about the Mercury sphere. If you compare what was said about the life of the soul when it has expanded to the Mercury sphere with what is contained in the book *Theosophy*

about the Region of Soul Light, you will realize that endeavours were
made to describe this region first from the aspect of inner influences
of the soul, and then from the aspect of the great macrocosmic conditions through which the soul passes.

If you read what is said in *Theosophy* about the Region of Active
Soul Force, you will realize that the inner experiences undergone in
that region are in keeping with what is decisive during the passage
through the Venus sphere. It has been said that if the soul is to pass
in the right way through the Venus sphere, it must have developed
certain religious impulses during earthly life. In order to progress
through the Venus sphere with companionship and not in compul-
sory isolation, the soul must be imbued with certain religious concepts. Compare what was said about this with the description given
in the book *Theosophy* of the Region of Active Soul Force and you
will find that they agree, that in one case the inner aspect of the conditions was described, in the other, the outer aspect.

The highest Region of Soul Life, the region of pure soul life, is
experienced by the soul in passing through the region of the Sun.
So we can say that the sphere of existence in Kamaloka extends
to and somewhat beyond the Moon sphere; then the more luminous regions of the soul world begin and extend to the sphere of
the Sun. The soul experiences in the Sun sphere the region of true
psychic life. We know that in the Sun sphere after death the soul
comes into contact with the Light-Spirit, with Lucifer, who on Earth
has become the tempter, the corrupter. When the soul has expanded
into the cosmos, it comes more and more closely into contact with
those forces that now enable it to develop what is needed for the
next incarnation on Earth. Not until the soul has passed through
the region of the Sun has it finished with the last earthly incarnation. As far as the Region of Liking and Disliking is concerned,
that is to say the region between the Moon and Mercury, the soul
is still burdened inwardly with yearning for the last life on Earth;
moreover, even in the regions of Mercury, Venus, and the Sun, the
soul is not yet completely free from the ties of the last incarnation. But then it must finally have finished even with everything
that transcends merely personal experience; in the Mercury region

Spiritland - directly above Earth
Tolkien's "faery" realm accessed
from Earth via
Imagination

with whatever moral concepts have or have not been acquired, in the region of Venus with whatever religious conceptions have been developed, in the region of the Sun with whatever understanding has been acquired of the 'universally human' quality in existence—that which is not confined to any particular religious creed, but is concerned with a religious life befitting all humanity. Thus it is even the higher interests that can develop in the further evolution of humanity with which the soul has finished by the time it enters into the region of the Sun.

Then the soul passes into cosmic, spiritual life and finds its place in the Mars region. This region corresponds with what is described in *Theosophy* as the first sphere of the spiritland. This description portrays the inner aspect of the fact that the soul is spiritual to the extent of being able to behold as something external to itself the 'archetype', as it were, of the physical bodily organization and of physical conditions on the Earth in general. The archetypes of physical life on Earth appear as a kind of 'continental' mass of the spiritland. The external configurations of all our different incarnations are inscribed in this 'continental' region. There we have a picture of what, in terms of cosmic existence, the human soul has to experience in the Mars region. It might seem strange that this Mars region which has repeatedly been described in these lectures as a region of strife, of aggressive impulses until the beginning of the seventeenth century, should be said to be the first region of Devachan, of the true spiritland. Nevertheless this is the case. Everything that on Earth belongs to the actual material realm and causes the mineral kingdom to appear as a purely material realm is due to the fact that on Earth the forces are engaged in perpetual conflict among themselves. This also led to the result that at the time when materialism was in its prime and material life was assumed to be the sole reality, the 'struggle for existence' was regarded as the only valid law of life on Earth. That is, of course, an error, because material existence is not the only form of existence evolving on Earth. But when we humans assume embodiment on Earth, we can only enter into the form of existence that has its archetypes in the lowest region of what is, for the Earth, the spiritland. Read the description of the lowest region of spiritland as given in the book *Theosophy*. I want to quote this particular chapter today in connection with our present studies. Towards the beginning of the description of the spiritland you will find the following passage:

> The development of the spirit in spiritland takes place in consequence of man's entering completely into the life of the various regions of this land. [p. 114]

Thus as the result of our studies in the course of the winter we could now say that from the Mars region onwards the human soul begins to live more deeply into spiritual conditions of existence.

To continue:

> His own life dissolves, as it were, into these regions successively and he takes on, for the time being, their characteristics. Through this they penetrated his being with theirs in order that he may be able to work, strengthened by theirs, in his earthly life.
>
> In the *first region* of spiritland man is surrounded by the spiritual archetypes of earthly things. During life on earth he learns to know only the shadows of these archetypes that he grasps in his thoughts. What is merely thought on earth is in this region experienced, lived. Man moves among thoughts, but those thoughts are real beings. [p. 114]

Again, a little later:

> Our own embodiments dissolve here into a unity with the rest of the world. Thus man here looks upon the archetypes of the physical corporeal reality as a unity to which he has belonged himself. He learns, therefore, gradually to know his relationship, his unity with the surrounding world by observation. He learns to say to it, 'What is here spread out around thee, thou wert that.' This is one of the fundamental thoughts of ancient Indian Vedanta wisdom. The sage acquires, even during his earthly life, what others experience after death, namely, the ability to grasp the thought that he himself is related to all things—the thought, 'Thou art that.' In earthly life this is an ideal to which the thought life can be devoted. In the land of the spirit it is an immediate fact, one that grows ever clearer to us through spiritual experience, and man himself comes to

know ever more clearly in this land that in his own inner being he belongs to the spirit world. He perceives himself to be a spirit among spirits, a member of the primordial spirits, feeling within himself the word of the primordial Spirit, 'I am the Primal Spirit.' The wisdom of the Vedanta says, 'I am Brahman,' that is, I belong as a member to the primordial being in whom all beings have their origin. [pp. 115-116]

From this passage it is clear that when, during the life between death and rebirth we enter into the Mars region, we grasp the full significance of the saying, '*Tat tvam asi*', 'Thou art that', and of the other saying, 'I am Brahman'. '*Tat tvam asi*', 'Thou art that', is only an earthly rendering that resounds in the soul of what is a self-evident experience in the Mars region, the lowest region of spiritland. If we now ask whence the wisdom of Ancient India derived the deeply significant affirmations, '*Tat tvam asi*', 'Thou art that', 'I am Brahman', we have now identified the region in question and those teachers in Ancient India are revealed to us as beings belonging to the Mars region, but transferred to the Earth. To what was said years ago in the book *Theosophy* about the Mars region, the lowest region of Devachan, there can now be added what we have heard in these lectures, namely, that at the dawn of the modern age the Buddha was transferred to this same region, the Mars region. Half a millennium before the Mystery of Golgotha, the Buddha—regarded as one who was to prepare spiritually for this Mystery—had come to the Earth, to the territory where Mars wisdom had been proclaimed since times primeval. And centuries after the Mystery of Golgotha he was, as we know, sent by an act of Rosicrucian wisdom to the Mars region in order to continue working there.[79] In ancient times, Brahmanism belonged intrinsically to the Mars region of the cosmos. At the beginning of the seventeenth century after the Mystery of Golgotha, Brahmanism passed over into the impulse of Buddha, and the reflection of this on Earth was the absorption of Brahmanism into Buddhism in the cultural life of India.

What takes place on Earth, therefore, is in a broad and grandiose sense an image of happenings in the heavens.

If you have read the chapter in *Theosophy* which deals with what you now know to be the Mars region, and in which a self-evident expression is the 'I am Brahman', you will be able, if you read that chapter again, to picture how an event here on Earth is also an event in a region of the cosmos, how this event can be understood, and how the impulse of Buddha as a cosmic happening is related to the circumstances described in the relevant chapter of that book. We shall realize that our studies during the winter were closely linked with the theosophical work we began more than ten years ago. We then described the spiritland and a 'continental' mass of spiritland; the lowest region of spiritland was characterized in relation to the inner life of the soul. The description given was such that if you have understood it, you will realize that the impulse of Buddha has its place in the lowest region of spiritland as described in these lectures. Here is an example of how the details of spiritual research harmonize with each other.

If we now pass on to consider the cosmic aspects of the second region of spiritland as described from the inner point of view of the soul, we shall find that this second region, the 'oceanic' region of spiritland, corresponds with the Jupiter region. Further, if we pass to the third region of Devachan, the 'airy' region of spiritland, we shall find that it corresponds with the influences of the Saturn region. What was described in *Theosophy* as the fourth region of spiritland already extends beyond our planetary system. There the soul expands into still wider spaces, into the starry firmament itself. From the descriptions that were given from the inner standpoint of the soul, it will be quite clear to you that the experiences of the soul in the fourth region of spiritland could not be undergone in any realm where the spatial relationship to the Earth is still the same as that of the planetary system. There is something so utterly foreign in what is conveyed by the fourth region of spiritland that it can never correspond with what can be experienced even within the outermost planetary sphere, the Saturn sphere.

Therefore, the soul passes into the starry firmament, that is to say into distances more and more remote both from the Earth and also from the Sun. These distant realms are described in the account of the three highest regions of spiritland traversed by the soul before it begins to draw together again and to pass, in the reverse order, through all the preceding conditions. On this journey the soul acquires the forces by means of which it can build up a new life on Earth.

In general, it can be said that when the soul has passed through the region of the Sun, it has finished with every element of 'personality'. What is experienced beyond the solar region, beyond the Region of Soul Life in the true sense, is spiritual; it transcends everything that is personal. What the soul then experiences as 'Thou art that'— and especially in our time as the impulse of Buddha in the Mars region—is something that seems strange here on Earth, though it is not so on Mars; it is the impulse denoted by the word 'Nirvana'. This means liberation from everything that is significant on the Earth, for the soul begins to realize the great cosmic significance of universal space. In living through all this, the soul emancipates itself entirely from the element of personality. In the Mars region, the lowest region of spiritland, where the soul acquires understanding of the 'Thou art that', or, as we should put it today, receives the impulse of Buddha, it frees itself from everything that is earthly. After the soul has become inwardly free of this—and the Christ-Impulse is needed here—it also liberates itself spiritually by recognizing that all ties of blood are forged on Earth and therefore belong by nature to the Earth. But the soul then passes on to new conditions.

[margin handwriting: Shift from blood kinship to spiritual kinship]

In the Jupiter region, conditions which force the soul into some particular creed are dissolved. We have heard that the soul can pass through the Venus region with companionship only if it had adopted a creed; without religion in some form, it would be lonely and isolated. We have also heard that the soul can pass through the solar region only when it has learnt to understand the creeds of all religions on the Earth. In the Jupiter region, however, the soul must liberate itself entirely from the particular creed to which it belonged during life on Earth. This was not an essentially personal attachment, but something into which it was born and was shared in company with other souls. Thus, the soul can pass through the Venus region only if it has acquired religious ideas in earthly life; it can pass through the solar region only if it has developed some measure of understanding of all such beliefs. The soul can pass through the region of Jupiter only if it is able to liberate itself from the particular confession to which it belonged on Earth; merely to understand the others is not enough. For during the passage through the Jupiter region it will be decided whether in the next life the soul will have to be connected with the same creed as before, or whether it has experienced everything that can be offered by one particular creed. In the Venus sphere, the soul garners the fruits of a particular faith; in the solar sphere, the fruits of an understanding of all forms of religious life; but when it reaches the region of Jupiter, the soul must be able to lay the foundation for a new relationship to religion during the next life on Earth.

These are three stages experienced by the soul between death and the new birth: first it experiences inwardly the fruits of the faith to which it belonged in the last life; then the fruits of having developed the capacity to appreciate the value of all other religious beliefs; and then it must free itself so completely from the beliefs held in the last life that it can wholeheartedly adopt a different religion. This cannot be achieved by attaching equal value to all creeds; and we know that on its return journey through these regions the soul comes once again into the region of Jupiter and there prepares the traits enabling it to live in the fullest sense in a different religion in the next life. In this way, the forces which the soul needs in order to shape a new life are gradually impressed into it.

If you now read what is said in the book *Theosophy* about the third region of the spiritland, the 'airy' or 'atmospheric' region, you will find again what has been said here in connection with the region of Saturn. In this region, companionship and the avoidance of terrible loneliness is possible only for souls already able to exercise a certain degree of genuine self-knowledge, of completely unbiased self-knowledge. Only by being able to put self-knowledge into practice can the soul find entrance to the regions beyond Saturn, therefore even beyond our solar system and leading into that cosmic life from which souls must bring the qualities that ensure progress on the Earth. If souls were never able to live in companionship in realms beyond the region of Saturn, progress on Earth would not be possible. Think, for example, of the individuals sitting here today. If the souls incarnated in the world at the present time had never passed beyond the Saturn region between death and rebirth, culture on Earth would still be at the stage reached, for example, in the epoch of Ancient India. The Ancient Indian culture was able to progress to that of Ancient Persia only because in the intervening periods souls had passed beyond the Saturn region; and again, the progress from Ancient Persian culture to Egypto-Chaldean culture was made possible by impulses for progress brought into the Earth from the realms beyond the region of Saturn. What human beings have contributed to the progress of culture on Earth has been gathered by their souls from realms beyond the region of Saturn.

The external progress of humanity originates in the new impulses brought from beyond the region of Saturn; in this way the various cultural epochs progress and new impulses take effect. But as well as this there is the stream of inner experiences which is to be distinguished from the progress of external culture and has its 'centre of gravity' in the Mystery of Golgotha. When we know that the stream of experiences in our inner life of soul on Earth has its centre of gravity in the Mystery of Golgotha, while on the other hand this Mystery of Golgotha is connected with the solar region, a question arises; it is a question that might well occupy our minds for a very long time, but we will at least consider it today. It is good that on the basis of what can already be found in lectures and courses of lectures, we should be able to form our own thoughts about such questions—thoughts which can then be rectified by reports of investigations given here.

On the one hand, we have the fact that Christ is the Sun Spirit who united Himself with the life of the Earth through the Mystery of Golgotha. You will find the most detailed account of this in the courses of lectures entitled *The Gospel of St John and Its Relation to the Other Gospels*,[80] given in Kassel, and *From Jesus to Christ*. And now we have heard of the other fact, namely that all external progress on Earth from one cultural epoch to the next is dependent upon influences from beyond the region of Saturn. A question thus arises here. Progress on Earth from one cultural epoch to another is dependent upon influences connected with a world beyond the sphere of Saturn—a world altogether different from the one where progress is brought about by the stream of spirituality that flows through the evolution of humanity, that approached humanity in ancient times, has its centre of gravity in the Mystery of Golgotha and thereafter took its course in the way often described. How do these two facts harmonize? The truth is that they harmonize completely.

You need only picture to yourself that our Earth evolution as it is today was preceded by the earlier incarnation of the Earth, namely Old Moon. Now think of Old Moon as we have often described it, followed by the present Earth. Midway in the process of evolution between Old Moon and Earth something like a condition of cosmic sleep took place. During the transition from Old Moon to Earth, everything that had existed on Old Moon passed into a kind of germinal state from which, at a later stage, everything in existence on Earth came forth. But all the planetary spheres also came forth from that cosmic sleep. During the epoch of Old Moon, therefore, the planetary spheres were not in the state in which they exist today. Old Moon passes into the cosmic sleep and out of this condition the planetary spheres develop into what they now are. Everything that evolved in the cosmos between the era of Old Moon and that of the Earth is contained within the range of the sphere of Saturn. The Christ-Impulse, however, does not belong to what evolved in the cosmos during the period of transition from Old Moon to Earth; rather, it already belonged to the Old Sun and remained in the sphere of the Sun when Old Moon eventually separated from it. The Christ-Impulse continued to evolve onwards towards the Earth, but remained united with the sphere of the Sun after the sphere of Saturn, the sphere of Jupiter and so forth, had separated from it. And so, in addition to what the human soul was, before the Mystery of Golgotha, it now has within it something that is more than all that is contained in the planetary spheres, something that is founded in the depths of the cosmos, that does indeed come over from Sun to Earth, but belongs to far deeper regions of the spiritual world than do the planetary spheres. For these planetary spheres are a product of what took place when Old Moon evolved to become Earth. What streams to us from the Christ-Impulse, however, comes from Old Sun, which preceded Old Moon.

From this we realize that external culture on Earth is connected with the cosmos, whereas the inner life of soul is connected in a much deeper sense with the Sun. Thus in all these connections—in their spiritual aspect, too—there is something of which the following can be said. When we look out into the stellar spheres there is revealed to us, as it were, outspread in space, a world that is embodied in culture on Earth because human souls have entered into these stellar spheres between death and rebirth; but when we gaze at the Sun we behold something that has become what it is today because behind it there is an infinitely long period of evolution. In an age when it was not yet possible to speak of a connection between culture on Earth and the stellar worlds as can be done today, even then the Sun was already united with the Christ-Impulse. It was a relationship, in primordial times, in which one still could not speak of a connection between the Earth and the world of stars. Thus everything brought from the stellar worlds for the promotion of culture on the Earth is to be regarded as a kind of Earth-body which needed to be—and actually was—ensouled by what came to the Earth from the Sun, namely by the Christ-Impulse. The Earth was ensouled when the Mystery of Golgotha took place; it was then that culture on Earth received its 'soul'.

'The death on Golgotha' was only seemingly a death; in reality it was the birth of the soul of the Earth. And everything that can be brought to the Earth from cosmic expanses, also from beyond the sphere of Saturn, is related to the sphere of the Earth as the body of the Earth is related to the soul of the Earth.

These reflections can show us that the presentation given in the book *Theosophy*—in rather different words and from a different point of view—contains what has been described as the cosmic aspect in the lectures given this winter. You need only to be reminded that in the one case the account is given from the point of view of the soul, and in the other from that of the great cosmic conditions, and you will find that the two descriptions are in complete harmony.

The conclusion which I would like to be able to draw from these lectures is that you realize how vast is the range of anthroposophy, and that its method must be to gather from every possible side whatever can throw light on the nature of the spiritual world. Even when additions are made to what had been said years ago, there need be no contradiction, for what is said is not the outcome of any philo-sophical argument or reflective thinking, but of occult investigation. Yellow today will still be yellow ten years hence, even though the essential quality of yellow as a colour is grasped for the first time ten years later. What was said years ago still holds good, although light is shed upon it from the new points of view which it has been possible to contribute during last winter.

The death on Golgotha was only seemingly a death; in reality it was the birth of the soul of the earth."

APPENDICES

Appendix 1

AHRIMAN AND LUCIFER

Rudolf Steiner spoke often about the dual nature of evil, ascribing its source to supersensible beings he calls Lucifer and Ahriman. Lucifer might be termed the 'red devil,' who tempts humans to sin on the side of *superbia*: pride, anger, egotism, erotic passions, etc. 'Ahriman' is a traditional name for a black demon, beginning with the Zoroastrian figure Angra Mainyu, opponent of the Sun God Ahura Mazda. Ahriman's temptations are those of *acedia*: laziness, greed, and denial of the Spirit generally.

Lucifer incarnated in the third millennium BCE, in the distant East. Ahriman will incarnate in the twenty-first century, in the West. Lucifer wants us to live in the past, while Ahriman cuts us off from the past. Lucifer wants us to flee the Earth; Ahriman wants to bind us to the Earth. Lucifer is responsible for the glories of pagan culture, which however provided no moral impulses. He longs for his cosmic home, which is the planet Venus. Ahriman seeks to subvert culture by promoting materialism, utility, nationalism, and literalism. He wants to reduce the freedom of the spiritual-cultural sphere to politics and economics. He wants to reduce all qualities to quantities.

Steiner argues that the assaults of these beings are providential: only by overcoming their resistance and holding them in proper balance can humanity become inwardly strong enough to develop genuine freedom, knowledge and love. Both figures are represented in Steiner's monumental sculpture 'The Group' (from which these photos have been taken). In 'The Group,' Christ as the Representative of Humanity shows us how to hold the balance: he does not vanquish Lucifer and Ahriman, but he keeps each in their place, restricting their activity.

For an excellent discussion of Steiner's ideas as applied to Goethe's *Faust*, see Alan P. Cottrell, *Goethe's View of Evil and the Search for a New Image of Man in our Time* (Edinburgh: Floris Press, 1982). Mephistopheles in Goethe's *Faust* exhibits traits of both beings by turns, and Steiner was critical of Goethe for having conflated them. Lucifer and Ahriman also appear as characters in Steiner's own expressionist *Mystery Dramas* (1910-1913): see GA 14, Rudolf Steiner, *Four Mystery Dramas*, trans. Ruth and Hans Pusch (Great Barrington, MA: SteinerBooks, 2007).

Ahriman

Lucifer

Appendix 2

ROSICRUCIANISM

'Rosicrucianism is a spiritual and cultural movement which arose in Europe in the early 17th century after the publication of several texts which purported to announce the existence of a hitherto unknown esoteric order to the world and made seeking its knowledge attractive to many. ...

The manifestos do not elaborate extensively on the matter, but clearly combine references to Kabbalah, Hermeticism, alchemy, and Christian mysticism. The Rosicrucian manifestos heralded a 'universal reformation of humanity', through a science allegedly kept secret for decades until the intellectual climate might receive it. ...

Between 1614 and 1617, three anonymous manifestos were published, first in Germany and later throughout Europe, These were the *Fama Fraternitatis RC* (*The Fame of the Brotherhood of RC*, 1614), the *Confessio Fraternitatis* (*The Confession of the Brotherhood of RC*, 1615), and the *Chymical Wedding of Christian Rosicross anno 1459* (1617).' [*Wikipedia*]

See Frances Yates, *The Rosicrucian Enlightenment* (London: Routledge, 1972); Paul Allen, ed., *A Christian Rosenkreutz Anthology* (Great Barrington, Massachusetts: Lindesfarne, 1996); Rudolf Steiner, *The Secret Stream: Christian Rosenkreutz and Rosicrucianism*, edited by Christopher Bamford (Great Barrington, Massachusetts: Anthroposophic Press, 2000); and CW 233a; Rudolf Steiner, *Rosicrucianism and Modern Initiation* (Forest Row: Rudolf Steiner Press, 2020).

Appendix 3

THE HIERARCHIES

Steiner's complex and highly esoteric ontology affirms the long-standing spiritual teaching that humans occupy a developmental stage between animals 'beneath' and angelic beings 'above' us. ('Beneath' and 'above' are meant to indicate relatively lower and higher levels of consciousness, developmental complexity, and power.) Arthur O. Lovejoy's eponymous study of 1936, which is widely viewed as the founding document of modern intellectual history, called this idea 'The Great Chain of Being', and that is now the conventional term for this set of ideas. This idea is in keeping with a Christian tradition extending back through Thomas Aquinas to Dionysius the Areopagite (late fifth or early sixth century CE; now referred to as 'Pseudo-Dionysius' to distinguish him from his much-earlier namesake), and ultimately to St Paul. In his treatise *On the Celestial Hierarchy* (Pseudo-Dionysius, *The Complete Works* [Mahwah, NJ: Paulist Press, 1987], pp. 143-192), Pseudo-Dionysius had distinguished nine ranks of beings 'above' humans in the spiritual or intelligible world: in ascending order, he terms them 'Angels', 'Archangels', and 'Principalities' (together the 'Third Hierarchy'); 'Authorities', 'Powers', and 'Dominions' (among other current translations; together the 'Second Hierarchy'); and 'Thrones', 'Cherubim', and 'Seraphim' (together the First Hierarchy). Steiner tends to refer to the Third and Second Hierarchies by their Greek names: 'Angeloi', 'Archangeloi', 'Archai'; 'Exousiai', 'Dynameis', and 'Kyriotetes'. Another set of terms Steiner often employs is 'Spirits of Form' (rather than 'Exousiai'), 'Spirits of Movement' (rather than 'Dynameis'), 'Spirits of Wisdom' (rather than 'Kyriotetes'), and 'Spirits of Will' (rather than 'Thrones'). Among Steiner's many discussions of the hierarchies, the most fundamental are Ch. 4 of CW 13: *An Outline of Esoteric Science*, trans. Catherine E. Creeger (Great Barrington, MA: SteinerBooks, 1997); CW 136: *Spiritual Beings in the Heavenly Bodies and in the Kingdoms of Nature* (Great Barrington, MA: SteinerBooks, 2012); and CW 110: *The Spiritual Hierarchies and the Physical World: Zodiac, Planets and Cosmos*, trans. René M. Querido (Great Barrington, NY: SteinerBooks, 2008).

APPENDIX 4

REPRESENTATION

Translators' introductions or notes invariably comment on the difficulty of translating *vorstellen*/*Vorstellung* and a few other German philosophical and psychological terms such as *Geist*, *Anschauung*, and *Gemüt*. Tellingly, in the title of Schopenhauer's magnum opus, *Die Welt als Wille und Vorstellung*, has been translated three different ways: initially as 'Representation', but then more recently as 'Idea' and finally as 'Presentation'. Both Michael Wilson's translation of Steiner's *Philosophy of Freedom* and Owen Barfield's *Case for Anthroposophy*[81] begin their discussions by noting that the standard translation of this Kantian philosophical term is 'representation'. But then Wilson goes on to argue (rightly) that this is too technical a term for most contexts, and that 'representation' has other, distracting meanings outside of philosophy, which led him to translate *Vorstellung* and its variants as 'mental picture'. Barfield chooses 'representation', which is understandable given that the context is Steiner's discussion of Brentano's neo-Kantian treatise. The reasons why this term is so very difficult to translate are (1) that it encompasses many different kinds of mental acts; (2) it refuses any sharp distinction between subjective and objective; (3) it can refer to a faculty, the activity of a faculty, or the result of that activity; (4) it often has a distinctly visual quality, but it can also refer to abstract concepts; and (5) it straddles the conventional divide between philosophy and psychology.

APPENDIX 5

MICHELANGELO AND THE MEDICI TOMBS
(BY MARGOT AMRINE)

MICHELANGELO Buonarroti (1475-1564), the artist and the human being, has fascinated royalty, scholars, artists, and travellers for centuries. His stunning technique serves great expressive goals; his life as a multifaceted, but solitary, genius continues to inspire and amaze. Biographers were hard at work before he died, and many others followed. Like most Renaissance artists, he worked as a painter, sculptor, and architect. One of the three 'Renaissance Triumvirate' (along with

Leonardo and Raphael), he is considered one of the three greatest Italian sculptors of *all* times, joining Donatello and Bernini. A short list of excellent books on his life and works follows.

Let us focus briefly on four topics: Renaissance ideals, tomb sculptures, the Medici family, and the phenomenon of the *'non-finito'*. A separate section that follows will address the Medici tombs specifically.

Renaissance ideals overlapped with some of the cherished ideals of the Middle Ages, but included a new emphasis on civic pride and responsibility, and they were informed by the ideals of antiquity. There was a renewed interest in the literature, philosophy, and art of Greco-Roman culture. When antique sculptures were found and excavated, there was tremendous excitement. Sadly, these works had lost the bright pigmentation and adornment they originally possessed, but the ancient understanding of the beauty of the human being was admired and celebrated. Renaissance writers moved to extol the dignity of each individual, and the meaning of life balanced between 'active' and 'contemplative' states.

Tomb sculptures were richly resonant of these ideals. Tomb sculptures memorialized the individual's life and agency, even if the portraits were not true likenesses. Often, Neoplatonic themes informed the sculptor's (or patron's) choices as well.

The Medici family was closely linked to Michelangelo's destiny. They are impossible to sum up. They were humanists, poets, republicans, despots, plotters, civic-minded, power-hungry, and more. They were certainly patrons of the arts, and they left a glorious legacy: among a multitude of gifts, they donated the entire Uffizi Museum to the public in 1743. The Medici patronized Michelangelo from his early teens.

Michelangelo was reluctant to finish his work. About two thirds of his sculptures are unfinished. This was a very rare occurrence before Michelangelo. Hence, the term *'non-finito,'* specifically with regard to him. Did he want his works to be more expressive? Was the mental activity of sculpting more important than craftsmanship? Was the process, rather than the product, paramount? These are questions to ponder when considering the Medici tombs.

The Medici Tombs

Not far from Brunelleschi's soaring and incomparable dome, the iconic symbol of Florence, is the Medici church of San Lorenzo. The façade is unfinished to this day. It was to have held 24 sculptures by Michelangelo, but the contract was annulled. Michelangelo was instead asked to create tomb sculptures for Lorenzo ('the Magnificent'), Giuliano ('the Magnificent'), and two younger Medici dukes with the same names. All four lie in rest in the 'New Sacristy of San Lorenzo', otherwise known as the Medici Chapel.

Although Michelangelo worked on many sketches, only the tombs of the two younger dukes were sculpted.[82] One hesitates to write 'completed', because of Michelangelo's characteristic '*non-finito*' style. The statue of Lorenzo shows a thoughtful, contemplative individual, while that of Giuliano reflects an active life. However, the faces are not portraits, and some have suggested the titles are reversed. Below each is a pair of reclining figures resting on a curved sarcophagus lid, probably intended to suggest the arc of life, rising and falling, according to Dante.

Let us consider these four reclining figures. 'Night' is the most famous. She seems to withdraw into herself, with symbols of death nearby: the owl, poppies, and an exceptional mask. At the same time he was sculpting 'Night', Michelangelo was painting 'Leda and the Swan' (now lost, but which we know from a copy by Cornelis Bos). The poses are strikingly similar. Michelangelo wrote about 'Night': 'Do not wake me: pass with bated breath.' 'Night' is highly polished, glistening. Opposite is 'Day', a male figure very much unfinished, twisting towards us. The other pair seem more subtle. 'Dawn' is sensual, a Venus-type who seems as though she might rise. 'Dusk' is also a transitional figure, but male and less finished than 'Dawn'.

What do these figures mean? Why these powerful nudes in the Sacristy, where communion is prepared? Do they represent the seasons, time and death, the four humours? In what way do they offer a picture of Neoplatonism? Does the Chapel relate to the Florentine cult of the Magi?

Not surprisingly, Rudolf Steiner's insights are original. He reads each of the four figures as a portrayal of one part of the fourfold human being. 'Night' presents the etheric body; 'Day' the ego; 'Dusk' the physical body; and 'Dawn' the astral body. Steiner asserts that artists are inspired by the spiritual world. Looking at the statues, Steiner's scheme makes sense. 'Day' is the least finished, just as our human ego is, and when we are confronted by his rough, yet piercing face, we wake up!

The Medici Chapel evokes wonder, questions, meditative thoughts. As we go to press in 2021, it has also become a very trendy topic. Why? The Chapel badly needed restoration, and an experimental technique succeeded. As reported in the *New York Times* (May 31, 2021),[83] a team of six Italian women (scientists, art restorers, art historians) used specific, nonhazardous strains of bacteria to eat the grime of centuries. The splendid Carrara marble, personally chosen by Michelangelo, has been renewed. The artist's genius shines forth. In one of his sonnets, Michelangelo wrote: 'The finest artist cannot conceive a thought that the marble itself does not bind within its shell, waiting to be brought out by the hand that serves the artist's mind.' The restorers left one small patch untouched (behind the sarcophagus of Giuliano) to show the contrast with the cleaned marble. A little nod to the *non-finito* perhaps.

Bibliography

- Beck, James. *Three Worlds of Michelangelo*. W. W. Norton, 1999.
- Gill, Anton. *Il Gigante*. St Martin's Press, 2002.
- Goffen, Rona. *Renaissance Rivals*. Yale, 2002.
- King, Ross. *Michelangelo and the Pope's Ceiling*. Walker, 2003.
- Pope-Hennessy, John. *Italian High Renaissance and Baroque Sculpture*. Phaidon, 1996.
- Scigliano, Eric. *Michelangelo's Mountain*. Free Press, 2005.

I am indebted to the late Ward Bissell, whose course on Renaissance sculpture at the University of Michigan was life changing. Thankfully, I took good notes, and kept them.

Appendix 6

THE ETHERIC AND THE ASTRAL BODIES

'E THERIC body' is Steiner's early, theosophical term for the subtle body of supra-physical forces that sustains life. Later he would also refer to it variously as 'the life body', or the 'formative forces body', or (echoing Spinoza's distinction between *natura naturans* and *natura naturata*) the realm of 'living working' as opposed to the physical realm of 'finished work'.

The etheric body is known through Imaginaton, and first reveals itself to strengthened thinking as supra-sensible pictures. The etheric body consists of centrifugal forces, expresses itself in all aqueous processes, and flows in great currents through the cosmos. The etheric is a 'time body'; here time becomes space. It is a unity that is always there as a temporal totality, right up to the present moment.

The individual etheric body is precipitated out of a vast cosmic ether. It can be subdivided further into warmth ether, light ether, chemical or tone ether, and life ether. Theodor Schwenk's *Sensitive Chaos: The Creation of Flowing Forms in Water and Air* (London: Rudolf Steiner Press, 1996) is a scientifically compelling and aesthetically beautiful exploration of these forces.

'Astral body' is Steiner's early, theosophical term for the subtle body that corresponds generally to 'soul' or 'psyche'. Like Freud and Jung, he sees it as internally differentiated and gradually transformed by the activity of the higher faculty of the 'I' or 'ego'. The astral body reveals itself to Inspiration, and emerges in a sense from behind Imagination. The traditional concept of the Music of the Spheres is an experience of macrocosmic astrality. It consists of centripetal forces, and expresses itself in breathing and in the airy element generally. It also expresses itself as the human nervous system. The astral body has remained behind in time, and casts its beams forward into the present incarnation; it remains in the spiritual world before conception and birth.

The *locus classicus* for both of these bodies among Steiner's introductory works is the uncharacteristically schematic and static description in his early book *Theosophy* (1904; many English editions are available, including now very inexpensive ebook editions). A much more dynamic (but also much more difficult) account is to be found in the middle four lectures of Rudolf Steiner, *A Psychology of Body, Soul, & Spirit* (New York: SteinerBooks, 1999), which includes a valuable Introduction by Robert Sardello. See also Lecture 5 (2 February 1924) of the cycle GA 234; *Anthroposophy and the Inner Life,* trans. and intro. Owen Barfield (Bristol: Rudolf Steiner Press, 1992).

APPENDIX 7

FRIEDRICH SCHILLER

FRIEDRICH Schiller (1759-1805) is best known in the German-speaking world as a dramatist. As a young man, he was the *enfant terrible* of the German stage, the leader of a movement called *Sturm und Drang*—'Storm and Stress'. To call the young Schiller politically and culturally 'radical' is an understatement: the epigraph to his first drama was *'In tyrannos'*—'tyrants up against the wall!' The leaders of the French Revolution named him the first honorary citizen of the new French Republic. Schiller started out as a combination of Elvis and Malcolm X, but then you then have to imagine that pair morphing into a professor of history, next into a first-rate philosopher , and finally into Arthur Miller : then you've got Schiller. A fascinating man who is sadly neglected in the English-speaking world.

Even in the German-speaking world, Schiller is not well known as a philosopher, but that may be his greatest claim to fame in the long run. Right from the moment it was published in 1794, Schiller's treatise *On the Aesthetic Education of Man* was recognized by his contemporaries as a masterpiece. Hegel pronounced it the greatest philosophical work of the German nation, which is saying a lot considering what Kant had just accomplished. And yet when Rudolf Steiner took up Schiller's essay at the end of the nineteenth century and used it as one of the main foundations for anthroposophy, he was like an archaeologist who had unearthed a treasure long buried and forgotten. Over the course of those few decades, intellectual life in Central Europe had descended so deeply into materialism and positivism that it could no longer recognize the value of Schiller's treatise. And it is really only since the publication of Wilkinson and Willoughby's edition and English translation by Oxford University Press in 1967 that Schiller's essay has again entered the mainstream of intellectual history.

Appendix 8

COSMIC EVOLUTION

S TEINER's account of cosmic evolution is grand beyond all imagining. Steiner affirmed the reality of evolution, but not as Darwin understood it. He honoured Darwin's theory, which was the inspiration and the precondition for Steiner's own research into what one might better term evolutionary cosmology. The same process Darwin describes from an earthly perspective as a gradually *ascending* evolution of increasingly complex biological forms, Steiner describes from a spiritual perspective as a gradual *descent* of spiritual entities into ever more adequate material vessels. In other places, Steiner offers additional perspectives on his cosmology, complementing the 'outer' view of the finished products in *Esoteric Science*, for example, with an especially sublime cycle of five short lectures offering, as it were, an 'Elohim's-eye view' of the same unfolding process.

In Steiner's account, humanity was created from the top down, but it has evolved from the bottom up, over successive 'incarnations' of Earth evolution proper, which was preceded by Saturn, Sun, and Moon. Evolution allows us to approach multiple goals: over many eons, we have been guided from simplicity toward complexity, from unconsciousness toward consciousness, from passivity toward activity, and from necessity toward freedom. Having received the gift of wisdom, our task is now to internalize that wisdom and transform it into active love. The paradox of freedom implies that the further we progress towards these goals, the less certain is the outcome of the process, which will increasingly be placed into our own hands.

The central texts are:

- Chapter 4 of CW 13, *An Outline of Esoteric Science* (Great Barrington, MA: SteinerBooks, 1997);
- CW 132, *Inner Experiences of Evolution* (Great Barrington, Massachusetts: SteinerBooks, 2009);
- CW 136, *Spiritual Beings in the Heavenly Bodies and in the Kingdoms of Nature* (Great Barrington, Massachusetts: SteinerBooks, 2012);
- CW 110, *The Spiritual Hierarchies and the Physical World: Zodiac, Planets and Cosmos*, trans. René M. Querido (Great Barrington, NY: Steiner-Books, 2008);
- and GA 122, *Genesis: Secrets of Creation* (2002; London: Rudolf Steiner Press, 2012).

APPENDIX 9

PLATONISM AND ARISTOTELIANISM

P LATO (428-347 BCE) was a Greek philosopher. He founded the first public school of Philosophy in Athens, the Academy, and he introduced into the discipline both dialogue and dialectics. His importance is hard to overestimate: indeed, Alfred North White-head wrote of the European philosophical tradition that it was nothing but a succession of footnotes to Plato. He is exceptional in that his full *oeuvre* seems to have been transmitted down through the ages intact. His immediate teacher was Socrates, and Aristotle was his student.

Aristotle (384-322 BCE) was also a Greek philosopher, and one of the greatest philosophers who ever lived. 'A prodigious researcher and writer, Aristotle left a great body of work, perhaps numbering as many as two-hundred treatises, from which approximately thirty-one survive. His extant writings span a wide range of disciplines, from logic, metaphysics and philosophy of mind, through ethics, political theory, aesthetics and rhetoric, and into such primarily non-philosophical fields as empirical biology, where he excelled at detailed plant and animal observation and description.' [*Stanford Encyclopedia of Philosophy*] He was the teacher of Alexander the Great.

Platonism inspired a large number of Neo-Platonists, the greatest being Plotinus. Plotinus (c. 204-270 CE) 'was a Platonic philosopher born in Lycopolis, Egypt. Although the story of his life was written down by his student Porphyry, few biographical details are included because Plotinus rejected the physical world of appearances in favor of the realm of the mind and considered trivialites such as his birth date, family, ancestry and personal endeavors unworthy of mention. At the age of 28 he began a course of study with the Platonist Ammonius Saccas that deeply impacted his life. Already a student of philosophy, Plotinus devoted himself fully to the discipline, absorbing Plato's *Dialogues* and his teacher's commentary on them. Plotinus' concept of the Divine Mind and the purpose of mortal existence exerted tremendous influence on all three of the world's great monotheistic religions and, for this reason, many consider him the most significant philosopher of the ancient world. He is the founder of the school of thought known as Neo-Platonism; a significant number of famous ancient writers, theologians, politicians, generals, and philosophers are now recognized as Neo-Platonists, although they would not have referred to themselves by that label. Plotinus' philosophy was recorded in the *Enneads* by Porphyry; he wrote nothing himself. He died in Rome at the age of 66.' [*ancient.eu*]

The School of Chartres revived a form of Platonism, and thus can be called Neo-Platonic. In the Renaissance, the Florentine philosopher Marsilio Ficino (1433-1499) translated Plato into Latin, and was himself heavily influenced by Plato as a philosopher, as was Giovanni Pico della Mirandola (1463–1494). Indeed, the pair headed a philosophical school that is referred to as Florentine Neo-Platonism.

The most important Aristotelians were the Scholastics, and especially Thomas Aquinas. Among modern philosophers, Leibniz (1646-1716) and Hegel (1770-1831) stand out for their strong, if heavily modified, Aristotelianism.

Appendix 10

NICHOLAS OF CUSA

Nicholas of Cusa (1401–1464) (also Nicholas von Kues and Nicolaus Cusanus) was the most important German thinker of the fifteenth century. He was also a theologian, jurist, and astronomer. He was appointed Cardinal for meritorious service to the Church in 1448. The most important of his many writings was *De Docta ignorantia* (*On Learned Ignorance*) of 1440. Nicholas later would claim that he decided to write the book as the result of a divine illumination he received aboard ship while returning from Constantinople.

Nicholas is a watershed figure, perched between ancient Neoplatonism and scholasticism, and modern metaphorical and conjectural thought. His writings about Christianity are deeply mystical, arguing that we can only know God in the mystical sense by *not* knowing him with our intellects. Yet he also anticipated many later ideas in mathematics, cosmology, astronomy and experimental science: for example, he advocated using conjectures or surmises to better approximate the truth, and he speculated about the possibility of a plurality of worlds. Most striking of all, perhaps, was his counting of the pulse against an external, objective measure, which had never been done before. 'He emphasized knowledge through experimentation and anticipated the work of the astronomer Copernicus by discerning a movement in the universe that did not centre in the Earth, although the Earth contributed to that movement. Cusa's study of plant growth, from which he concluded that plants absorb nourishment from the air, was the first modern formal experiment in biology and the first proof that air has weight. Numerous other developments, including a map of Europe, can also be traced to Cusa.'

Moreover, his theology was strikingly tolerant for the time. In 1453, he wrote a treatise imagining a summit meeting in heaven of all nations and religions. He argued that Christianity was a single faith, but represented in different rites, as for example those of the Eastern and Western Church. But he also showed respect for non-Christian religions.

An exceptional facet of *On Learned Ignorance* is his use of geometrical metaphors 'to provide his readers some object lessons designed to teach how we might reach for the unlimited even while we are aware that we cannot grasp what the infinite God may be. For instance, we are to imagine a circle and a straight line or tangent that meets the circle. From a certain perspective, as the diameter or circumference of the circle increases, its circumference approaches the straight line and appears less and less curved. If we then imagine and extrapolate the circumference to the infinite, we can almost "see" that both straight tangent and curved circumference should coincide—a kind of "coincidence of opposites" that is a figure of how we may think beyond limited things toward the transcendent One.'

It is telling that Nicholas of Cusa was barely understood in his own day, and, except for Giordano Bruno, his reception began only in the nineteenth century.

[sources: *Wikipedia*, *The Stanford Encyclopedia of Philosophy*; Introduction to Jasper Hopkins, ed., *Complete Philosophical and Theological Treatises on Nicholas of Cusa*, 2 vols. (Minneapolis: Banning, 2001); *Britannica*]

APPENDIX 11

EMIL DU BOIS-REYMOND

EMIL du Bois-Reymond (1818-1896) was an important German scientist who is credited with having founded the discipline of electrophysiology. Du Bois-Reymond gave the famous and influential address, 'On the Limits of Science' [*'Über die Grenzen des Naturerkennens'*], before the German Association of Doctors and Scientists on 14 August 1872, in Leipzig. See also Lecture 1 (27 September 1920) in GA 322, *The Boundaries of Science*, translated by Frederick Amrine and Konrad Oberhuber, Introduction by Saul Bellow (Keryx, 2017), where Steiner refers to this address as a symptom of the failure of late nineteenth century sceptical positivism. Indeed, the title of this lecture-cycle seems to be an ironic reference to the physiologist's speech.

Du Bois-Reymond is notorious among Goethe scholars for the inaugural address he gave in 1882 as the *Rektor* (roughly, President) of the University of Berlin, 'Goethe and More Goethe' ['*Goethe und kein Ende*']. There he expresses puzzlement at Goethe's Faust, and wishes aloud that he had just married Gretchen, legitimized his child, and gotten on with the serious business of inventing vacuum pumps and such.

Yet another famous and influential address, 'The Seven World Riddles', was given by du Bois-Reymond before the Berlin Academy of Sciences in 1880. Regarding such issues as 'simple sensation', 'the ultimate nature of matter and force', and 'the origin of motion', he declared '*ignoramus et ignorabimus*': 'we do not know and we shall not ever know'.

In 1842, the German medical students Emil du Bois-Reymond and Ernst Brücke (both of whom would go on to become lead-ing figures within nineteenth-century science) made a formal pact that has come to be called 'the Reymond-Brücke oath', which began '[We pledge] to put in power this truth: no other forces than the common physical-chemical ones are active within the organism.' The oath then became a shibboleth within the school of Helmholtz. See Henry A. Murray and Robert W. White, *The Study of Lives: Essays on Personality in Honor of Henry A. Murray* (Piscataway, NJ: Aldine Trans-action, 2006), pp. 372-375.

Appendix 12

PIERRE-SIMON, MARQUIS DE LAPLACE

PIERRE-SIMON, Marquis de Laplace (1749-1827) was a great French mathematician and astronomer who extended the Newtonian paradigm in his five-volume *Celestial Mechanics* (1799-1825) and other writings. Indeed, he was referred to as 'the French Newton'. The son of a peasant farmer, he revealed his mathematical abilities at an early age. He is best known for his investigations into the stability of the solar system. 'He developed a *conceptual* view of evolutionary change in the structure of the solar system. He also demonstrated the usefulness of probability for interpreting scientific data.'

Many English translations are available of his *System of the World* (1796); this popular presentation of the material that would later be presented in more rigorous, mathematical form in his *Celestial Mechanics* is considered a masterpiece of French prose. 'The book included his "nebular hypothesis"—attributing the origin of the solar system to cooling and contracting of a gaseous nebula—which strongly influenced future thought on planetary origin.'

In *Celestial Mechanics*, 'he offered a complete mechanical interpretation of the solar system by devising methods for calculating the motions of the planets and their satellites and their perturbations, including the resolution of tidal problems. The book made him a celebrity.'

[sources: *Britannica*]

Notes

Textual source:

The lectures were stenographed by the Berlin branch member, Walter Vegelahn (1880-1959), although his original stenograms have been lost.

('GA' refers to the original edition of Rudolf Steiner's works in German.)

1   Peter Staudenmaier, *Between Occultism and Nazism: Anthroposophy and the Politics of Race in the Fascist Era.* Leiden/Boston: Brill, 2014.

2   The most striking quote to this effect is on page 150 of C. G. Jung's autobiography, *Memories, Dreams, Reflections* (New York: Vintage, 1989): 'I can still recall vividly how Freud said to me, "My dear Jung, promise me never to abandon the sexual theory. That is the most essential thing of all. You see, we must make a dogma of it, an unshakable bulwark." … In some astonishment I asked him, "A bulwark—against what?" To which he replied, "Against the black tide of mud"—and here he hesitated for a moment, then added—"of occultism".'

3   From 25-31 August, 1912, eight lectures were presented with the following general title: *On Initiation, Eternity and the Passing Moment: On Spiritual Light and Darkness of Life* [GA 138] (New York: Anthroposophic Press, 1980).

4   Rudolf Steiner wrote and directed four Mystery Dramas: *The Portal of Initiation* (1910), *The Soul's Probation* (1911), *The Guardian of the Threshold* (1912) and *The Souls' Awakening* (1913). See GA 14, Rudolf Steiner, *Four Mystery Dramas*, trans. Ruth and Hans Pusch (Great Barrington, MA: SteinerBooks/Anthroposophic Press, 2007); also *The Four Mystery Plays*, trans. Adam Bittleston (London: Rudolf Steiner Press, 1982). All four were performed originally in Munich, which had become the centre of the artistic avant-garde in Central Europe, and they are in many ways typically Expressionist. Kandinsky and Schönberg among many others experienced the Mystery Dramas and were influenced by them during these last years leading up to World War I.

5   See Appendix 1.

6   *The Gospel of St Mark* (Anthroposophic Press, 1986).

7   'The Mystery of Golgotha' is Steiner's favoured term for all that is more con-
    ventionally referred to as the Incarnation, the Passion, and the Resurrection.
    One of Steiner's earliest publications, his book *Christianity as Mystical Fact*, situ-
    ates Christianity squarely within the context of ancient mystery religions (rather
    than mysticism, which the title might seem to imply). This important text is now
    volume 8 of Steiner's *Complete Works* in English, and the latest edition (New
    York: Anthroposophic Press, 1997) was both translated and introduced by a
    scholar and anthroposophist of great stature, Andrew Welburn. In the same
    spirit, Steiner also refers to 'the Easter Mystery'.

8   CW 8; *Christianity as Mystical Fact and the Mysteries of Antiquity*, trans. Andrew Wel-
    burn, ed. Christopher Bamford (Great Barrington: SteinerBooks, 2006).

9   *Gemüt* is a word with no precise English equivalent that refers simultaneously to
    our thinking, feeling, sensibility, and temperament, all bundled up together.

10 GA 140; *Okkulte Untersuchungen über das Leben zwischen Tod und neuer Geburt: Die leb-
    endige Wechselwirkung zwischen Leben und Tod* [*Esoteric Investigation into the Life Between
    Death and New Birth: The Living Interaction Between Life and Death*]. The volume has
    only partly been translated into English.

11 Kali Yuga is the age of darkness, or more properly the age of strife, which ended
    in 1899. Since then, the doors of the spiritual world are beginning to open, and
    there is a new possibility of enlightenment. The phrase is taken from ancient
    Hindu scriptures, but its meaning has been modified considerably by Steiner.

12 St Norbert (c. 1085–1134), the chaplain of Henry V. In 1121 founded the Order
    of Norbertines. In 1126 he became Archbishop of Magdeburg.

13 See Appendix 2.

14 See Appendix 3.

15 See Appendix 4.

16 See Appendix 4.

17 Kamaloka is the period after death when the soul is freeing itself from its incli-
    nation toward physical existence in order to follow the laws of the spiritual
    world. See CW 9; *Theosophy* (1904; many English editions are available, including
    very inexpensive ebook editions), Chapter 3, or Chapter 3 of CW 13; *An Outline
    of Esoteric Science*, trans. Catherine E. Creeger (Great Barrington, MA: Steiner-
    Books, 1997). (Also available as *Occult Science, An Outline*, Forest Row: Rudolf
    Steiner Press, 2011.)

18 Homer (ninth or eighth century BCE) was the author of foundational epics the
    Iliad and the *Odyssey*.

19 See Appendix 5.

20 See Appendix 6.

21 Arthur Schopenhauer (1788-1860), a post-Kantian German philosopher known especially for his profound pessimism. Although Schopenhauer's magnum opus, *The World as Will and Idea* [*Die Welt als Wille und Vorstellung*] was first published in 1819, it was only decades later that Schopenhauer became widely read and influential.

22 Not *monotheism* but rather the (figurative) religion of *monism*, which is to say, materialism.

23 This complex thought has some steps missing. Presumably, what Steiner means is that monism/materialism can call forth only an abstract morality, and any number of abstract platitudes based on that form of morality will have little real effect.

24 Steiner means the planetary sphere of Venus as experienced between incarnations, and not the metamorphosis of Earth itself in the very distant future.

25 Genesis 14: 17-20.

26 'Impulse' is one of Steiner's favourite words. It crops up everywhere, and it is always (but only mildly) metaphorical. Because the term is so resolutely mechanistic, but its referent is invariably spiritual or cultural, the effect can be jarring. As is so easily done in German, Steiner will frequently coin new terms by conjoining them with other words, e.g. 'Faust-impulse,' 'Resurrection-impulse,' and 'I-impulse.' 'Christ-impulse' occurs very frequently, and it makes sense in the context of Steiner's view of Christianity as a cosmic event unfolding over eons, of which even the Incarnation is but a single chapter.

27 Fortunately, this has changed dramatically in the interim, and in the direction Steiner would have hoped.

28 Acts 26:23.

29 Matthew 18:20.

30 John 10:34.

31 Genesis 3:5.

32 The Akashic Record is a symbolic, spiritual script in which everything is recorded that has ever happened on Earth. It can be read by an initiate, and this is how the spiritual researcher can speak of things about which no historical records survive. Ervin László in *Science and the Akashic Field: An Integral Theory of Everything* (2004), based on ideas by Rudolf Steiner, posits 'a field of information' as the substance of the cosmos, which he calls 'Akashic field' or 'A-field'.

33 This is Steiner's term for the traditional poet-patriarchs of the Vedic religion. Steiner refers to them frequently as the founders of the Ancient Indian cultural epoch, and he asserts that they were real, historical personages rather than mythic figures.

[34] 'From the perspective of anthroposophy Rudolf Steiner asserts that the Lower Devachan (or the Heavenly World) and Higher Devachan (or the World of Reason) are two "supersensible" realms, above the astral realm, associated with emotions and will impulse, respectively. In comparison, the mental realm is associated with thought'. [*Wikipedia*]

[35] 'Maya' is a theosophical term that Steiner uses frequently. It is a contraction of the Sanskrit terms *maha* [great], *a* [not or non-, like 'alpha privative' in Ancient Greek; cf. 'apolitical'], and *ya* [being]; hence, 'maya' means literally 'the great non-being'. It is illusory because it seems to exist, but ultimately does not.

[36] The *Titanic* was a British ocean liner that notoriously sank on 15 April, 1912 after striking an iceberg.

[37] See Appendix 7.

[38] The earliest instance of the allegory is by the poet Jacopone da Todi (ca. 1230-1306).

[39] Jakob Balde (1604-1668), a lyric poet of the seventeenth century. He entered the Order of Jesuits in 1624. Balde was widely acclaimed during his life, but was neglected as a poet after his death until the end of the eighteenth century. Herder translated many of Balde's neo-Latin lyrics and brought his genius to the notice of scholars.

[40] See Appendix 8.

[41] Translated as CW 13; *An Outline of Esoteric Science*, trans. Catherine E. Creeger (Great Barrington, MA: SteinerBooks, 1997). An otherwise excellent earlier translation by George Adams bore the unfortunate title *Occult Science*. At the time of writing, Steiner was the head of the Theosophical Society in Germany, and the word *Geheimwissenschaft* in his title was meant to echo Blavatsky's tome, *The Secret Doctrine*. CW 13 is now considered one of the four 'basic books' of anthroposophy.

[42] In the *Vedas*, 'soma' is a ritual drink that calls forth immortality.

[43] See Appendix 8.

[44] 'The Egypto-Chaldean period' is Steiner's theosophical term for a long epoch he sees as having ended ca. 747 BCE. He also calls it the third post-Atlantean epoch or age. The implication of the term is that the Egyptian, Sumerian and Babylonian cultures were in the vanguard of human cultural evolution during that period—quite a conventional notion after all, despite the idiosyncrasy of the label. Because it has become a standard anthroposophical term, 'Chaldean' stands here rather than Sumerian and/or Babylonian, which would be more conventional in English.

[45] See Appendix 8.

46   See Appendix 9.

47   See Appendix 9.

48   Kant pronounced the German mathematician and astronomer Johannes Kepler (1571-1630) the most rigorous thinker who ever lived. He is most famous for discovering and mathematically modelling the elliptical motions of the planets, and for major contributions toward the theory of gravitation eventually formalized by Newton.

49   Nicolaus Copernicus (1473-1543) was the first astronomer to publish a comprehensive and persuasive heliocentric account of the universe, *On the Revolutions of the Heavenly Spheres* (1543).

50   See Kepler's report of 1613 in *Gesammelte Werke*, Vol. 5 (München: C. H. Beck, 1953), pp. 127-201.

51   See Kepler, *De Stella Nova in pede Serpentarii* [*On the New Star in the Foot of the Serpent Handler*], and *Bericht vom Neuen Stern* [*Report on the New Star*] in *Gesammelte Werke*, Vol. 1 (München: C. H. Beck, 1938), pp. 147-399.

52   See Appendix 2.

53   The Buddha's 'First Sermon', delivered at the deer park in Benares, sets out the doctrine of the Four Noble Truths, a key concept of Buddhist thought. The First Noble Truth is that old age, illness, and death are all forms of human suffering, and that there are many other ways in which people suffer. The Second Noble Truth is that suffering is closely linked to desire, a desire for being which leads from birth to death and involve ageing, illness, and mortality. The Third Noble Truth is that suffering can be dispelled by the abandonment of all desires. The last of the Four Noble Truths holds that such abandonment of desires can be achieved by following the Noble Eightfold Path. [*age-of-the-sage.com*]

54   See GA 114; *According to Luke: The Gospel of Compassion and Love Revealed* (Great Barrington, Massachusetts: SteinerBooks, 2001).

55   Luke 2:13-14.

56   Saint Francis of Assisi (1181/1182-1226) was a Catholic friar, preacher, and mystic. He founded the Franciscan Order, and is one of the most venerated figures in Christian history. Saint Francis was, among many other things, the first person to receive the stigmata of Christ.

57   See Appendix 10.

58   CW 10; *How to Know Higher Worlds: A Modern Path of Initiation*, trans. Christopher Bamford, Classics in Anthroposophy (Great Barrington, MA: Anthroposophic Press, 1994). (Also available as *Knowledge of the Higher Worlds*, Forest Row: Rudolf Steiner Press, 2011.)

59   CW 149; *Christ and the Spiritual World and the Search for the Holy Grail* (1963; Forest Row: Rudolf Steiner Press, 2008).

60   See Appendix 3.

61   Presumably Steiner means the 'whirling' Dervishes, who seek union with God through ecstatic dancing.

62   See Appendix 4.

63   GA 293 and 66; *The Education of the Child and Early Lectures on Education* (Great Barrington, Massachusetts: SteinerBooks, 1996).

64   GA 15; *The Spiritual Guidance of the Individual and Humanity*, Classics in Anthroposophy (Hudson, New York: Anthroposophic Press, 1991). This beautiful booklet, worked up from three lectures Steiner had given earlier, is one of the best introductions to anthroposophy.

65   See especially 1 Corinthians 15:45.

66   GA 131; *From Jesus to Christ* (Forest Row, Sussex: Rudolf Steiner Press, 2005).

67   See GA 114; *According to Luke: The Gospel of Compassion and Love Revealed* (Great Barrington, Massachusetts: SteinerBooks, 2001).

68   Johann Wolfgang von Goethe (1749-1832), author of *Faust* and *Wilhelm Meister*, is widely regarded as the greatest German poet. He was also an extraordinary scientist: see his *Metamorphosis of Plants* (1790) and his *Theory of Colours* (1810) especially.

69   Robert Sommer, *Goethe im Lichte der Vererbungslehre* [*Goethe in the Light of the Theory of Inheritance*], Leipzig, 1908.

70   Tr. Anna Swanwick, L.L.D., *Bohn's Standard Library*.

71   See Appendix 11.

72   See Appendix 12.

73   Ludwig Büchner (1824-1899) was a German philosopher and scientist who became one of the most popular exponents of nineteenth-century materialism. He was the younger brother of the famous playwright, Georg Büchner. His principal work was *Force and Matter* (1855), which was so blatantly materialistic that he had to resign his position at the University of Tübingen over it.

74   Karl Christoph Vogt (1817-1895) was a German scientist, philosopher, and politician, who published in zoology, geology, and physiology. He was a strong proponent of atheism and scientific materialism.

75   See Lectures Three, Five and Six of GA 114; *According to Luke* (Great Barrington, MA: SteinerBooks, 2001).

76   Leonardo da Vinci (1452-1519) was an Italian painter, draftsman, sculptor, architect, and engineer whose genius, perhaps more than that of any other figure, epitomized the Renaissance humanist ideal. His *Last Supper* (1495–98) and

Mona Lisa (*c*. 1503–19) are among the most widely popular and influential paint-ings of the Renaissance.

77   CW 9; *Theosophy* (1904; many English editions are available, including now very inexpensive ebook editions). This early work presents the basics of Steiner's spiritual psychology using the terminology of theosophy. A much more dynamic (but also much more difficult) account is to be found in the middle four lectures of Rudolf Steiner, *A Psychology of Body, Soul, & Spirit* (New York: SteinerBooks, 1999), which includes a valuable Introduction by Robert Sardello.

78   All passages and terms from *Theosophy* in this lecture will be quoted from the 1971 edition published by Anthroposophic Press.

79   See Lecture 5.

80   CW 112; *The Gospel of St John and Its Relation to the Other Gospels*, edited by Stewart C. Easton, translated by Maria St Goar (Hudson, New York: Anthroposophic Press, 1982).

81   This is an older, partial translation. For a newer translation, see Rudolf Steiner, CW 21; *On The Enigmas of the Soul*, trans. Frederick Amrine and Owen Barfield, commentary by Frederick Amrine (Keryx 2017).

82   The Chapel also holds Michelangelo's startling, mysterious, expressive *Madonna and Child*, which will not be discussed here.

83   The article is fascinating, but if you do happen upon it, please keep an open mind regarding Alessandro.

Rudolf Steiner's Collected Works

The German Edition of Rudolf Steiner's Collected Works (the *Gesamtausgabe* [GA] published by Rudolf Steiner Verlag, Dornach, Switzerland) presently runs to 354 titles, organized either by type of work (written or spoken), chronology, audience (public or other), or subject (education, art, etc.). For ease of comparison, the Collected Works in English [CW] follows the German organization exactly. A complete listing of the CWs follows with literal translations of the German titles. Other than in the case of the books published in his lifetime, titles were rarely given by Rudolf Steiner himself, and were often provided by the editors of the German editions. The titles in English are not necessarily the same as the German; and, indeed, over the past 75 years have frequently been different, with the same book sometimes appearing under different titles.

For ease of identification and to avoid confusion, we suggest that readers looking for a title should do so by CW number. Because the work of creating the Collected Works of Rudolf Steiner is an ongoing process, with new titles being published every year, we have not indicated in this listing which books are presently available. To find out what titles in the Collected Works are currently in print, please check our website at www.rudolfsteinerpress.com (or www.steinerbooks.org for US readers).

Written Work

CW 1   Goethe: Natural-Scientific Writings, Introduction, with Footnotes and Explanations in the text by Rudolf Steiner

CW 2   Outlines of an Epistemology of the Goethean World View, with Special Consideration of Schiller

CW 3   Truth and Science

CW 4   The Philosophy of Freedom

CW 4a   Documents to 'The Philosophy of Freedom'

CW 5   Friedrich Nietzsche, A Fighter against His Time

CW 6   Goethe's Worldview

CW 6a   Now in CW 30

CW 7   Mysticism at the Dawn of Modern Spiritual Life and Its Relationship
         with Modern Worldviews

CW 8   Christianity as Mystical Fact and the Mysteries of Antiquity

CW 9   Theosophy: An Introduction into Supersensible World Knowledge
         and Human Purpose

CW 10   How Does One Attain Knowledge of Higher Worlds?

CW 11   From the Akasha-Chronicle

CW 12   Levels of Higher Knowledge

CW 13   Occult Science in Outline

CW 14   Four Mystery Dramas

CW 15   The Spiritual Guidance of the Individual and Humanity

CW 16   A Way to Human Self-Knowledge: Eight Meditations

CW 17   The Threshold of the Spiritual World. Aphoristic Comments

CW 18   The Riddles of Philosophy in Their History, Presented as an Outline

CW 19   Contained in CW 24

CW 20   The Riddles of the Human Being: Articulated and Unarticulated in the
         Thinking, Views and Opinions of a Series of German and Austrian
         Personalities

CW 21   The Riddles of the Soul

CW 22   Goethe's Spiritual Nature and its Revelation in 'Faust' and through the
         'Fairy Tale of the Snake and the Lily'

CW 23   The Central Points of the Social Question in the Necessities of Life in
         the Present and the Future

CW 24   Essays Concerning the Threefold Division of the Social Organism
         and the Period 1915-1921

CW 25   Cosmology, Religion and Philosophy

CW 26   Anthroposophical Leading Thoughts

CW 27   Fundamentals for Expansion of the Art of Healing according to
         Spiritual-Scientific Insights

CW28   The Course of My Life

CW 29   Collected Essays on Dramaturgy, 1889-1900

CW 30   Methodical Foundations of Anthroposophy: Collected Essays on Phi-
         losophy, Natural Science, Aesthetics and Psychology, 1884-1901

CW 31   Collected Essays on Culture and Current Events, 1887-1901

CW 32   Collected Essays on Literature, 1884-1902

CW 33   Biographies and Biographical Sketches, 1894-1905

CW 34   Lucifer-Gnosis: Foundational Essays on Anthroposophy and Reports
         from the Periodicals 'Lucifer' and 'Lucifer-Gnosis,' 1903-1908

CW 35   Philosophy and Anthroposophy: Collected Essays, 1904-1923

CW 36   The Goetheanum-Idea in the Middle of the Cultural Crisis of the Pres-
         ent: Collected Essays from the Periodical 'Das Goetheanum,' 1921-1925

CW 78   Anthroposophy, Its Roots of Knowledge and Fruits for Life
CW 79   The Reality of the Higher Worlds
CW 80   Public lectures in various cities, 1922
CW 81   Renewal-Impulses for Culture and Science—Berlin College Course
CW 82   So that the Human Being Can Become a Complete Human Being
CW 83   Western and Eastern World-Contrast. Paths to Understanding It through Anthroposophy
CW 84   What Did the Goetheanum Intend and What Should Anthroposophy Do?

Lectures to the Members of the Anthroposophical Society
CW 88   Concerning the Astral World and Devachan
CW 89   Consciousness—Life—Form. Fundamental Principles of a Spiritual-Scientific Cosmology
CW 90   Participant Notes from the Lectures during the Years 1903-1905
CW 91   Participant Notes from the Lectures during the Years 1903-1905
CW 92   The Occult Truths of Ancient Myths and Sagas
CW 93   The Temple Legend and the Golden Legend
CW 93a Fundamentals of Esotericism
CW 94   Cosmogony. Popular Occultism. The Gospel of John. The Theosophy in the Gospel of John
CW 95   At the Gates of Theosophy
CW 96   Origin-Impulses of Spiritual Science. Christian Esotericism in the Light of New Spirit-Knowledge
CW 97   The Christian Mystery
CW 98   Nature Beings and Spirit Beings—Their Effects in Our Visible World
CW 99   The Theosophy of the Rosicrucians
CW 100 Human Development and Christ-Knowledge
CW 101 Myths and Legends. Occult Signs and Symbols
CW 102 The Working into Human Beings by Spiritual Beings
CW 103 The Gospel of John
CW 104 The Apocalypse of John
CW 104a From the Picture-Script of the Apocalypse of John
CW 105 Universe, Earth, the Human Being: Their Being and Development, as well as Their Reflection in the Connection between Egyptian Mythology and Modern Culture
CW 106 Egyptian Myths and Mysteries in Relation to the Active Spiritual Forces of the Present
CW 107 Spiritual-Scientific Knowledge of the Human Being
CW 108 Answering the Questions of Life and the World through Anthroposophy
CW 109 The Principle of Spiritual Economy in Connection with the Question of Reincarnation. An Aspect of the Spiritual Guidance of Humanity
CW 110 The Spiritual Hierarchies and Their Reflection in the Physical World. Zodiac, Planets and Cosmos

CW 278	Eurythmy as Visible Song
CW 279	Eurythmy as Visible Speech
CW 280	The Method and Nature of Speech Formation
CW 281	The Art of Recitation and Declamation
CW 282	Speech Formation and Dramatic Art
CW 283	The Nature of Things Musical and the Experience of Tone in the Human Being
CW 284/285	Images of Occult Seals and Pillars. The Munich Congress of Whitsun 1907 and Its Consequences
CW 286	Paths to a New Style of Architecture. 'And the Building Becomes Human'
CW 287	The Building at Dornach as a Symbol of Historical Becoming and an Artistic Transformation Impulse
CW 288	Style-Forms in the Living Organic
CW 289	The Building-Idea of the Goetheanum: Lectures with Slides from the Years 1920–1921
CW 290	The Building-Idea of the Goetheanum: Lectures with Slides from the Years 1920–1921
CW 291	The Nature of Colours
CW 291a	Knowledge of Colours. Supplementary Volume to 'The Nature of Colours'
CW 292	Art History as Image of Inner Spiritual Impulses
CW 293	General Knowledge of the Human Being as the Foundation of Pedagogy
CW 294	The Art of Education, Methodology and Didactics
CW 295	The Art of Education: Seminar Discussions and Lectures on Lesson Planning
CW 296	The Question of Education as a Social Question
CW 297	The Idea and Practice of the Waldorf School
CW 297a	Education for Life: Self-Education and the Practice of Pedagogy
CW 298	Rudolf Steiner in the Waldorf School
CW 299	Spiritual-Scientific Observations on Speech
CW 300a	Conferences with the Teachers of the Free Waldorf School in Stuttgart, 1919 to 1924, in 3 Volumes, Vol. 1
CW 300b	Conferences with the Teachers of the Free Waldorf School in Stuttgart, 1919 to 1924, in 3 Volumes, Vol. 2
CW 300c	Conferences with the Teachers of the Free Waldorf School in Stuttgart, 1919 to 1924, in 3 Volumes, Vol. 3
CW 301	The Renewal of Pedagogical-Didactical Art through Spiritual Science
CW 302	Knowledge of the Human Being and the Forming of Class Lessons
CW 302a	Education and Teaching from a Knowledge of the Human Being
CW 303	The Healthy Development of the Human Being
CW 304	Methods of Education and Teaching Based on Anthroposophy
CW 304a	Anthroposophical Knowledge of the Human Being and Pedagogy

SIGNIFICANT EVENTS IN THE LIFE OF
RUDOLF STEINER

1829:   June 23: birth of Johann Steiner (1829–1910)—Rudolf Steiner's father—in Geras, Lower Austria.

1834:   May 8: birth of Franciska Blie (1834–1918)—Rudolf Steiner's mother—in Horn, Lower Austria. 'My father and mother were both children of the glorious Lower Austrian forest district north of the Danube.'

1860:   May 16: marriage of Johann Steiner and Franciska Blie.

1861:   February 25: birth of *Rudolf Joseph Lorenz Steiner* in Kraljevec, Croatia, near the border with Hungary, where Johann Steiner works as a telegrapher for the South Austria Railroad. Rudolf Steiner is baptized two days later, February 27, the date usually given as his birthday.

1862:   Summer: the family moves to Modling, Lower Austria.

1863:   The family moves to Pottschach, Lower Austria, near the Styrian border, where Johann Steiner becomes station master. 'The view stretched to the mountains . . . majestic peaks in the distance and the sweet charm of nature in the immediate surroundings.'

1864:   November 15: birth of Rudolf Steiner's sister, Leopoldine (d. November 1, 1927). She will become a seamstress and live with her parents for the rest of her life.

1866:   July 28: birth of Rudolf Steiner's deaf-mute brother, Gustav (d. May 1, 1941).

1867:   Rudolf Steiner enters the village school. Following a disagreement between his father and the schoolmaster, whose wife falsely accused the boy of causing a commotion, Rudolf Steiner is taken out of school and taught at home.

1868:   A critical experience. Unknown to the family, an aunt dies in a distant town. Sitting in the station waiting room, Rudolf Steiner sees her 'form,' which speaks to him, asking for help. 'Beginning with this experience, a new soul life began in the boy, one in which not only the outer trees and mountains spoke to him, but also the worlds that lay behind them. From this moment on, the boy began to live with the spirits of nature . . .'

1869: The family moves to the peaceful, rural village of Neudorfl, near Wiener Neustadt in present-day Austria. Rudolf Steiner attends the village school. Because of the 'unorthodoxy' of his writing and spelling, he has to do 'extra lessons'.

1870: Through a book lent to him by his tutor, he discovers geometry: 'To grasp something purely in the spirit brought me inner happiness. I know that I first learned happiness through geometry.' The same tutor allows him to draw, while other students still struggle with their reading and writing. 'An artistic element' thus enters his education.

1871: Though his parents are not religious, Rudolf Steiner becomes a 'church child,' a favourite of the priest, who was 'an exceptional character.' 'Up to the age of ten or eleven, among those I came to know, he was far and away the most significant.' Among other things, he introduces Steiner to Copernican, heliocentric cosmology. As an altar boy, Rudolf Steiner serves at masses, funerals, and Corpus Christi processions. At year's end, after an incident in which he escapes a thrashing, his father forbids him to go to church.

1872: Rudolf Steiner transfers to grammar school in Wiener-Neustadt, a five-mile walk from home, which must be done in all weathers.

1873–75: Through his teachers and on his own, Rudolf Steiner has many wonderful experiences with science and mathematics. Outside school, he teaches himself analytic geometry, trigonometry, differential equations, and calculus.

1876: Rudolf Steiner begins tutoring other students. He learns bookbinding from his father. He also teaches himself stenography.

1877: Rudolf Steiner discovers Kant's *Critique of Pure Reason*, which he reads and rereads. He also discovers and reads von Rotteck's *World History*.

1878: He studies extensively in contemporary psychology and philosophy.

1879: Rudolf Steiner graduates from high school with honours. His father is transferred to Inzersdorf, near Vienna. He uses his first visit to Vienna 'to purchase a great number of philosophy books'—Kant, Fichte, Schelling, and Hegel, as well as numerous histories of philosophy. His aim: to find a path from the 'I' to nature.

October
1879–1883: Rudolf Steiner attends the Technical College in Vienna—to study mathematics, chemistry, physics, mineralogy, botany, zoology,

biology, geology, and mechanics—with a scholarship. He also attends lectures in history and literature, while avidly reading philosophy on his own. His two favourite professors are Karl Julius Schröer (German language and literature) and Edmund Reitlinger (physics). He also audits lectures by Robert Zimmermann on aesthetics and Franz Brentano on philosophy. During this year he begins his friendship with Moritz Zitter (1861–1921), who will help support him financially when he is in Berlin.

1880: Rudolf Steiner attends lectures on Schiller and Goethe by Karl Julius Schröer, who becomes his mentor. Also 'through a remarkable combination of circumstances,' he meets Felix Koguzki, a 'herb gatherer' and healer, who could 'see deeply into the secrets of nature'. Rudolf Steiner will meet and study with this 'emissary of the Master' throughout his time in Vienna.

1881: January: '... I didn't sleep a wink. I was busy with philosophical problems until about 12:30 a.m. Then, finally, I threw myself down on my couch. All my striving during the previous year had been to research whether the following statement by Schelling was true or not: *Within everyone dwells a secret, marvellous capacity to draw back from the stream of time—out of the self clothed in all that comes to us from outside— into our innermost being and there, in the immutable form of the Eternal, to look into ourselves.* I believe, and I am still quite certain of it, that I discovered this capacity in myself; I had long had an inkling of it. Now the whole of idealist philosophy stood before me in modified form. What's a sleepless night compared to that!'

Rudolf Steiner begins communicating with leading thinkers of the day, who send him books in return, which he reads eagerly.

July: 'I am not one of those who dives into the day like an animal in human form. I pursue a quite specific goal, an idealistic aim— knowledge of the truth! This cannot be done offhandedly. It requires the greatest striving in the world, free of all egotism, and equally of all resignation.'

August: Steiner puts down on paper for the first time thoughts for a 'Philosophy of Freedom.' 'The striving for the absolute: this human yearning is freedom.' He also seeks to outline a 'peasant philosophy,' describing what the worldview of a 'peasant'—one who lives close to the earth and the old ways—really is.

1881–1882: Felix Koguzki, the herb gatherer, reveals himself to be the envoy of another, higher initiatory personality, who instructs Rudolf Steiner to penetrate Fichte's philosophy and to master modern scientific thinking as a preparation for right entry into the spirit. This 'Master' also teaches him the double (evolutionary and involutionary) nature of time.

1882:   Through the offices of Karl Julius Schröer, Rudolf Steiner is asked by Joseph Kürschner to edit Goethe's scientific works for the *Deutschen National-Literatur* edition. He writes 'A Possible Critique of Atomistic Concepts' and sends it to Friedrich Theodor Vischer.

1883:   Rudolf Steiner completes his college studies and begins work on the Goethe project.

1884:   First volume of Goethe's *Scientific Writings* (CW 1) appears (March). He lectures on Goethe and Lessing, and Goethe's approach to science. In July, he enters the household of Ladislaus and Pauline Specht as tutor to the four Specht boys. He will live there until 1890. At this time, he meets Josef Breuer (1842–1925), the co-author with Sigmund Freud of *Studies in Hysteria*, who is the Specht family doctor.

1885:   While continuing to edit Goethe's writings, Rudolf Steiner reads deeply in contemporary philosophy (Eduard von Hartmann, Johannes Volkelt, and Richard Wahle, among others).

1886:   May: Rudolf Steiner sends Kürschner the manuscript of *Outlines of Goethe's Theory of Knowledge* (CW 2), which appears in October, and which he sends out widely. He also meets the poet Marie Eugenie Delle Grazie and writes 'Nature and Our Ideals' for her. He attends her salon, where he meets many priests, theologians, and philosophers, who will become his friends. Meanwhile, the director of the Goethe Archive in Weimar requests his collaboration with the *Sophien* edition of Goethe's works, particularly the writings on colour.

1887:   At the beginning of the year, Rudolf Steiner is very sick. As the year progresses and his health improves, he becomes increasingly 'a man of letters,' lecturing, writing essays, and taking part in Austrian cultural life. In August–September, the second volume of Goethe's *Scientific Writings* appears.

1888:   January–July: Rudolf Steiner assumes editorship of the 'German Weekly' *(Deutsche Wochenschrift)*. He begins lecturing more intensively, giving, for example, a lecture titled 'Goethe as Father of a New Aesthetics.' He meets and becomes soul friends with Friedrich Eckstein (1861–1939), a vegetarian, philosopher of symbolism, alchemist, and musician, who will introduce him to various spiritual currents (including Theosophy) and with whom he will meditate and interpret esoteric and alchemical texts.

1889:   Rudolf Steiner first reads Nietzsche *(Beyond Good and Evil)*. He encounters Theosophy again and learns of Madame Blavatsky in the theosophical circle around Marie Lang (1858–1934). Here he also meets well-known figures of Austrian life, as well as esoteric figures like the occultist Franz Hartmann and Karl Leinigen-Billigen (translator of C.G. Harrison's *The Transcendental Universe*). During this period, Steiner first reads A.P. Sinnett's *Esoteric Buddhism* and Mabel Collins's *Light on the Path*. He also begins travelling, visiting Budapest, Weimar, and Berlin (where he meets philosopher Eduard von Hartmann).

1890:   Rudolf Steiner finishes Volume 3 of Goethe's scientific writings. He begins his doctoral dissertation, which will become *Truth and Science* (CW 3). He also meets the poet and feminist Rosa Mayreder (1858–1938), with whom he can exchange his most intimate thoughts. In September, Rudolf Steiner moves to Weimar to work in the Goethe-Schiller Archive.

1891:   Volume 3 of the Kürschner edition of Goethe appears. Meanwhile, Rudolf Steiner edits Goethe's studies in mineralogy and scientific writings for the *Sophien* edition. He meets Ludwig Laistner of the Cotta Publishing Company, who asks for a book on the basic question of metaphysics. From this will result, ultimately, *The Philosophy of Freedom* (CW 4), which will be published not by Cotta but by Emil Felber. In October, Rudolf Steiner takes the oral exam for a doctorate in philosophy, mathematics, and mechanics at Rostock University, receiving his doctorate on the twenty-sixth. In November, he gives his first lecture on Goethe's 'Fairy Tale' in Vienna.

1892:   Rudolf Steiner continues work at the Goethe-Schiller Archive and on his *Philosophy of Freedom*. *Truth and Science,* his doctoral dissertation, is published. Steiner undertakes to write Introductions to books on Schopenhauer and Jean Paul for Cotta. At year's end, he finds lodging with Anna Eunike, née Schulz (1853–1911), a widow with four daughters and a son. He also develops a friendship with Otto Erich Hartleben (1864–1905) with whom he shares literary interests.

1893:   Rudolf Steiner begins his habit of producing many reviews and articles. In March, he gives a lecture titled 'Hypnotism, with Reference to Spiritism.' In September, volume 4 of the Kürschner edition is completed. In November, *The Philosophy of Freedom* appears. This year, too, he meets John Henry Mackay (1864–1933), the anarchist, and Max Stirner, a scholar and biographer.

1894:   Rudolf Steiner meets Elisabeth Fürster Nietzsche, the philosopher's sister, and begins to read Nietzsche in earnest, beginning with the as yet unpublished *Antichrist*. He also meets Ernst Haeckel (1834–1919). In the fall, he begins to write *Nietzsche, A Fighter against His Time* (CW 5).

1895:   May, *Nietzsche, A Fighter against His Time* appears.

1896:   January 22: Rudolf Steiner sees Friedrich Nietzsche for the first and only time. Moves between the Nietzsche and the Goethe-Schiller

Archives, where he completes his work before year's end. He falls out with Elisabeth Förster Nietzsche, thus ending his association with the Nietzsche Archive.

1897: Rudolf Steiner finishes the manuscript of *Goethe's Worldview* (CW 6). He moves to Berlin with Anna Eunike and begins editorship of the *Magazin für Literatur*. From now on, Steiner will write countless reviews, literary and philosophical articles, and so on. He begins lecturing at the 'Free Literary Society.' In September, he attends the Zionist Congress in Basel. He sides with Dreyfus in the Dreyfus affair.

1898: Rudolf Steiner is very active as an editor in the political, artistic, and theatrical life of Berlin. He becomes friendly with John Henry Mackay and poet Ludwig Jacobowski (1868–1900). He joins Jacobowski's circle of writers, artists, and scientists—'The Coming Ones' (*Die Kommenden*)—and contributes lectures to the group until 1903. He also lectures at the 'League for College Pedagogy.' He writes an article for Goethe's sesquicentennial, 'Goethe's Secret Revelation,' on the 'Fairy Tale of the Green Snake and the Beautiful Lily.'

1898–99: 'This was a trying time for my soul as I looked at Christianity. . . . I was able to progress only by contemplating, by means of spiritual perception, the evolution of Christianity. . . . Conscious knowledge of real Christianity began to dawn in me around the turn of the century. This seed continued to develop. My soul trial occurred shortly before the beginning of the twentieth century. It was decisive for my soul's development that I stood spiritually before the Mystery of Golgotha in a deep and solemn celebration of knowledge.'

1899: Rudolf Steiner begins teaching and giving lectures and lecture cycles at the Workers' College, founded by Wilhelm Liebknecht (1826–1900). He will continue to do so until 1904. Writes: *Literature and Spiritual Life in the Nineteenth Century; Individualism in Philosophy; Haeckel and His Opponents; Poetry in the Present;* and begins what will become (fifteen years later) *The Riddles of Philosophy* (CW 18). He also meets many artists and writers, including Kothe Kollwitz, Stefan Zweig, and Rainer Maria Rilke. On October 31, he marries Anna Eunike.

1900: 'I thought that the turn of the century must bring humanity a new light. It seemed to me that the separation of human thinking and willing from the spirit had peaked. A turn or reversal of direction in human evolution seemed to me a necessity.' Rudolf Steiner finishes *World and Life Views in the Nineteenth Century* (the second part of what will become *The Riddles of Philosophy*) and dedicates it to

Ernst Haeckel. It is published in March. He continues lecturing at *Die Kommenden,* whose leadership he assumes after the death of Jacobowski. Also, he gives the Gutenberg Jubilee lecture before 7,000 typesetters and printers. In September, Rudolf Steiner is invited by Count and Countess Brockdorff to lecture in the Theosophical Library. His first lecture is on Nietzsche. His second lecture is titled 'Goethe's Secret Revelation.' October 6, he begins a lecture cycle on the mystics that will become *Mystics after Modernism* (CW 7). November–December: 'Marie von Sivers appears in the audience. . . .' Also in November, Steiner gives his first lecture at the Giordano Bruno Bund (where he will continue to lecture until May, 1905). He speaks on Bruno and modern Rome, focusing on the importance of the philosophy of Thomas Aquinas as monism.

1901: In continual financial straits, Rudolf Steiner's early friends Moritz Zitter and Rosa Mayreder help support him. In October, he begins the lecture cycle *Christianity as Mystical Fact* (CW 8) at the Theosophical Library. In November, he gives his first 'theosophical lecture' on Goethe's 'Fairy Tale' in Hamburg at the invitation of Wilhelm Hubbe-Schleiden. He also attends a gathering to celebrate the founding of the Theosophical Society at Count and Countess Brockdorff's. He gives a lecture cycle, 'From Buddha to Christ,' for the circle of the *Kommenden.* November 17, Marie von Sivers asks Rudolf Steiner if Theosophy needs a Western–Christian spiritual movement (to complement Theosophy's Eastern emphasis). 'The question was posed. Now, following spiritual laws, I could begin to give an answer. . . .' In December, Rudolf Steiner writes his first article for a theosophical publication. At year's end, the Brockdorffs and possibly Wilhelm Hubbe-Schleiden ask Rudolf Steiner to join the Theosophical Society and undertake the leadership of the German section. Rudolf Steiner agrees, on the condition that Marie von Sivers (then in Italy) work with him.

1902: Beginning in January, Rudolf Steiner attends the opening of the Workers' School in Spandau with Rosa Luxemburg (1870–1919). January 17, Rudolf Steiner joins the Theosophical Society. In April, he is asked to become general secretary of the German Section of the theosophical Society, and works on preparations for its founding. In July, he visits London for a theosophical congress. He meets Bertram Keightly, G.R.S. Mead, A.P. Sinnett, and Annie Besant, among others. In September, *Christianity as Mystical Fact* appears. In October, Rudolf Steiner gives his first public lecture on Theosophy ('Monism and Theosophy') to about three hundred people at the Giordano Bruno Bund. On October 19–21, the

German Section of the Theosophical Society has its first meeting; Rudolf Steiner is the general secretary, and Annie Besant attends. Steiner lectures on practical karma studies. On October 23, Annie Besant inducts Rudolf Steiner into the Esoteric School of the Theosophical Society. On October 25, Steiner begins a weekly series of lectures: 'The Field of Theosophy.' During this year, Rudolf Steiner also first meets Ita Wegman (1876–1943), who will become his close collaborator in his final years.

1903: Rudolf Steiner holds about 300 lectures and seminars. In May, the first issue of the periodical *Luzifer* appears. In June, Rudolf Steiner visits London for the first meeting of the Federation of the European Sections of the Theosophical Society, where he meets Colonel Olcott. He begins to write *Theosophy* (CW 9).

1904: Rudolf Steiner continues lecturing at the Workers' College and elsewhere (about 90 lectures), while lecturing intensively all over Germany among theosophists (about 140 lectures). In February, he meets Carl Unger (1878–1929), who will become a member of the board of the Anthroposophical Society (1913). In March, he meets Michael Bauer (1871–1929), a Christian mystic, who will also be on the board. In May, *Theosophy* appears, with the dedication: 'To the spirit of Giordano Bruno.' Rudolf Steiner and Marie von Sivers visit London for meetings with Annie Besant. June: Rudolf Steiner and Marie von Sivers attend the meeting of the Federation of European Sections of the Theosophical Society in Amsterdam. In July, Steiner begins the articles in *Luzifer-Gnosis* that will become *How to Know Higher Worlds* (CW 10) and *Cosmic Memory* (CW 11). In September, Annie Besant visits Germany. In December, Steiner lectures on Freemasonry. He mentions the High Grade Masonry derived from John Yarker and represented by Theodore Reuss and Karl Kellner as a blank slate 'into which a good image could be placed'.

1905: This year, Steiner ends his non-theosophical lecturing activity. Supported by Marie von Sivers, his theosophical lecturing—both in public and in the Theosophical Society—increases significantly: 'The German Theosophical Movement is of exceptional importance.' Steiner recommends reading, among others, Fichte, Jacob Boehme, and Angelus Silesius. He begins to introduce Christian themes into Theosophy. He also begins to work with doctors (Felix Peipers and Ludwig Noll). In July, he is in London for the Federation of European Sections, where he attends a lecture by Annie Besant: 'I have seldom seen Mrs Besant speak in so inward and heartfelt a manner... Through Mrs Besant I have found the way to H.P. Blavatsky.' September to October, he gives a course of 31 lectures for a small group of esoteric students. In October, the annual meeting of the German Section of the Theosophical Society, which still remains very small, takes place. Rudolf Steiner reports membership has risen from 121 to 377 members. In November, seeking to establish esoteric 'continuity,' Rudolf Steiner and Marie von Sivers participate in a 'Memphis-Misraim' Masonic ceremony. They pay 45 marks for membership. 'Yesterday, you saw how little remains of former esoteric institutions.' 'We are dealing only with a "framework" . . for the present, nothing lies behind it. The occult powers have completely withdrawn.'

1906:   Expansion of theosophical work. Rudolf Steiner gives about 245 lectures, only 44 of which take place in Berlin. Cycles are given in Paris, Leipzig, Stuttgart, and Munich. Esoteric work also intensifies. Rudolf Steiner begins writing *An Outline of Esoteric Science* (CW 13). In January, Rudolf Steiner receives permission (a patent) from the Great Orient of the Scottish A & A Thirty-Three Degree Rite of the Order of the Ancient Freemasons of the Memphis-Misraim Rite to direct a chapter under the name 'Mystica Aeterna.' This will become the 'Cognitive-Ritual Section' (also called 'Misraim Service') of the Esoteric School. (See: *Freemasonry and Ritual Work: The Misraim Service,* CW 265.) During this time, Steiner also meets Albert Schweitzer. In May, he is in Paris, where he visits Édouard Schuré. Many Russians attend his lectures (including Konstantin Balmont, Dimitri Mereszkovski, Zinaida Hippius, and Maximilian Woloshin). He attends the General Meeting of the European Federation of the Theosophical Society, at which Col. Olcott is present for the last time. He spends the year's end in Venice and Rome, where he writes and works on his translation of H.P. Blavatsky's *Key to Theosophy.*

1907:   Further expansion of the German Theosophical Movement according to the Rosicrucian directive to 'introduce spirit into the world'—in education, in social questions, in art, and in science. In February, Col. Olcott dies in Adyar. Before he dies, Olcott indicates that 'the Masters' wish Annie Besant to succeed him: much politicking ensues. Rudolf Steiner supports Besant's candidacy. April–May: preparations for the Congress of the Federation of European Sections of the Theosophical Society—the great, watershed Whitsun 'Munich Congress,' attended by Annie Besant and others. Steiner decides to separate Eastern and Western (Christian–Rosicrucian) esoteric schools. He takes his esoteric school out of the Theosophical Society (Besant and Rudolf Steiner are 'in harmony' on this). Steiner makes his first lecture tours to Austria and Hungary. That summer, he is in Italy. In September, he visits Édouard Schuré, who will write the Introduction to the French edition of *Christianity as Mystical Fact* in Barr, Alsace. Rudolf Steiner writes the autobiographical statement known as the 'Barr Document.' In *Luzifer-Gnosis*, 'The Education of the Child' appears.

1908:   The movement grows (membership: 1,150). Lecturing expands. Steiner makes his first extended lecture tour to Holland and Scandinavia, as well as visits to Naples and Sicily. Themes: St John's Gospel, the Apocalypse, Egypt, science, philosophy, and logic. *Luzifer-Gnosis* ceases publication. In Berlin, Marie von Sivers (with Johanna Mücke (1864–1949) forms the *Philosophisch-Theosophisch* (after 1915 *Philosophisch-Anthroposophisch) Verlag* to publish Steiner's work. Steiner gives lecture cycles titled *The Gospel of St John* (CW 103) and *The Apocalypse* (104).

1909:   *An Outline of Esoteric Science* appears. Lecturing and travel continues. Rudolf Steiner's spiritual research expands to include the polarity of Lucifer and Ahriman; the work of great individualities in history; the Maitreya Buddha and the Bodhisattvas; spiritual economy (CW 109); the work of the spiritual hierarchies in heaven and on earth (CW 110). He also deepens and intensifies his research into the Gospels, giving lectures on the Gospel of St Luke (CW 114) with the first mention of two Jesus children. Meets and becomes friends with Christian Morgenstern (1871–1914). In April, he lays the foundation stone for the Malsch model—the building that will lead to the first Goetheanum. In May, the International Congress of the Federation of European Sections of the Theosophical Society takes place in Budapest. Rudolf Steiner receives the Subba Row medal for *How to Know Higher Worlds*. During this time, Charles W. Leadbeater discovers Jiddu Krishnamurti (1895–1986) and proclaims him the future 'world teacher,' the bearer of the Maitreya Buddha and the 'reappearing Christ.' In October, Steiner delivers seminal lectures on 'anthroposophy,' which he will try, unsuccessfully, to rework over the next years into the unfinished work, *Anthroposophy (A Fragment)* (CW 45).

1910:   New themes: *The Reappearance of Christ in the Etheric* (CW 118); *The Fifth Gospel; The Mission of Folk Souls* (CW 121); *Occult History* (CW 126); the evolving development of etheric cognitive capacities. Rudolf Steiner continues his Gospel research with *The Gospel of St Matthew* (CW 123). In January, his father dies. In April, he takes a month-long trip to Italy, including Rome, Monte Cassino, and Sicily. He also visits Scandinavia again. July–August, he writes the first mystery drama, *The Portal of Initiation* (CW 14). In November, he gives 'psychosophy' lectures. In December, he submits 'On the

Psychological Foundations and Epistemological Framework of Theosophy' to the International Philosophical Congress in Bologna.

1911: The crisis in the Theosophical Society deepens. In January, 'The Order of the Rising Sun,' which will soon become 'The Order of the Star in the East,' is founded for the coming world teacher, Krishnamurti. At the same time, Marie von Sivers, Rudolf Steiner's co-worker, falls ill. Fewer lectures are given, but important new ground is broken. In Prague, in March, Steiner meets Franz Kafka (1883–1924) and Hugo Bergmann (1883–1975). In April, he delivers his paper to the Philosophical Congress. He writes the second mystery drama, *The Soul's Probation* (CW 14). Also, while Marie von Sivers is convalescing, Rudolf Steiner begins work on *Calendar 1912/1913*, which will contain the 'Calendar of the Soul' meditations. On March 19, Anna (Eunike) Steiner dies. In September, Rudolf Steiner visits Einsiedeln, birthplace of Paracelsus. In December, Friedrich Rittelmeyer, future founder of the Christian Community, meets Rudolf Steiner. The *Johannes-Bauverein*, the 'building committee,' which would lead to the first Goetheanum (first planned for Munich), is also founded, and a preliminary committee for the founding of an independent association is created that, in the following year, will become the Anthroposophical Society. Important lecture cycles include *Occult Physiology* (CW 128); *Wonders of the World* (CW 129); *From Jesus to Christ* (CW 131). Other themes: esoteric Christianity; Christian Rosenkreutz; the spiritual guidance of humanity; the sense world and the world of the spirit.

1912: Despite the ongoing, now increasing crisis in the Theosophical Society, much is accomplished: *Calendar 1912/1913* is published; eurythmy is created; both the third mystery drama, *The Guardian of the Threshold* (CW 14) and *A Way of Self-Knowledge* (CW 16) are written. New (or renewed) themes included life between death and rebirth and karma and reincarnation. Other lecture cycles: *Spiritual Beings in the Heavenly Bodies and in the Kingdoms of Nature* (CW 136); *The Human Being in the Light of Occultism, Theosophy, and Philosophy* (CW 137); *The Gospel of St Mark* (CW 139); and *The Bhagavad Gita and the Epistles of Paul* (CW 142). On May 8, Rudolf Steiner celebrates White Lotus Day, H.P. Blavatsky's death day, which he had faithfully observed for the past decade, for the last time. In August, Rudolf Steiner suggests the 'independent association' be called the 'Anthroposophical Society.' In September, the first eurythmy course takes place. In October, Rudolf Steiner declines recognition of a Theosophical Society lodge dedicated to the Star of the East and decides to expel all Theosophical Society members belonging to the order.

Also, with Marie von Sivers, he first visits Dornach, near Basel, Switzerland, and they stand on the hill where the Goetheanum will be built. In November, a Theosophical Society lodge is opened by direct mandate from Adyar (Annie Besant). In December, a meeting of the German section occurs at which it is decided that belonging to the Order of the Star of the East is incompatible with membership in the Theosophical Society. December 28: informal founding of the Anthroposophical Society in Berlin.

1913:   Expulsion of the German section from the Theosophical Society. February 2–3: Foundation meeting of the Anthroposophical Society. Board members include: Marie von Sivers, Michael Bauer, and Carl Unger. September 20: Laying of the foundation stone for the *Johannes Bau* (Goetheanum) in Dornach. Building begins immediately. The third mystery drama, *The Soul's Awakening* (CW 14), is completed. Also: *The Threshold of the Spiritual World* (CW 147). Lecture cycles include: *The Bhagavad Gita and the Epistles of Paul* and *The Esoteric Meaning of the Bhagavad Gita* (CW 146), which the Russian philosopher Nikolai Berdyaev attends; *The Mysteries of the East and of Christianity* (CW 144); *The Effects of Esoteric Development* (CW 145); and *The Fifth Gospel* (CW 148). In May, Rudolf Steiner is in London and Paris, where anthroposophical work continues.

1914:   Building continues on the *Johannes Bau* (Goetheanum) in Dornach, with artists and co-workers from seventeen nations. The general assembly of the Anthroposophical Society takes place. In May, Rudolf Steiner visits Paris, as well as Chartres Cathedral. June 28: assassination in Sarajevo ('Now the catastrophe has happened!'). August 1: War is declared. Rudolf Steiner returns to Germany from Dornach—he will travel back and forth. He writes the last chapter of *The Riddles of Philosophy*. Lecture cycles include: *Human and Cosmic Thought* (CW 151); *Inner Being of Humanity between Death and a New Birth* (CW 153); *Occult Reading and Occult Hearing* (CW 156). December 24: marriage of Rudolf Steiner and Marie von Sivers.

1915:   Building continues. Life after death becomes a major theme, also art. Writes: *Thoughts during a Time of War* (CW 24). Lectures include: *The Secret of Death* (CW 159); *The Uniting of Humanity through the Christ Impulse* (CW 165).

1916:   Rudolf Steiner begins work with Edith Maryon (1872–1924) on the sculpture 'The Representative of Humanity' ('The Group'— Christ, Lucifer, and Ahriman). He also works with the alchemist Alexander von Bernus on the quarterly *Das Reich*. He writes *The Riddle of Humanity* (CW 20). Lectures include: *Necessity and Freedom in World History and Human Action* (CW 166); *Past and Present in the*

Human Spirit (CW 167); *The Karma of Vocation* (CW 172); *The Karma of Untruthfulness* (CW 173).

1917: Russian Revolution. The U.S. enters the war. Building continues. Rudolf Steiner delineates the idea of the 'threefold nature of the human being' (in a public lecture March 15) and the 'threefold nature of the social organism' (hammered out in May–June with the help of Otto von Lerchenfeld and Ludwig Polzer-Hoditz in the form of two documents titled *Memoranda*, which were distributed in high places). August–September: Rudolf Steiner writes *The Riddles of the Soul* (CW 20). Also: commentary on 'The Chymical Wedding of Christian Rosenkreutz' for Alexander Bernus (*Das Reich*). Lectures include: *The Karma of Materialism* (CW 176); *The Spiritual Background of the Outer World: The Fall of the Spirits of Darkness* (CW 177).

1918: March 18: peace treaty of Brest-Litovsk—'Now everything will truly enter chaos! What is needed is cultural renewal.' June: Rudolf Steiner visits Karlstein (Grail) Castle outside Prague. Lecture cycle: *From Symptom to Reality in Modern History* (CW 185). In mid-November, Emil Molt, of the Waldorf-Astoria Cigarette Company, has the idea of founding a school for his workers' children.

1919: Focus on the threefold social organism: tireless travel, countless lectures, meetings, and publications. At the same time, a new public stage of Anthroposophy emerges as cultural renewal begins. The coming years will see initiatives in pedagogy, medicine, pharmacology, and agriculture. January 27: threefold meeting: 'We must first of all, with the money we have, found free schools that can bring people what they need.' February: first public eurythmy performance in Zurich. Also: 'Appeal to the German People' (CW 24), circulated March 6 as a newspaper insert. In April, *Towards Social Renewal* (CW 23) appears—'perhaps the most widely read of all books on politics appearing since the war'. Rudolf Steiner is asked to undertake the 'direction and leadership' of the school founded by the Waldorf-Astoria Company. Rudolf Steiner begins to talk about the 'renewal' of education. May 30: a building is selected and purchased for the future Waldorf School. August–September, Rudolf Steiner gives a lecture course for Waldorf teachers, *The Foundations of Human Experience (Study of Man)* (CW 293). September 7: Opening of the first Waldorf School. December (into January): first science course, the *Light Course* (CW 320).

1920: The Waldorf School flourishes. New threefold initiatives. Founding of limited companies *Der Kommende Tag* and *Futurum A.G.* to infuse spiritual values into the economic realm. Rudolf Steiner also focuses on the sciences. Lectures: *Introducing Anthroposophical*

Medicine (CW 312); *The Warmth Course* (CW 321); *The Boundaries of Natural Science* (CW 322); *The Redemption of Thinking* (CW 74). February: Johannes Werner Klein—later a co-founder of the Christian Community—asks Rudolf Steiner about the possibility of a 'religious renewal,' a 'Johannine church.' In March, Rudolf Steiner gives the first course for doctors and medical students. In April, a divinity student asks Rudolf Steiner a second time about the possibility of religious renewal. September 27–October 16: anthroposophical 'university course.' December: lectures titled *The Search for the New Isis* (CW 202).

1921:　Rudolf Steiner continues his intensive work on cultural renewal, including the uphill battle for the threefold social order. 'University' arts, scientific, theological, and medical courses include: *The Astronomy Course* (CW 323); *Observation, Mathematics, and Scientific Experiment* (CW 324); the *Second Medical Course* (CW 313); *Colour.* In June and September–October, Rudolf Steiner also gives the first two 'priests' courses' (CW 342 and 343). The 'youth movement' gains momentum. Magazines are founded: *Die Drei* (January), and—under the editorship of Albert Steffen (1884–1963)—the weekly, *Das Goetheanum* (August). In February–March, Rudolf Steiner takes his first trip outside Germany since the war (Holland). On April 7, Steiner receives a letter regarding 'religious renewal,' and May 22–23, he agrees to address the question in a practical way. In June, the Klinical-Therapeutic Institute opens in Arlesheim under the direction of Dr Ita Wegman. In August, the Chemical-Pharmaceutical Laboratory opens in Arlesheim (Oskar Schmiedel and Ita Wegman are directors). The Clinical Therapeutic Institute is inaugurated in Stuttgart (Dr Ludwig Noll is director); also the Research Laboratory in Dornach (Ehrenfried Pfeiffer and Gunther Wachsmuth are directors). In November–December, Rudolf Steiner visits Norway.

1922:　The first half of the year involves very active public lecturing (thousands attend); in the second half, Rudolf Steiner begins to withdraw and turn toward the Society—'The Society is asleep.' It is 'too weak' to do what is asked of it. The businesses—*Der Kommende Tag* and *Futurum A.G.*—fail. In January, with the help of an agent, Steiner undertakes a twelve-city German lecture tour, accompanied by eurythmy performances. In two weeks he speaks to more than 2,000 people. In April, he gives a 'university course' in The Hague. He also visits England. In June, he is in Vienna for the East–West Congress. In August–September, he is back in England for the Oxford Conference on Education. Returning to Dornach, he gives the lectures *Philosophy, Cosmology, and Religion*

(CW 215), and gives the third priests' course (CW 344). On September 16, The Christian Community is founded. In October–November, Steiner is in Holland and England. He also speaks to the youth: *The Youth Course* (CW 217). In December, Steiner gives lectures titled *The Origins of Natural Science* (CW 326), and *Humanity and the World of Stars: The Spiritual Communion of Humanity* (CW 219). December 31: Fire at the Goetheanum, which is destroyed.

1923: Despite the fire, Rudolf Steiner continues his work unabated. A very hard year. Internal dispersion, dissension, and apathy abound. There is conflict—between old and new visions—within the Society. A wake-up call is needed, and Rudolf Steiner responds with renewed lecturing vitality. His focus: the spiritual context of human life; initiation science; the course of the year; and community building. As a foundation for an artistic school, he creates a series of pastel sketches. Lecture cycles: *The Anthroposophical Movement; Initiation Science* (CW 227) (in Wales at the Penmaenmawr Summer School); *The Four Seasons and the Archangels* (CW 229); *Harmony of the Creative Word* (CW 230); *The Supersensible Human* (CW 231), given in Holland for the founding of the Dutch society. On November 10, in response to the failed Hitler-Ludendorff putsch in Munich, Steiner closes his Berlin residence and moves the *Philosophisch-Anthroposophisch Verlag* (Press) to Dornach. On December 9, Steiner begins the serialization of his *Autobiography: The Course of My Life* (CW 28) in *Das Goetheanum*. It will continue to appear weekly, without a break, until his death. Late December–early January: Rudolf Steiner re-founds the Anthroposophical Society (about 12,000 members internationally) and takes over its leadership. The new board members are: Marie Steiner, Ita Wegman, Albert Steffen, Elisabeth Vreede, and Gunther Wachsmuth. (See *The Christmas Meeting for the Founding of the General Anthroposophical Society,* CW 260.) Accompanying lectures: *Mystery Knowledge and Mystery Centres* (CW 232); *World History in the Light of Anthroposophy* (CW 233). December 25: the Foundation Stone is laid (in the hearts of members) in the form of the 'Foundation Stone Meditation.'

1924: January 1: having founded the Anthroposophical Society and taken over its leadership, Rudolf Steiner has the task of 'reforming' it. The process begins with a weekly newssheet ('What's Happening in the Anthroposophical Society') in which Rudolf Steiner's 'Letters to Members' and 'Anthroposophical Leading Thoughts' appear (CW 26). The next step is the creation of a new esoteric class, the 'first class' of the 'University of Spiritual Science' (which was to have been followed, had Rudolf Steiner lived longer, by two more advanced classes). Then comes a new language for

Anthroposophy—practical, phenomenological, and direct; and Rudolf Steiner creates the model for the second Goetheanum. He begins the series of extensive 'karma' lectures (CW 235–40); and finally, responding to needs, he creates two new initiatives: biodynamic agriculture and curative education. After the middle of the year, rumours begin to circulate regarding Steiner's health. Lectures: January–February, *Anthroposophy* (CW 234); February: *Tone Eurythmy* (CW 278); June: *The Agriculture Course* (CW 327); June–July: *Speech Eurythmy* (CW 279); *Curative Education* (CW 317); August: (England, 'Second International Summer School'), *Initiation Consciousness: True and False Paths in Spiritual Investigation* (CW 243); September: *Pastoral Medicine* (CW 318). On September 26, for the first time, Rudolf Steiner cancels a lecture. On September 28, he gives his last lecture. On September 29, he withdraws to his studio in the carpenter's shop; now he is definitively ill. Cared for by Ita Wegman, he continues working, however, and writing the weekly installments of his *Autobiography* and *Letters to the Members/ Leading Thoughts* (CW 26).

1925:   Rudolf Steiner, while continuing to work, continues to weaken. He finishes *Extending Practical Medicine* (CW 27) with Ita Wegman. On March 30, around ten in the morning, Rudolf Steiner dies.

INDEX